Frommer's®

W9-BXM-190

Venice
day BY day™

2nd Edition

by Stephen Brewer

WILEY

Wiley Publishing, Inc.

Contents

Published by:

Wiley Publishing, Inc.

111 River St.
Hoboken, NJ 07030-5774

ISBN 978-0-470-38439-8

Editor: Emil J. Ross
Production Editor: Suzanna R. Thompson and Heather Wilcox
Photo Editor: Richard Fox, with Photo Affairs
Cartographer: Andrew Murphy
Production by Wiley Indianapolis Composition Services

For information on our other products and services or to obtain technical support, please contact our Customer Care Department within the U.S. at 800/762-2974, outside the U.S. at 317/572-3993 or fax 317/572-4002.

Wiley also publishes its books in a variety of electronic formats. Some content that appears in print may not be available in electronic formats.

Manufactured in China

5 4 3 2 1

A Note from the Editorial Director

Organizing your time. That's what this guide is all about.

Other guides give you long lists of things to see and do and then expect you to fit the pieces together. The Day by Day guides are different. These guides tell you the best of everything, and then they show you how to see it *in the smartest, most time-efficient way*. Our authors have designed detailed itineraries organized by time, neighborhood, or special interest. And each tour comes with a bulleted map that takes you from stop to stop.

Hoping to tour the Gallerie dell'Accademia, or to cruise up the Grand Canal in a gondola? Planning a walk through the Piazza San Marco, or side trips to Padua and Verona? Whatever your interest or schedule, the Day by Days give you the smartest routes to follow. Not only do we take you to the top attractions, hotels, and restaurants, but we also help you access those special moments that locals get to experience—those "finds" that turn tourists into travelers.

The Day by Days are also your top choice if you're looking for one complete guide for all your travel needs. The best hotels and restaurants for every budget, the greatest shopping values, the wildest nightlife—it's all here.

Why should you trust our judgment? Because our authors personally visit each place they write about. They're an independent lot who say what they think and would never include places they wouldn't recommend to their best friends. They're also open to suggestions from readers. If you'd like to contact them, please send your comments our way at feedback@frommers.com, and we'll pass them on.

Enjoy your Day by Day guide—the most helpful travel companion you can buy. And have the trip of a lifetime.

Warm regards,

Kelly Regan

Kelly Regan
Editorial Director
Frommer's Travel Guides

About the Author

Stephen Brewer stepped off a train in Venice many years ago, took one look at the Grand Canal, and decided he agreed with Marcel Proust in thinking, "When I went to Venice, my dream became my address." He enjoys many other beautiful places, too, and often writes about them. He is the coauthor of *Frommer's Best Day Trips from London* and the author of *The Unofficial Guide to England* and *The Unofficial Guide to Ireland*.

Acknowledgments

I would like to thank the patient people at the Piazza San Marco and Giardinetti Reale branches of the Venice tourist office, who never seem to tire of handing out maps and brochures and telling me which vaporetto to take. Likewise, thanks to the many kindly Venetians who treat us visitors well and are always willing and able to give directions and advice. Thanks, especially, to Stefano and Eleanora and the other Venetian friends who have provided lodging over the years and introduced me to the wonders of their city, and to Emil Ross, my talented editor at Frommer's, who guided me through a dream of an assignment.

An Additional Note

Please be advised that travel information is subject to change at any time—and this is especially true of prices. We therefore suggest that you write or call ahead for confirmation when making your travel plans. The authors, editors, and publisher cannot be held responsible for the experiences of readers while traveling. Your safety is important to us, however, so we encourage you to stay alert and be aware of your surroundings.

Star Ratings, Icons & Abbreviations

Every hotel, restaurant, and attraction listing in this guide has been ranked for quality, value, service, amenities, and special features using a **star-rating system.** Hotels, restaurants, attractions, shopping, and nightlife are rated on a scale of zero stars (recommended) to three stars (exceptional). In addition to the star-rating system, we also use a **kids icon** to point out the best bets for families. Within each tour, we recommend cafes, bars, or restaurants where you can take a break. Each of these stops appears in a shaded box marked with a coffee-cup-shaped bullet ☕.

The following **abbreviations** are used for credit cards:

AE	American Express	DISC	Discover	V	Visa
DC	Diners Club	MC	MasterCard		

Frommers.com

Now that you have this guidebook to help you plan a great trip, visit our website at **www.frommers.com** for additional travel information on more than 4,000 destinations. We update features regularly to give you instant access to the most current trip-planning information available. At Frommers.com, you'll find scoops on the best airfares, lodging rates, and car rental bargains. You can even book your travel online through our reliable travel booking partners. Other popular features include:

- Online updates of our most popular guidebooks
- Vacation sweepstakes and contest giveaways
- Newsletters highlighting the hottest travel trends
- Podcasts, interactive maps, and up-to-the-minute events listings
- Opinionated blog entries by Arthur Frommer himself
- Online travel message boards with featured travel discussions

A Note on Prices

In the "Take a Break" and "Best Bets" sections of this book, we have used a system of dollar signs to show a range of costs for 1 night in a hotel (the price of a double-occupancy room) or the cost of an entree at a restaurant. Use the following table to decipher the dollar signs:

Cost	Hotels	Restaurants
$	under $100	under $10
$$	$100–$200	$10–$20
$$$	$200–$300	$20–$30
$$$$	$300–$400	$30–$40
$$$$$	over $400	over $40

An Invitation to the Reader

In researching this book, we discovered many wonderful places—hotels, restaurants, shops, and more. We're sure you'll find others. Please tell us about them, so we can share the information with your fellow travelers in upcoming editions. If you were disappointed with a recommendation, we'd love to know that, too. Please write to:

Frommer's Venice Day by Day, 2nd Edition
Wiley Publishing, Inc. • 111 River St. • Hoboken, NJ 07030-5774

10 Favorite
Moments

10 Favorite **Moments**

0 | 1/8 Mi
0 | 200 meters

Madonna dell'Orto
Pal. Contarini dal Zaffo
Torcello
Casa di Tintoretto
Sacca della Misericordia

CANNAREGIO
GHETTO

Cappella d. Volto Santo
S. Marziale
Scuola Vécchia d. Misericordia
S. Maria d. Misericordia
Ex Convento e Chiesa di S. Caterina
Fondamenta Nove
Pal. Donà
Fond. Nove

S. Marcuola
Pal. Diedo
La Maddalena
Pal. Lezze
Pal. Vendramin
Gesuiti

S. Marcuola
Pal. Vendramin Calergi
Pal. Molin
S. Fosca
Pal. Papafava
Ex Convento
Pal. Seriman

Riva da Biásio
Fond. d. Turchi
Ca' Tron
S. Stae
S. Felice
Strada di S. Felice

S. Zan Degola
S. Stae
Pal. Boldù
Ca' d'Oro
S. Sofia
Rio di Ca' d'Oro

S. Giacomo dell'Orio
Palazzo Mocenigo
S. Maria Máter Domini
Palazzo Brandolin
Ca' d'Oro
Ss. Apóstoli
S. Canciano
Pal. Widman
Ospedale Civile

SANTA CROCE
Pal. Zane
Pal. Grioni
S. Cassiano
Pescaria
Fábbriche Nuove
Ca' da Mosto
Pal. Mangilli
Teatro Málibran
Pal. Soranzo-Van Axel
Ss. Giovanni e Paolo (S. Zanipolo)

Pal. Muti Baglioni
Pal. Civran
Pal. Pisani

SAN POLO
Palazzo Dieci Savi
Fóndaco D. Tedeschi
S. Bartolomeo
Pal. Contarini
Palazzo Ruzzini
Palazzo Dona
Pal. Vitturi

Pal. Cornèr
Campo S. Polo
Ponte di Rialto
Rialto
S. Maria Formosa

Palazzo Morolin
S. Silvestro
Palazzo Dólfin-Manin
Pal. Gussoni
Campo dei Frari
S. Polo
S. Silvestro
S. Salvador
Pal. Tasca Papafáva

Campo dei Frari
S. Maria G. dei Frari
Pal. Centani
Palazzo Grimani
Pal. Dándolo
Ca'Farsetti
Ex Convento
Palazzo Soranzo
Pal. Querini Stampalia

S. Tomà
S. Tomà
Palazzo Volpi
Pal. Loredàn
SAN MARCO
S. Giovanni Novo

Pal. Balbi
Palazzo Mocenigo
Palazzo Cornèr Spinelli
Palazzo Fortuny
Cinema Rossini

Ca' Foscari
Campo S. Ángelo
Ateneo Véneto
Pal. Contarini del Bovolo
Palazzo Patriarcale
Basilica di San Marco

Ca' Rezzonico
S. Stefano
S. Gallo
Piazza San Marco
Pal. d. Prigioni
Palazzo Dándolo

S. Samuele
Teatro La Fenice
S. Fantin
Museo Correr
Palazzo Ducale
S. Zaccaria

Ca' Rezzonico
Palazzo Loredàn
S. Maurizio
S. Moisè

Ca' del Duca
Pal. Falier
Palazzo Morosini
S. Maria d. Giglio
Palazzo Giustinián
S. Marco

Accademia
Palazzo Pisani
Palazzo Cornèr della Ca' Granda
Pal. Gritti
Pal. Ferro Fini
Palazzo Tiépolo

Ponte dell'Accademia
S. Maria d. Giglio
Pal. Sálute
Bacino di San Marco

Gallerie dell'Accademia
Pal. Venier dei Leoni (Guggenheim)
Pal. Genovese
S. Maria d. Salute
Dogana da Mar

S. Agnese
Ex Ospizio

Gesuati
Spirito Santo
Fondam. Záttere ai Saloni

Canale della Giudecca

Isola della Giudecca

Redentore

Il Redentore
Ex Chiesa della Croce

Previous page: The San Marco Basilica and Campanile, built in the 11th century.

Venice, city of visual delights, fires up the imagination. The colors, the many exotic domes and mosaics, the omnipresence of water, the rich history that's almost palpable in the streets and squares—best simply to let yourself be overwhelmed by it all. If you have to choose, though, you can't miss with the activities below.

1 Cruising on the Grand Canal. Even though the craft is a humble *vaporetto* (one of the city's boat buses) and the trip is an everyday routine for many Venetians, the experience never fails to be exhilarating. No matter how many times I've taken to the canal here, I'm still in awe of the dreamy water world that is Venice. *See p 18.*

2 Savoring the Piazza San Marco. This civilized square is, as Napoleon called it, the "drawing room" of Europe. The Piazza, as it's simply known, is where Venetians and their visitors converge to sip a cappuccino or cocktail on the outdoor terraces of some of Europe's grandest cafes. *See p 7,* **5**.

3 Being dazzled by the mosaics in the Basilica di San Marco. Step into this cathedral and let the shimmering brilliance of thousands of mosaics sweep you away. Then take a close look at the glass tiles that cover the floors, walls, and domes. Saints, sinners, angels, and mere mortals have been touchingly and painstakingly depicted here. *See p 23,* **5**.

Palazzi line the 3.8km-long (2.4-mile) Grand Canal.

4 Sipping a cappuccino in Campo Santi Giovanni e Paolo. Grab an outdoor table at **Rosa Salva** (p 80), a venerable cafe, and soak in the scene. Verrocchio's equestrian statue of Bartolomeo Colleoni stands guard over the neighborhood, and the formidable facade of the Chiesa di Santi Giovanni e Paolo hints at the treasures that await you. *See p 15,* **4**.

5 Strolling through the Rialto markets. Exotic sea creatures from the Adriatic, artichokes from the island of Sant' Erasmo in the lagoon, and freshly picked pears from the Veneto seem especially appetizing with the Grand Canal flowing past. The sheer bustle of this place, the commercial heart of Venice for more than 1,000 years, brings to mind old Shylock's oft-quoted question in *The Merchant of Venice:* "What news on the Rialto?" *See p 42,* **10**.

A fruit stand at the wholesale and retail Rialto market.

The Basilica di Santa Maria Assunta on the island of Torcello is an example of Venetian-Byzantine architecture.

6 Standing in front of your favorite painting in the Accademia (or in any other museum or *scuola*, for that matter). You'll soon find the canvas that captivates you. Some worthy candidates are Giorgione's mysterious *Temptest* or Carpaccio's rich *Story of Saint Ursula* and *Miracle of the Relic of the True Cross*. If you're anything like me, you'll find yourself mesmerized by more than one. *See p 34.*

7 Looking over the Grand Canal and Bacino di San Marco from the Dogana da Mar, the Customs house. On this point of land where ships once moored to be inspected, with the sea lanes stretching in front of you, it's easy to imagine Venice as a seafaring power and the crossroads between East and West. Magnificent relics of the trading wealth that once poured into the city—in the form of *palazzi* (palaces) lining the banks—complete the view. *See p 11,* **2**.

8 Crossing the lagoon to Torcello. Part of the charm of Torcello is the ghostlike presence of the

20,000 souls who once inhabited this all-but-deserted little island; they left behind the glorious, mosaic-paved Basilica di Santa Maria Assunta, one of the few remaining signs of civilization. Past grandeur aside, Torcello is also a perfectly nice place to escape from the bustle of Venice for an afternoon. *See p 45,* **7**.

9 Taking a *passeggiata* on the Zattere. Many Venetians couldn't imagine ending a day without an "evening stroll" on this broad promenade along the Giudecca Canal, and you should join them. Ocher-colored houses capture the last rays of the sun, a tangy sea breeze stirs the air, and the church of Il Redentore across the canal provides a stage-set backdrop. *See p 90,* **2**.

10 Standing on the Ponte di Rialto at night. Who cares if the gondolas slipping beneath your feet are laden with sightseers and the strains of "'O Sole Mio" are taped? Fall under the spell of the shimmering reflections on the palazzi and imagine a time when the likes of Lord Byron and Casanova glided up the canal in the dark of a Venetian night. *See p 48,* **2**. ●

The 12th-century Ponte di Rialto is an architectural icon of Venice.

1 The Best Full-Day Tours

6

The Best **in One Day**

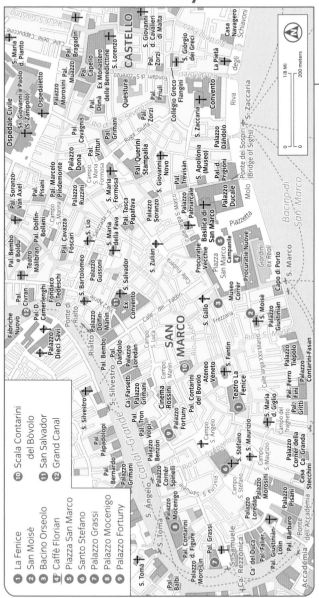

1 La Fenice
2 San Moisè
3 Bacino Orseolo
4 Caffè Florian
5 Piazza San Marco
6 Santo Stefano
7 Palazzo Grassi
8 Palazzo Mocenigo
9 Palazzo Fortuny
10 Scala Contarini del Bòvolo
11 San Salvador
12 Grand Canal

Previous page: The Campanile rises 98m (322 ft.) from Piazza San Marco.

The French novelist Marcel Proust said of his first trip [to] Venice, "My dream became my address." You may feel the [same] way as you begin to explore the city. Start in the San Marco section, not far from the Piazza San Marco, and take in the uniquely Venetian palaces and churches. Top off your tour with a cruise along one of the world's most storied waterways, the Grand Canal. START: Vaporetto to Santa Maria del Giglio.

1 ★★ **La Fenice.** The aptly named opera house (*fenice* means "phoenix") has burned several times, most recently in 1996, and risen from the ashes looking just as it has for centuries. Several Verdi operas, including *Rigoletto* and *La Traviata,* premiered in the sumptuous, newly restored house, and Maria Callas is among the stars who have graced the stage. ⏱ *15 min. See p 128.*

2 ★ **San Moisè.** In a city of beautiful churches, this baroque extravagance stands out as one of the ugliest. ⏱ *15 min. Campo San Moisè.* ☎ *041-5285840. Daily 9:30am–12:30pm. Vaporetto: San Marco/Vallaresso.*

3 ★★ **Bacino Orseolo.** One of the city's 11 gondola stands is a good place to get a close look at these uniquely Venetian craft—or to board one. ⏱ *15 min. Fondamenta Orseolo. Vaporetto: San Marco/Vallaresso.*

4 **Caffè Florian.** You'll pay dearly for your cappuccino on the terrace here, but you'll never sip coffee in

Piazza San Marco's pigeons are almost as famous as its architecture.

more atmospheric surroundings. *Piazza San Marco.* ☎ *041-5205641. See p 117.*

5 ★★★ **Piazza San Marco.** This square, the heart of the city for more than 1,000 years, combines the very old (the Basilica) with the relatively new (the 16th- and 17th-c. Procuratie Vecchie and Procuratie Nuove buildings on the north and south sides of the square), yet still manages to be harmonious.

Venice's glorious opera house, La Fenice ("The Phoenix") has been destroyed by fire three times.

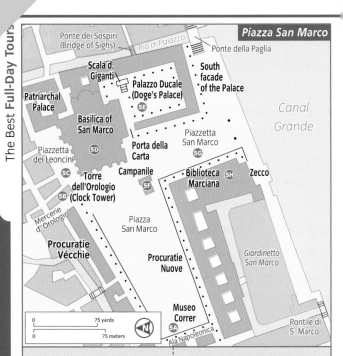

Piazza San Marco

The Piazza San Marco contains many of Venice's major attractions: In the **5A Museo Correr** (see p 31, ①), maps, coins, costumes, and, best of all, paintings by Vittore Carpaccio (room 38) and Jacopo Bellini (room 36) recall the days of the republic. Across the square, bronze Moors strike the bells of the **5B Torre dell'Orologio** to mark the time. During the feasts of the Ascension and Epiphany, statues of the Magi appear out of the clock on the hour, accompanied by a procession of angels. Below, in the **5C Piazzetta dei Leoncini,** marble lions stand guard over what was once a market-place. Next to this plaza is the **5D Basilica di San Marco** (see p 23, ⑤), which inspired 19th-century man of letters John Ruskin to exhale into his journals, "The crests of the arches break into a marble foam, and toss themselves into the blue sky in flashes and wreaths of sculpted spray"; less poetical observers will be similarly moved by its ornate Byzantine architecture. **5E Palazzo Ducale** (see p 37, ④), the palace where the doges lived and ruled, adjacent to the Basilica, is majestic but has a touch of whimsy as well. The city's tallest structure, the **5F Campanile** (see p 44, ②) or bell tower of the Basilica, in the center of the piazza, affords stunning views. Two columns, one topped by a winged lion and the other by Saint Theodore, frame the **5G Piazzetta San Marco,** the seaside extension of Piazza San Marco. Finally, don't miss one of Venice's great Renaissance monuments, the **5H ★ Biblioteca Marciana,** which was completed in the 16th century to house a precious hoard of Greek and Latin manuscripts. ⏱ 4–5 hr. San Marco. Vaporetto: San Marco.

⑥ ★ **Santo Stefano.** Beyond this church's 15th-century sculpted portal by Bartolomeo Bon is a wooden ceiling whose shape resembles the inverted hull of a ship, as well as two works by Tintoretto in the sacristy. ⏱ *30 min. Campo Santo Stefano.* ☎ *041-5225061. Sacristy 3€. Church daily 9am–7pm; sacristy Mon–Sat 10am–5pm. Vaporetto: San Samuele.*

⑦ ★★ **Palazzo Grassi.** One of the last of the great palaces to be built in Venice dates from 1749 and was stunningly converted in 2006 to house the contemporary art collections of French magnate François Pinault. ⏱ *45 min. San Marco 3231, San Samuele.* ☎ *041-5231680. www. palazzograssi.it. 10€. Daily 10am–7pm. Vaporetto: San Samuele.*

⑧ ★ **Palazzo Mocenigo.** One of the largest and grandest houses in Venice is actually four palaces that a succession of prominent residents combined over the centuries. Lord Byron lived here from 1818 to 1819—with enough pets to populate a small zoo, an army of servants, and his mistress. He often swam home across the lagoon from outings on the Lido. ⏱ *10 min. Calle Mocenigo. Not open to the public. Vaporetto: San Stae.*

⑨ ★ **Palazzo Fortuny.** The last resident of this 15th-century palazzo was textile designer and photographer Mariano Fortuny. The mansion now displays his distinctive work. *See p 37,* ②.

⑩ ★★ **Scala Contarini del Bòvolo.** The beautiful spiral staircase (*bòvolo,* or snail, in Venetian dialect) that this palazzo is named for climbs five stories from a lovely courtyard. Until lengthy restoration work is completed sometime in 2009, the staircase can be admired only from below in the courtyard; a reward for a climb to the top is a

The Scala Contarini del Bòvolo is undergoing restoration but remains a charming architectural flourish.

panoramic view over the rooftops of Venice. ⏱ *15 min. Corte di Contarini del Bòvolo.* ☎ *041-5322920. Vaporetto: Rialto.*

⑪ ★ **San Salvador.** The handsome white interior of this chapel provides refuge from the busy Mercerie, one of Venice's main shopping streets, as well as the chance to view some excellent paintings: two Titians (a *Transfiguration* and an *Annunciation*) and Carpaccio's *Disciples at Emmaus.* ⏱ *30 min. Campo San Salvador.* ☎ *041-2702464. Mon–Sat 9am–noon, 3–7:15pm; Sun 3–7:15pm. Vaporetto: Rialto.*

⑫ ★★★ **Grand Canal.** A cruise up one of the world's most beautiful waterways is the ideal way to end a long day of touring. Get off at the Ferrovia stop for the return trip. *See p 18. For details on the vaporetto, see p 167.*

The Best **in Two Days**

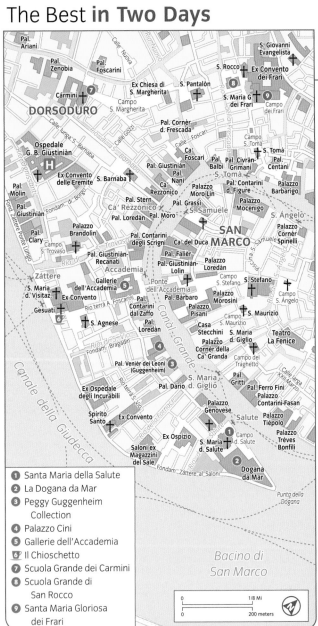

1 Santa Maria della Salute
2 La Dogana da Mar
3 Peggy Guggenheim
   Collection
4 Palazzo Cini
5 Gallerie dell'Accademia
6 Il Chioschetto
7 Scuola Grande dei Carmini
8 Scuola Grande di
   San Rocco
9 Santa Maria Gloriosa
   dei Frari

0   1/8 Mi
0   200 meters

Now it's time to explore the Dorsoduro, the quarters across the Grand Canal from San Marco. This is not a quiet neighborhood amble: Some of Venice's greatest masterpieces are here, and you'll discover one remarkable church and treasure-filled museum after another. START: **Vaporetto to Salute.**

① ★★ Santa Maria della Salute. The church of "Saint Mary of Health" was built in 1630, an offering of thanks to the Virgin Mary for bringing an end to a plague outbreak that killed a third of the city's population. The massive white-marble cathedral by architect Baldassare Longhena commands the entrance to the Grand Canal, and its high domes, suggestive of the Madonna's crown, mimic those of the Basilica di San Marco across the water. A suitably impressive collection of paintings hangs in the round, marble interior, including Tintoretto's *Wedding at Cana* and Titian's *Saint Mark Enthroned with Saints.* The Virgin is honored on the high altar with a Byzantine icon and a wonderfully dramatic marble sculptural group by Giusto Le Corte—an old hag representing the plague flees from a torch-bearing angel as the Virgin and a noblewoman, in the role of Venice, look on. ⏲ *30 min. Campo della Salute.* 📞 *041-5225558. Sacristy 2€. Apr–Sept daily 9am–noon, 3–6:30pm; Oct–Mar daily 9am–noon, 3–5:30pm. Vaporetto: Salute.*

② ★★ La Dogana da Mar. The 17th-century Customs house at the tip of the Dorsoduro resembles the hull of a ship and was once a mandatory stop for all vessels entering Venice. On the roof, a statue of Fortune stands over a gold globe, and looking out to sea from the landing stage, it's easy to imagine the time when Venetians felt they were indeed the lucky rulers of the waves. The modern world will

Gondolas moored in front of the octagonal church of Santa Maria della Salute, known simply as the Salute.

establish a beachhead here at the tip of the city in mid-2009 with the opening of the **Centro d'Arte Contemporanea de Punta della Dogana,** which will house works that include those from the collections of the Palazzo Grassi (see p 9, ⑦). ⏲ *30 min. Fondamenta Dogana alla Salute. Vaporetto: Salute.*

③ ★★★ Peggy Guggenheim Collection. The American heiress (1898–1979) spent much of her life collecting contemporary art, living up to her pledge to "buy a picture a day." In 1949, she found a home for herself and her paintings, the **Palazzo Venier dei Leoni,** that is as surreal as some of the works she preferred. Only the ground floor of the 18th-century palace was completed, providing distinctive surroundings

The Peggy Guggenheim Collection contains a canal-side sculpture garden.

for a collection that includes Giorgio De Chirico's *The Red Tower,* Rene Magritte's *Empire of Light,* and works by Jackson Pollock (whom Guggenheim discovered), Max Ernst (whom she married), and many others. The shady garden is filled with sculptures, as well as the graves of Guggenheim and her dogs. The waterside terrace provides sweeping views up and down the Grand Canal. ⏱ *1 hr. Palazzo Venier dei Leoni.*

Giovanni Bellini's Madonna of the Red Cherubs, *in the Gallerie dell'Accademia.*

☎ *041-2405411. www.guggenheim-venice.it. 10€. Wed–Mon 10am–6pm. Vaporetto: Accademia.*

④ ★★ **Palazzo Cini.** Industrialist Vittorio Cini (1885–1977) spent much of his fortune collecting religious art from Tuscany, and his small, intimate palace, open only for special events and exhibitions, is filled with works by Sandro Botticelli, Piero della Francesca, and others. **See p 37,** ①.

⑤ ★★★ **Gallerie dell'Accademia.** A walk through the galleries here can take the good part of a day and is a lesson in Venetian art from Carpaccio to Tiepolo. If time is tight or the temptation to be outdoors exploring the city too great, at least see the works by Titian, Tintoretto, and Veronese, and Carpaccio's colorful, action-filled *Story of Saint Ursula* cycle. **See p 34.**

⑥ **Il Chioschetto.** At this outdoor cafe, a panino and a glass of wine, well deserved after a morning of viewing art, come with a view of the Giudecca Canal. *Zattere Ponte Luongo.* ☎ 338-1174077.

Back to *Scuola*

Founded in the Middle Ages, the Venetian *scuole* (schools) were guilds that brought together merchants and craftspeople from certain trades (for example, the dyers of Scuola dei Carmini), as well as those who shared similar religious devotions (Scuola Grande di San Rocco). The guilds were social clubs, credit unions, and sources of spiritual guidance. Many commissioned elaborate headquarters and hired the best artists of the day to decorate them. The *scuole* that remain in Venice today house some of the city's finest art treasures.

⑦ ★★ Scuola Grande dei Carmini. The Carmelite order founded this *scuola* in the 17th century in association with the guild of dyers and hired the architect Baldassare Longhena to build their premises. The master's facades remain intact—as does much of the interior, little touched over the centuries. A painting by Tiepolo, *The Virgin in Glory Appearing to the Blessed Simon Stock,* flows over the ceiling of the salon. 🕐 *30 min. See p 32,* ⑧.

⑧ ★★★ Scuola Grande di San Rocco. San Rocco, the patron saint of the sick and a Venetian favorite, was especially popular for his alleged prowess at curing the plague. A *scuola* in his honor was begun in the early 16th century to house the saint's relics; it was lavishly decorated by Tintoretto. 🕐 *30 min. See p 32,* ⑨.

⑨ ★★★ Santa Maria Gloriosa dei Frari. One of the largest churches in Venice is also one of the city's great treasure troves of art, with masterworks by Titian and Giovanni Bellini. *See p 33,* ⑩.

The church of Santa Maria Gloriosa dei Frari contains dozens of works of art by Italian masters, including Donatello and Titian.

The Best in Three Days

1 Rialto
2 Alla Madonna
3 Traghetto
4 Campo Santi Giovanni e Paolo (San Zanipòlo)
5 Santa Maria dei Miracoli
6 Santi Apostoli
7 Strada Nuova
8 Ca d'Oro!
9 Galleria Franchetti
9 Campo di Ghetto Nuovo
10 Palazzo Labia

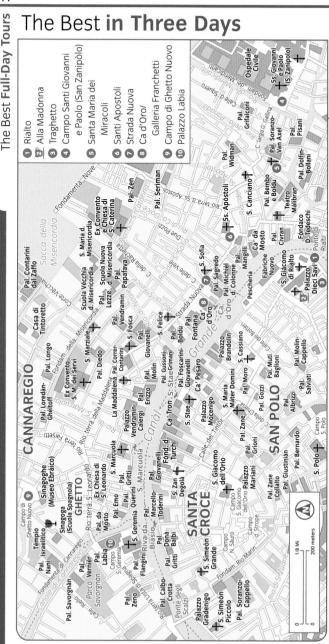

Everyday life in Venice begins at its busy marketplace, the Rialto, so you should, too. Continue your day by exploring the historic *sestieri* (districts) of Cannaregio and San Polo, neighborhoods where Venetians just go about their daily business. Along this route you'll also find a few more of the notable churches, palaces, galleries, and monuments with which the city is so liberally laced.

START: **Vaporetto to Rialto.**

① **★★ Rialto.** The markets and alleys of the Rialto are a good place to begin your walk. The name comes from *rivoaltus*, or "high bank," a geographic asset when settlers in the early 9th century were searching for dry ground to establish the city's first bazaar. (The Rialto has been a commercial center ever since.) Ships from around the globe once docked at the **Fondaco dei Tedeschi**—the Renaissance-style structure that now houses the main post office—and other neighborhood warehouses, and it was here that the Grand Canal was first spanned. See p 42, **⑩**.

② **Alla Madonna.** For an authentic taste of the Rialto markets, take a seat in this busy room and enjoy a seafood lunch. *Calle della Madonna.* ☎ 041-5223824. See p 102.

③ **★ Traghetto.** Enjoy a walk over the Ponte dei Rialto, Venice's oldest bridge over the Canal, then retrace your steps and make the crossing in one of the *traghetti* that run between the banks of the canal. A traghetto—basically, a large, plain gondola—provides a poor man's gondola ride (one-way passage is just .50€), but comes with a challenge: By tradition, passengers remain standing during the ride. ⏱ *10 min. Near the Rialto; traghetti run from Fondamente del Vin to Riva del Carbòn (Mon–Sat 8am–2pm) and the Pescaria to Santa Sofia (Mon–Sat 7:30am–8:30pm; Sun 8am–7pm).* See p 48, **②**, for more details on the Ponte di Rialto. *Vaporetto: Rialto.*

④ **★★ Campo Santi Giovanni e Paolo.** Bartolomeo Colleoni, a 15th-century mercenary, rides across one of Venice's most beautiful squares astride an equestrian monument by Verrocchio. The namesake basilica here (known as **San Zanipòlo** in Venetian dialect) is the final resting place of 25 doges, entombed in marble splendor. ⏱ *45 min. Castello. Vaporetto: Fondamenta Nuove.*

⑤ **★★★ Santa Maria dei Miracoli.** This small, beautiful church, inconspicuously tucked away on a small campo next to a canal, seems

Passengers typically stand during traghetto *(ferry) rides traversing the Grand Canal.*

The church of San Zanipòlo is the principal Dominican basilica in Venice.

almost like an apparition. *See p 66,* ⑩.

⑥ ★ **Santi Apostoli.** Venetian legend has it that the 12 apostles appeared to Saint Magnus and told him to build a church where he saw 12 cranes. The church's bell tower, a 17th-century addition, is topped with an onion dome and is a much-beloved landmark. Giambattista Tiepolo's rendering of Saint Lucy near the altar is eye-catching indeed—the martyr's eyes lie on the floor next to her, but she seems to be smiling all the same. ⏱ *30 min. Campo Santi Apostoli.* ☎ *041-5238297. Mon–Sat 8:30–noon, 5–7pm; Sun 4–7pm. Vaporetto: Ca' d'Oro.*

⑦ ★ **Strada Nuova.** One of the few straight paths in Venice (**Via Garibaldi**, *p 59,* ⑭, is another), this street was laid out in the 1860s to facilitate foot traffic to and from the then-new railway station.

⑧ ★★★ **Ca' d'Oro/Galleria Franchetti.** This 15th-century palazzo just off the Strada Nuova still bears the trappings of a cushy Renaissance lifestyle and is filled with works by Venetian masters. *See p 16,* ⑧.

⑨ ★★ **Campo di Ghetto Nuovo.** The Ghetto was once the only part of Venice where Jews were allowed to live. This large square and surrounding neighborhood occupy an island that was closed off at dusk and still feels remote. The houses on the square are higher than most in Venice, as stories were added to accommodate a population that expanded as the Jewish community prospered in trade and banking. ⏱ *15 min. Ghetto Nuovo, Cannaregio. Vaporetto: Ponte de Guglie.*

⑩ ★★ **Palazzo Labia.** One of the grandest palaces in Venice is set back from the Grand Canal—a sign that the Labias, a clan of Spanish traders, were never accepted by Venetian nobility. Giambattista Tiepolo painted a magnificent fresco of Anthony and Cleopatra for the Banqueting Hall in honor of the marriage of Maria Labia. ⏱ *30 min. Fondamenta Labia.* ☎ *041-5242812. Closed for restoration; normally open Wed–Fri 3–4pm, by appointment only (call or ask your hotel to make arrangements). Vaporetto: San Marcuola/Ponte de Guglie.* ●

Tiepolo's 18th-century fresco, The Meeting of Antony and Cleopatra, *in the Palazzo Labia.*

2 The Best Special-Interest Tours

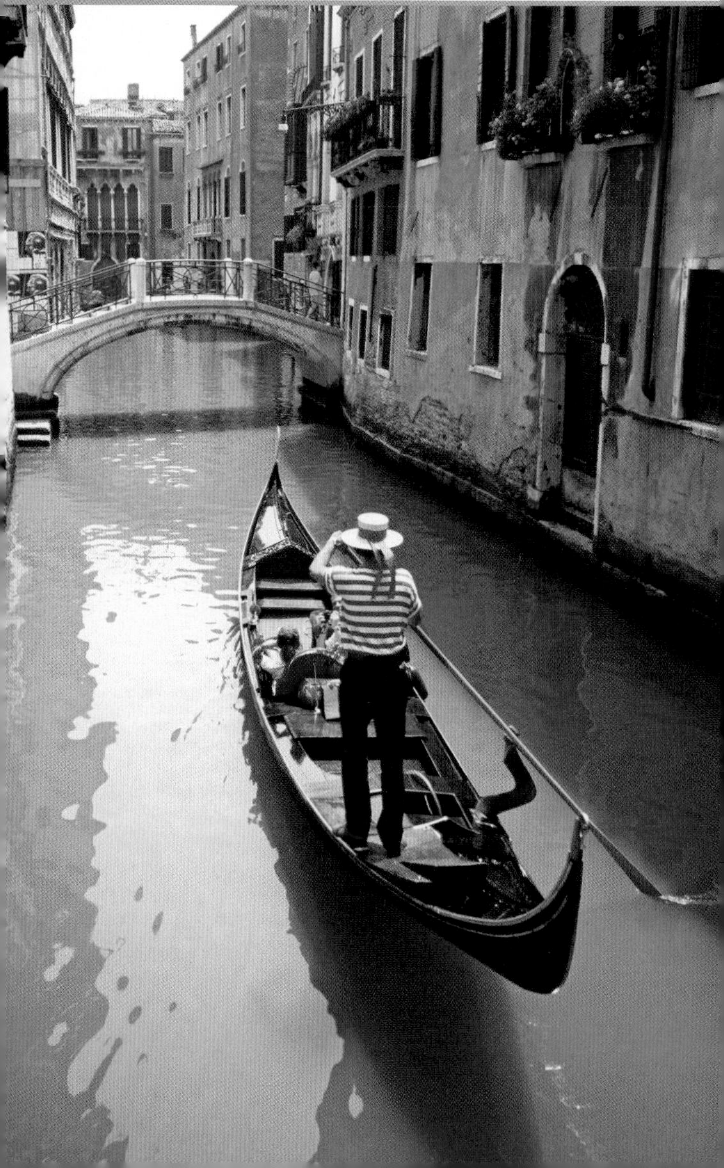

The Grand Canal

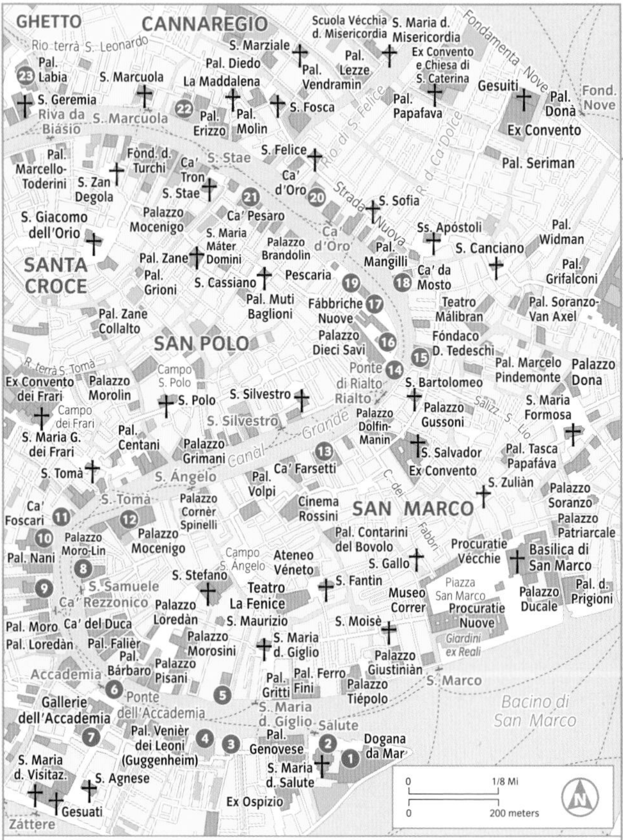

1. Dogana da Mar
2. Santa Maria della Salute
3. Ca' Dario
4. Palazzo Venier dei Leoni/ Peggy Guggenheim Collection
5. Palazzo Corner della Ca' Grande
6. Ponte dell'Accademia
7. Gallerie dell'Accademia
8. Palazzo Grassi
9. Ca' Rezzonico
10. Ca' Foscari
11. Palazzo Balbi
12. Palazzo Mocenigo
13. Palazzo Loredan and Palazzo Farsetti
14. Ponte di Rialto
15. Fondaco dei Tedeschi
16. Palazzo dei Camerlenghi
17. Fabbriche Vecchie and Fabbriche Nuove
18. Ca' da Mosto
19. Pescaria
20. Ca d'Oro
21. Ca' Pesaro
22. Palazzo Vendramin Calergi
23. Palazzo Labia

Previous page: A gondolier navigates one of the 150 shallow canals of Venice.

Main Street for Venetians is the Grand Canal, an S-shaped, 2-mile-long stretch of busy waterway between San Marco and the train station. Commerce has long thrived on the canal, and for centuries, nobility built their palaces on the banks. The half-hour vaporetto trip up the canal not only reveals the city's past grandeur, but also provides an exhilarating look at life in present-day Venice.
START: **Vaporetto from San Marco/Vallaresso toward Piazzale Roma.**

❶ ★ **Dogana da Mar.** The 15th-century triangular Customs house at the entrance to the Grand Canal was at one time a mandatory stop for all vessels entering Venice. Adjacent warehouses are now filled with the works of the **Centro d'Arte Contemporanea de Punta della Dogana.** See p 11, ❷.

❷ ★★ **Santa Maria della Salute.** A baroque fantasy in white marble, this church designed by Baldassare Longhena and built as an offering to end an outbreak of the plague hints at the architectural wonders that line the canal ahead. See p 11, ❶.

❸ ★ **Ca' Dario.** A long roster of former residents died under mysterious circumstances, endowing this small, 15th-century palazzo with a reputation of being cursed. Vaporetto: Salute.

❹ ★★★ **Palazzo Venier dei Leoni.** The Venier clan ran into fiscal straits while building their palazzo, but the ground floor—the only part completed—was well suited to the

Venice's canals serve as roads, and every form of transport in the central city is on water or by foot.

tastes of American heiress Peggy Guggenheim. Today the palazzo shows off the **Peggy Guggenheim Collection** of modern art, to ideal advantage. See p 11, ❸.

❺ ★ **Palazzo Corner della Ca' Grande.** Venice's police department is headquartered in this elegant, early Renaissance palazzo built in the 1590s. Vaporetto: Santa Maria del Giglio.

The Dogana da Mar and the church of Santa Maria della Salute welcome vessels to the Grand Canal.

Ca' Foscari is the main seat of the University of Venice.

6 ★ **Ponte dell'Accademia.** This prosaic wooden bridge dates from 1934 (though it replaced an iron structure erected in 1854)—until then, the Ponte di Rialto was the only span across the canal. *Vaporetto: Accademia.*

7 ★★★ **Gallerie dell'Accademia.** Three former religious buildings house the world's richest repository of Venetian art. *See p 34.*

8 ★ **Palazzo Grassi.** The last palazzo to be built on the Grand Canal dates from 1749. The salons are filled with contemporary art and surround a beautiful courtyard and frescoed staircase. *See p 9,* **7**.

9 ★ **Ca' Rezzonico.** The home of the **Museo del Settecento Veneziano** (Museum of 18th-Century Venice) has also been home to the poets Robert Browning and Elizabeth Barrett Browning, Cole Porter, and James McNeill Whistler. *See p 39,* **6**.

10 ★ **Ca' Foscari.** The home of a 15th-century doge houses the **Università Ca' Foscari Venezia** (University of Venice). *Vaporetto: Ca' Rezzonico.*

11 ★ **Palazzo Balbi.** Napoleon is among the legions of spectators who have sat on the balcony here to watch the many regattas that, since 1315, have crossed the finish line in front of the palazzo. *Vaporetto: San Tomà.*

12 ★ **Palazzo Mocenigo.** The Mocenigo clan produced seven doges; it also connected four adjacent palaces to create one of the grandest homes on the canal. In the early 19th century, one commodious wing accommodated Lord Byron and his menagerie. *Vaporetto: San Stae.*

13 ★ **Palazzo Loredan/Palazzo Farsetti.** Two of the first palazzi on the canal, built in the 13th century, now serve as Venice's city hall. Palazzo Loredan was home to the first woman to ever earn a college degree—she completed her studies at the University of Padua in 1678. *Vaporetto: Rialto.*

14 ★★★ **Ponte di Rialto.** Venice's most famous bridge, completed in 1590, was the first crossing over the Grand Canal. *See p 48,* **2**.

15 ★ **Fondaco dei Tedeschi.** Built in 1508 as a multipurpose warehouse, office space, and a hostelry for *Tedeschi* (Germans) working in Venice, this Renaissance-style structure is now Venice's main post office. *Vaporetto: Rialto.*

16 ★ **Palazzo dei Camerlenghi.** The world's first-known office building was completed in 1528 for Venice's financial magistrates—a function it still serves, as the headquarters of the financial court. *Vaporetto: Rialto.*

17 ★ **Fabbriche Vecchie/Fabbriche Nuove.** Both these elegant structures were actually built in the

15th century as warehouses. *Vaporetto: Rialto.*

18 ★ **Ca' da Mosto.** The oldest palace on the Grand Canal was completed in the 13th century for a family whose members included Alvise da Mosto, the 15th-century navigator who discovered the Cape Verde Islands. *Vaporetto: Ca d'Oro.*

19 ★ **Pescaria.** Venetians have bought their fish from this spot since the 14th century; the neo-Gothic market hall dates from the early 20th century. *Vaporetto: Rialto.*

20 ★★ **Ca' d'Oro.** Even without the gold leaf that graced the facade and lent the palazzo its name, this early-15th-century palazzo would be a glittering example of Venetian Gothic architecture. Inside are the Venetian masterpieces of the **Galleria Franchetti**. *See p 39,* **8**.

21 ★ **Ca' Pesaro.** The Pesaro family combined three Gothic houses to create one of Venice's largest palaces, now housing Asian and modern art collections. *See p 39,* **7**.

22 ★ **Palazzo Vendramin Calergi.** Past residents include the composer Richard Wagner, who completed *Tristan und Isolde* here in 1859. The Renaissance palazzo is the winter home of the city-operated casino. *Vaporetto: Santa Marcuola.*

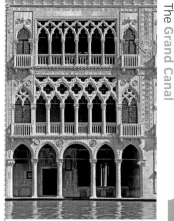

The exterior of the 15th-century palazzo Ca' d'Oro ("Golden House") was once decorated in gold leaf.

23 ★★ **Palazzo Labia.** The 17th-century home of a Spanish trading family now houses the Venice offices of RAI, the Italian national television network. The Labia clan left behind tales of legendary wealth and pretension—at their lavish galas, they would hurl gold dinnerware into the canal. (Concealed nets ensured easy retrieval.) Another legacy: the frescoes that Giambattista Tiepolo executed for the Banqueting Hall in honor of the marriage of Maria Labia in the 18th century. *See p 16,* **10**.

Mooring poles on the S-shaped Grand Canal.

Byzantine Venice

1. San Giacomo di Rialto
2. Museo dell'Istituto Ellenico
3. Sant'Apollonia
4. Gran Caffè Quadri
5. Basilica di San Marco
6. San Zan Degolà
7. San Giacomo dell'Orio
8. Santa Maria e San Donato
9. Santa Maria Assunta
10. Santa Fosca

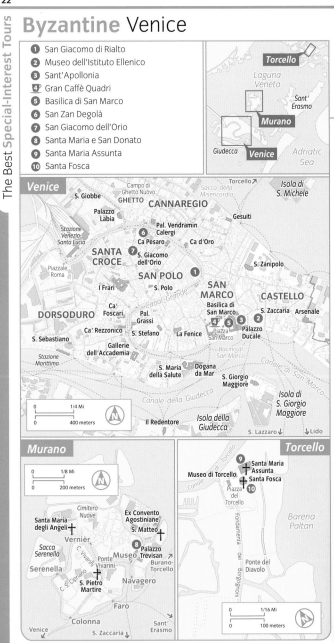

East and West come together in Venice, adding a hefty dose of exoticism to the city's cultural stew. Settlers and early traders from Constantinople (now Istanbul) brought with them arts, such as mosaic work, and architecture, primarily in the form of Greek-cross-shaped churches with arches and domes. The trail of the Venetian Byzantine leads from San Marco across the lagoon to the 7th-century settlement on the island of Torcello. START: **Rialto.**

① ★ San Giacomo di Rialto. The oldest church in Venice, founded in the 5th century and restored in the 11th century, retains the shape of a Greek cross and other telltale Byzantine elements. A lively fruit and vegetable market is just outside the door. ⏱ *1 hr. See p 127.*

② ★ Museo dell'Istituto Ellenico. Founded by Greeks who poured into Venice after the Turks took Constantinople in 1453, the incense-scented **Scuola di San Nicolo** building houses this museum's hoard of icons. Many are pure Byzantine works; others show the influence of Westernized styles of painting. Next door, the campanile of the church of San Giorgio dei Greci gently leans toward a canal, supplying a vista that is uniquely Venetian. ⏱ *1 hr. Ponte dei Greci.* ☎ *041-5226581. 4€. Mon–Sat 9am–12:30pm, 1–4:30pm; Sun 10am–5pm. Vaporetto: San Zaccaria.*

③ ★ Sant'Apollonia. Venice's only Romanesque cloisters date from the 14th century and were once part of a Benedictine convent. Inside are Byzantine carvings and other holdings of the **Museo Diocesano di Arte Sacra.** ⏱ *30 min. Ponte della Canonica.* ☎ *041-5229166. Mon–Sat 10:30am–12:30pm. Vaporetto: San Zaccaria.*

④ Gran Caffè Quadri. Can't get enough of the glorious mosaic facade of San Marco (below)? Here on the terrace of the favorite cafe of Proust and Stendahl, you can bask in the view while lingering over a coffee. *Piazza San Marco.* ☎ *041-522105.*

⑤ ★★★ Basilica di San Marco. Venice's Byzantine extravaganza is a shrine to the city's patron saint. Sometime around A.D. 800, or so the story goes, Venetian traders stole Mark's body from Alexandria, where he had been bishop, wrapped the remains in pork to deter Muslim guards from prying, and smuggled the prize back home. The saint soon became a symbol of the city's power—and the multidomed, mosaic-paved basilica built in the 11th century as the saint's resting place still evokes the might of the Venetian republic.

The spectacular ceiling mosaics of the Basilica di San Marco contain gold, bronze, and a variety of gemstones.

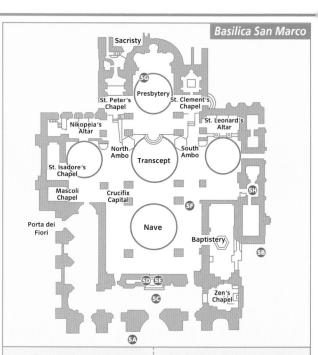

Basilica San Marco

Sacristy
Presbytery
5G
St. Peter's Chapel
St. Clement's Chapel
St. Leonard's Altar
Nikopeia's Altar
North Ambo
South Ambo
Transcept
St. Isadore's Chapel
Mascoli Chapel
Crucifix Capital
5F
5H
Porta dei Fiori
Nave
Baptistery
5B
5D 5E
5C
Zen's Chapel
5A

In the **5A main facade** of the Basilica di San Marco, the combined effect of glittering mosaics, domes, and double rows of arches is best appreciated from the center of the piazza. Some claim that the **5B Tetrarchs,** four figures depicting Byzantine emperors, are actually infidels turned to stone while pilfering church treasures. In the **5C atrium,** illiterate believers boned up on the Old Testament with lively mosaic depictions of the story of the Creation, Noah and the flood, and other biblical narratives. In the **5D Galleria,** make the climb for a close-up look at the atrium's ceiling mosaics; for the bird's-eye view of the piazza from the loggia; and to see the gilded bronze horses, loot from the 4th Crusade, in the **5E Museo Marciano.** (The horses on the loggia are copies.)

More than 3.8 sq. km (1½ sq. miles) of colorful glass-tile **5F mosaics** sparkle and bedazzle with rich renditions of an ascending Christ, saints, the apostles, and other religious rank and file. Byzantine goldsmiths fashioned the **5G Pala d'Oro** (Golden Altar), Saint Mark's final resting place, in the 10th century. Among the glittering prizes brought back from the Crusades now on view in the **5H Tesoro** (Treasury) are icons, censers (incense containers), and a relic of the true cross. ⏲ *2–3 hr. Piazza San Marco.* ☎ *041-5225205. Basilica: Mon–Sat 9:45am–5pm, Sun 2–5pm (until 4pm Nov–Easter). Museo Marciano: 3€. Daily 9:45am–5pm (until 4:30pm Oct–Mar). Pala d'Oro and Tesoro: 2.50€ Pala; 3€ Tesoro. Mon–Sat 9:45am–5pm, Sun 2–5pm (2–4pm Nov–Easter). Vaporetto: San Marco/Vallaresso.*

A mosaic of Saint Nicholas in the Basilica di San Marco is covered in real gold.

6 ★★ San Zan Degolà. One of Venice's oldest churches, built in A.D. 1007 to honor Saint John the Beheaded, yielded a treasure during recent renovations: Byzantine ceiling and wall frescoes of saints and evangelists from the 11th to 14th centuries. ⏱ *30 min. Campo San Zan Degolà.* ☎ *041-5240672. Mon–Sat 10am–noon. Vaporetto: Riva di Biasio.*

7 ★ San Giacomo dell'Orio. A 1225 renovation of this 10th-century church imparted such Byzantine/Romanesque flourishes as a charming campanile rising above the sleepy square shaded with plane trees. Byzantine capitals, frescoes, and statues are scattered about a 16th-century altarpiece, *The Madonna and Saints,* by Lorenzo Lotto and ceiling paintings by Veronese. ⏱ *30 min. Campo San Giacomo dell'Orio.* ☎ *041-2750462. 3€. Mon–Sat 10am–5pm. Vaporetto: Riva di Biasio.*

8 ★★ Santa Maria e San Donato, Murano. The exterior of the curved 12th-century apse of this church is showily Byzantine and richly decorated with arches, balconies, and columns. Inside, the multicolored mosaics are reminiscent of those in San Marco. Most haunting is a mosaic figure of the Virgin who looks over the apse from a shining field of gold. ⏱ *30 min. Campo San Donato.* ☎ *041-739056.*

Mon–Sat 8:30am–noon, 4–7pm; Sun 4–6pm. Vaporetto: 12 from Fondamenta Nuove to Murano–Museo.

9 ★★★ Santa Maria Assunta, Torcello. The oldest building on the Venetian lagoon dates from the 7th century and once served a population of 20,000. Torcello was abandoned 1,000 years ago, but Byzantine splendors—the campanile, paintings, and mosaics—remain intact. The apse has a simple mosaic of a Madonna and Child, while at the other end of the church, a fear-invoking mosaic cycle portrays the Last Judgment—with lurid images of sinners burning as Lucifer watches. ⏱ *1 hr. Campo San Donato.* ☎ *041-730084. Church: 3€. Mar–Oct daily 10:30am–6pm; Nov–Feb daily 10am–5pm. Campanile: 3€. Mar–Oct daily 10:30am–5:30pm (4:30pm Nov–Feb). Vaporetto: 12 from Murano to Torcello.*

10 ★ Santa Fosca, Torcello. A pentagonal portico surrounds the small and sparsely elegant church built to house the body of Saint Fosca, brought to Torcello in the 11th century. ⏱ *30 min. Campo San Donato.* ☎ *041-739056. Apr–Oct daily 10:30am–5:30pm; Nov–Mar daily 10am–5pm. Vaporetto: Torcello.*

The plain church of San Giacomo dell' Orio is located in a quiet residential area.

Venice's Best Churches

I n Venice's churches—rebuilt over the centuries, lavishly decorated by generations of masters, and often painstakingly restored—the city's history and artistic heritage unfolds. Step into one, and the temptation to see the treasures housed in so many others will probably be irresistible. START: **Piazza San Marco.**

1 ★★★ Basilica di San Marco. Venice merges its links to East and West in an arched, domed, and mosaic-paved Byzantine tour de force. See p 23, **5**.

2 ★★ San Zaccaria. A glorious *Madonna and Child with Saints* by Giovanni Bellini lights up the interior of this Renaissance church dedicated to the father of John the Baptist. See p 57, **1**.

3 ★★ San Francesco della Vigna. One of the finest Renaissance churches in Venice has a 15th-century facade by Andrea Palladio, paintings by Veronese and Giovanni Bellini, and lovely cloisters. See p 58, **11**.

4 ★★ Santi Giovanni e Paolo. The largest Gothic church in Venice, completed in 1430, is a showy bastion of the Dominican order and

The San Giacomo di Rialto clock tower was built in the 15th century, though the church itself is much older.

The church of San Zaccaria supposedly contains the body of John the Baptist's father.

an unofficial pantheon of doges, many of whom are buried there. See p 58, **8**.

5 ★★★ Santa Maria dei Miracoli. Sheathed in white marble and perfectly proportioned, this Renaissance creation looks like an ornamental jewelry box. See p 66, **10**.

6 ★ San Giacomo di Rialto. The oldest church in Venice was founded in the 5th century and restored in the 11th century. See p 23, **1**.

7 ★ San Giacomo dell'Orio. A distinctive ship's-keel ceiling from 1225 shelters the apse here, and ceiling paintings by Veronese decorate a chapel. See p 25, **7**.

The altar of Santa Maria dei Miracoli contains colored marble.

8 **Al Prosecco.** An equally well-known landmark next to San Giacomo dell'Orio, this *enoteca* (wine shop) serves the namesake sparkling white as well as many other wines by the glass. *Campo San Giacomo dell'Orio, Santa Croce.* ☎ *041-5240222.*

9 ★★ **San Zan Degolà.** Recent restorations of this church have revealed simple but exquisite Byzantine frescoes. *See p 25,* **6**.

10 ★★ **Santa Maria Gloriosa dei Frari.** The massive Italian Gothic edifice is a treasure house of remarkable paintings and sculptures by Titian, Donatello, Bellini, and others. *See p 33,* **10**.

11 ★★ **San Sebastiano.** Paolo Veronese's fresco cycle and huge canvases pay tribute to the namesake saint here. *See p 32,* **7**.

12 ★★ **Santa Maria della Salute.** The glimmering white basilica stands guard over the entrance to the Grand Canal. Inside is Tintoretto's *Wedding at Cana*, Titian's *Saint Mark Enthroned with Saints*, and other treasures. *See p 11,* **1**.

13 ★★★ **Il Redentore.** Built to assuage the plague of 1576, Andrea Palladio's graceful church is a stately presence on the islands of the Giudecca. *See p 46,* **1**.

14 **Palladio Garden Bar.** Contemplate Palladian restraint while enjoying a drink in the delightful garden of the former convent of **La Zitelle** (see p 46, **1**), now a worldly and elegant hotel. *Fondamenta delle Zitelle, Giudecca.* ☎ *041-5207022.*

The cloisters of San Giorgio Maggiore, a Benedictine monastery.

The exterior of the 12th-century Byzantine Santa Maria e San Donato, on Murano.

⑮ ★★★ San Giorgio Maggiore. An elegant church by architect Andrea Palladio graces this island directly across the lagoon from San Marco. *See p 46,* ②.

⑯ ★★ Santa Maria e San Donato, Murano. In the curved, 12th-century apse is a sea of multicolored mosaics. *See p 25,* ⑧.

⑰ ★★★ Santa Maria Assunta, Torcello. The oldest building on the Venetian lagoon is adorned with a glorious, fearsome mosaic cycle of *The Last Judgment. See p 25,* ⑨.

A mosaic of the Virgin and Child in the Basilica di Santa Maria Assunta, on the island of Torcello.

Master of Classicism

The most stately of Venice's churches are the work of Andrea Palladio (1508–80), who was born in Padua and spent most of his life in Venice. Perhaps the greatest architect of the Renaissance, Palladio studied the ruins of ancient Rome and turned to the classical elements of symmetry, proportion, and harmony for the villas he built for nobility on the mainland and the churches he designed in Venice. In such churches as Il Redentore and San Giorgio Maggiore, look for the telltale elements of Palladian style—tall columns, porticos like those on Roman temples, and domes.

Art in Venice

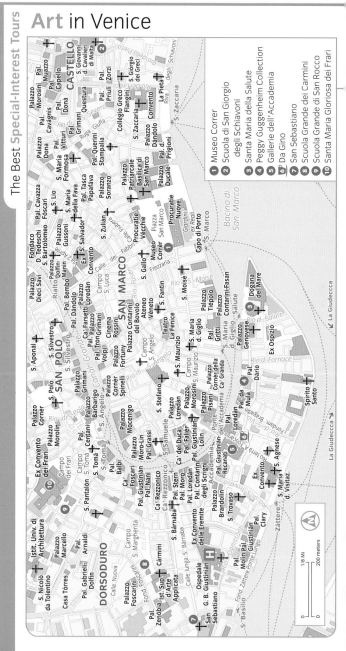

1 Museo Correr
2 Scuola di San Giorgio degli Schiavoni
3 Santa Maria della Salute
4 Peggy Guggenheim Collection
5 Gallerie dell'Accademia
6 Da Gino
7 San Sebastiano
8 Scuola Grande dei Carmini
9 Scuola Grande di San Rocco
10 Santa Maria Gloriosa dei Frari

Can you actually see the great works of Venetian art in a day? If you're ambitious and pressed for time, yes. But it's hard to resist the temptation to linger for hours in any number of the city's fine museums and churches. If you're on a more leisurely trip, you can do this tour over the course of several days. START: **Piazza San Marco.**

❶ ★ **Museo Correr.** The Museum of the City and Civilization of Venice provides some fascinating glimpses of Venetian life. In Carpaccio's *Two Venetian Ladies*, the bored subjects wait for their husbands to return from hunting. Among the other curiosities is a pair of sandals with 2-foot-tall heels upon which women of fashion once tottered. ⏱ *1 hr. Piazza San Marco.* ☎ *041-5225625. Single ticket not available; 12€ for entry to all civic museums. Easter–Nov daily 9am–7pm; Nov–Easter daily 9am–5pm.*

❷ ★★ **Scuola di San Giorgio degli Schiavoni.** Carpaccio spent 5 years painting his *Cycle of Saint George,* an homage to the patron saint of the Slavic members of this *scuola* (guild). The painter's lush colors and flair for storytelling bring dragon-slaying to vivid life; detailed depictions of decomposing bodies, ferocious dragons, and out-of-body experiences may captivate you for hours. ⏱ *30 min. Calle dei Furlani.* ☎ *041-2750642. 3€. Mon 2:45–6pm; Tues–Sat 9:15am–1pm, 2:45–6pm;*

A depiction of the 1380 Battle of Chioggia, in the Museo Correr.

Sun 9:15am–1pm. Vaporetto: San Zaccaria.

❸ ★★ **Santa Maria della Salute.** Turn your back on the water views and walk up the majestic staircase of this baroque church to admire Tintoretto's *Wedding at Cana,* Titian's *Saint Mark Enthroned with Saints,* and other masterworks. *See p 11,* ❶.

Carpaccio's Cycle of Saint George, *in the Scuola di San Giorgio degli Schiavoni.*

A detail from Veronese's Feast in the House of Levi, *in the Accademia.*

④ ★★★ Peggy Guggenheim Collection. Picassos, Klees, and Miròs hang in airy, light-filled galleries along the Grand Canal, all of it a refreshing antidote to the religious fervor that permeates most Venetian art. *See p 11,* ③.

⑤ ★★★ Gallerie dell'Accademia. Three former religious buildings house the city's major art collection, a vast repository of Venetian art from the Byzantine to the rococo. A contemplation of just a few of the masterpieces here—Bellini's *San Giobbi* altarpiece, Veronese's *Feast in the House of Levi,* and Titian's *Pietà,* for example—is an experience long remembered. *See p 34.*

⑥ Da Gino. At this handy stop on the well-worn path between the Guggenheim and the Accademia, take an outdoor table and linger over a glass of wine and one of the delicious panini. *Calle Nuova Sant'Agese, Dorsoduro.* ☎ *041-5285276.*

⑦ ★★ San Sebastiano. Paolo Veronese's frescoes of the church's namesake saint cover the walls, ceilings, even the organ doors. More striking than the saint's gruesome martyrdom, perhaps, is the artist's fascination with sumptuous colors and lavish costumes. ⏱ *30 min. Fondamenta di San Sebastiano.* ☎ *041-2750642. 3€. Mon–Sat 10am–5pm. Vaporetto: San Basilio.*

⑧ ★★ Scuola Grande dei Carmini. In this remarkably well-preserved *scuola* founded by the Carmelites in the 17th century, one of Giambattista Tiepolo's great masterpieces, *The Virgin in Glory Appearing to the Blessed Simon Stock,* flows across the ceiling of the upper salon. Mirrors provided to view the painting help visitors capture the drama of the Virgin handing the saint a scapular, a length of cloth draped over the shoulders as a sign of servitude. ⏱ *30 min. See p 13,* ⑦.

⑨ ★★ Scuola Grande di San Rocco. When the affluent school dedicated to San Rocco wanted to entrust an artist with the decoration, Tintoretto one-upped the competition and presented a completed painting rather than a sketch as a sample design. He spent the next 23 years filling the interior with depictions of the saint and his heavenly consorts that reveal the painter's masterly command of light and perspective. ⏱ *30 min. See p 13,* ⑧.

Titian's Assumption of the Virgin, *in Santa Maria Gloriosa dei Frari.*

⑩ ★★ Santa Maria Gloriosa dei Frari. By the time the massive Italian Gothic edifice was completed—around 1440—this was one of the largest churches in Venice; the campanile is the second highest on the lagoon, outstripped only by that of San Marco. The church is filled with remarkable paintings and sculpture.

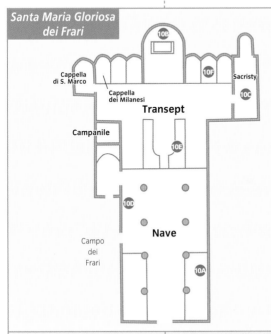

Santa Maria Gloriosa dei Frari

Cappella di S. Marco

Cappella dei Milanesi

Sacristy

Transept

Campanile

Nave

Campo dei Frari

A Titian's tomb is a banal monument to the artist who bathed the church in bold colors. Titian succumbed to the plague in 1576 at age 90; the monument was put up 300 years later. In Titian's powerful rendition of the **B Assumption of the Virgin,** Mary ascends from a crowd of awe-struck apostles amid a swirl of *putti* (cherubs). Giovanni Bellini's triptych, the **C Madonna Enthroned with Saints,** is filled with lute-playing angels. Elsewhere, Titian painted **D Madonna di Ca' Pesaro** in honor of Captain Jacopo Pesaro, whose papal fleet had just defeated the Turks. A refined Renaissance sculptural grouping, the **E Monuments to Doge Nicolò Tron and Doge Francesco Foscari,** rises above the tomb of Doge Tron. Foscari, interred across from Tron, died of a broken heart when his son Jacopo was exiled in 1547 on bribery and corruption charges. It's also hard not to feel a pang of sympathy for **F John the Baptist,** who in Donatello's amazingly lifelike rendering is decidedly scrawny and bedraggled. 🕐 *1 hr. Campo dei Frari.* 📞 *041-5222637. 1.55€. Mon–Sat 9am–6pm; Sun 1–6pm. Vaporetto: San Tomà.*

The Gallerie dell'Accademia

Christ in the House of Levi
4

WC

Gift Shop

Courtyard

2

1

3

Story of St. Ursula
7

6

5

Courtyard

8

Former Church of La Carità

Entrance

1 Room 2
2 Room 5
3 Room 7
4 Room 10
5 Room 17
6 Room 20
7 Room 21
8 Room 24

Painting locations subject to change

Venice's largest museum was founded in the 19th century to house art from churches and convents suppressed by Napoleon. Today's galleries occupy a complex including the monastery of the Lateran Canons, the church of La Carità, and the Scuola Santa Maria della Carità. A visit is a stroll through the great periods of Venetian art. ***Please note:*** Because of ongoing renovations, paintings may be relocated within the galleries. START: **Vaporetto to Accademia.**

1 **Room 2.** Among eight magnificent altarpieces is Giovanni Bellini's *Virgin and Child with Saints,* often known as the ★★★ *Pala di San Giobbe* (for the Venetian church that commissioned the piece).

2 **Room 5.** The symbolism of ★★ *The Tempest* by Giorgione, a portrayal of a woman suckling her infant in an eerie cast of green light, has evaded scholars for centuries, adding to the work's appealing

mystery. The artist's *Old Woman,* hanging nearby, evokes the brevity of life—made all the more poignant by the fact that the painter died of the plague at age 35.

3 **Room 7.** Lorenzo Lotto's bold, stark ★★ *Portrait of a Young Gentleman in His Study* suggests that moodiness, self-absorption, and psychic unrest are not uniquely modern-day preoccupations.

4 Room 10. Three great 16th-century masters convene in one room. Veronese painted his ★★ *Feast in the House of Levi* as a *Last Feast*, but church authorities found the ribaldry and Venetian setting heretical, so he changed the name. Titian, at 90, painted the *Pietà* for his tomb but died before finishing it. Tintoretto's ★★ **Saint Mark cycle** includes some of his finest works, illustrating, among other moments, the theft of the saint's body.

5 Room 17. Canaletto's views of the Grand Canal, Francesco Guardi's *Isola di San Giorgio,* and other pleasant 18th-century Venetian scenes may be familiar. What you may not have seen before are the works of a female artist, Rosalba Carriera.

6 Room 20. In the 15th and 16th centuries, the Scuola di San Giovanni Evangelista commissioned Venetian painters to illustrate *Miracles of the Relic of the True Cross*. Carpaccio's effort is a fascinatingly detailed look at Venice in that distant past, when a wooden bridge crossed the Grand Canal at the Rialto.

7 Room 21. Carpaccio's ★★ **Story of Saint Ursula** is a color-saturated, action-packed

Hans Memling's Portrait of a Young Man before a Landscape, *in the Accademia.*

medieval travelogue in which the Breton princess and her English betrothed, Hereus, travel to Rome so the groom-to-be can be converted to the true faith.

8 Room 24. Titian painted his *Presentation of the Virgin to the Temple* for this room, the former *albergo* (hostel) of the Scuola della Carità. This elegant rendering is a graceful endnote to our visit. 🕐 *2–3 hr. Campo Carità.* ☎ *041-5222247. €6.50. Mon 8:15am–2pm; Tues–Sun 8:15am–7:15pm. Vaporetto: Accademia.*

Arrival of the English Ambassadors, *by Carpaccio, in the Accademia.*

Great Palazzi of Venice

0 1/8 Mi
0 200 meters

CANNAREGIO

GHETTO
Sinagoghe
(Museo Ebráico)

Scuola dei Mercanti
Madonna dell'Orto
Casino dei Spiriti
Pal. Arrigoni
Pal. Mastelli
Pal. Contarini dal Zaffo
Casa di Tintoretto
Sacca della Misericordia
Ex Convento S. M. dei Servi
Cappella d. Volto Santo
S. Marziale
Scuola Vécchia d. Misericordia
S. Maria d. Misericordia
Ex Convento e Chiesa di S. Caterina
Gesuiti
Pal. Donà
Fond. Nove
Pal. Seriman
Pal. Labia
S. Marcuola
Pal. Diedo
La Maddalena
Pal. Lezze
Vendramin
Pal. Papafava
Ex Convento
S. Geremia
Riva da Biásio
Pal. Erizzo
Pal. Molin
S. Fosca
Rio terra S. Leonardo
Fond. d. Turchi
Ca' S. Stae
S. Felice
Rio di S. Felice
S. Sofia
Ss. Apóstoli
S. Canciano
Pal. Widman
Pal. Marcello-Toderini
S. Zan Degola
S. Stae
Palazzo Mocenigo
Ca' d'Oro
Strada Nuova
Ca' d'Oro
Pal. Mangilli
Ca' da Mosto
Pal. Grifalconi
Pal. Soranzo-Van Axel
SANTA CROCE
S. Giacomo dell'Orio
S. Maria Máter Domini
Pal. Zane Domini
Ca' Pesaro
Palazzo Brandolin
Pescaria
Fábbriche Nuove
Pal. Civran
Teatro Málibran
Pal. Grioni
S. Cassiano
Pal. Muti Baglioni
Palazzo Dieci Savi
Ponte di Rialto
Fóndaco D. Tedeschi
S. Bartolomeo
Pal. Marcelo Pindemonte
Palazzo Dona
Pal. Zane Collalto
SAN POLO
Campo S. Polo
S. Polo
S. Silvestro
Rialto
Palazzo Dolfin-Manin
Palazzo Gussoni
S. Maria Formosa
Ex Convento dei Frari
Palazzo Morolin
Pal. Centani
Palazzo Grimani
Pal. Dándolo
Pal. Farsetti
Pal. Loredán
S. Salvador
Ex Convento
S. Zuliàn
Pal. Tasca Papafáva
S. Maria G. dei Frari
S. Tomà
S. Angelo
Pal. Volpi
Cinema Rossini
SAN MARCO
Palazzo Soranzo
Pal. Balbi
S. Tomà
Palazzo Corner Spinelli
Pal. Contarini del Bovolo
Procuratie Vécchie
Palazzo Patriarcale
Ca' Foscari
Palazzo Mocenigo
Palazzo Moro-Lin
Campo S. Angelo
Ateneo Véneto
S. Gallo
S. Stefano
S. Fantin
Museo Correr
Procuratie Nuove
Basilica di San Marco
Pal. Nani
Pal. Grassi
S. Samuele
Palazzo Loredàn
Teatro La Fenice
S. Maurizio
Piazza San Marco
Pal. d. Prigioni
Pal. Moro
Ca' del Duca
Pal. Falièr
Palazzo Morosini
S. Moisè
Palazzo Ducale
Pal. Loredàn
Accademia
Bárbaro Pisani
Palazzo Corner della Ca' Granda
S. Maria d. Giglio
Palazzo Giustiniàn
Giardini ex Reali
Gallerie dell'Accademia
Ponte dell'Accademia
Pal. Ferro Fini
Pal. Gritti
Palazzo Tiépolo
S. Marco
S. Maria d. Visitaz.
S. Agnese
Pal. Venier dei Leoni (Guggenheim)
Pal. Genovese
S. Maria d. Salute
Dogana da Mar
Bacino di San Marco
Gesuati
Ex Ospizio
Záttere
Spirito Santo
Fond. Záttere ai Saloni
Canale della Giudecca
Palanca
Fónd. S. Giacomo
Ísola della Giudecca
Redentore
Il Redentore
Ex Chiesa della Croce

1 Palazzo Cini
2 Museo Fortuny
3 Museo della Fondazione Querini Stampalia
4 Palazzo Ducale
5 Pizzeria Accademia
6 Ca' Rezzonico/Museo del Settecento Veneziano
7 Ca' Pesaro
8 Ca' d'Oro

Venetian nobility began building elaborate palaces as early as the 1st century. The best address, of course, was on the Grand Canal, though none of the residences built along this busy waterway or elsewhere in the city were technically known as palaces—the term *palazzo* was reserved for the home and headquarters of the doge. Many of these palazzi now house exquisite collections of art, making a visit doubly rewarding. START: **Piazza San Marco.**

1 ★★ Palazzo Cini. A collector's eye is much in evidence in the home of industrialist Vittorio Cini (1885–1977), who filled the rooms with religious works by Sandro Botticelli, Piero della Francesca, and other Tuscan painters. ⏱ *45 min. Campo Carità.* ☎ *041-5222247. Open only for special events and exhibitions; prices and times vary. Vaporetto: Accademia.*

2 ★ Museo Fortuny. Mariano Fortuny (1871–1949), the Spanish artist and textile designer, bought and restored this 15th-century palazzo. The exotic fashions he created for the rich and famous using medieval dyeing and threading techniques are now on display in the salons. ⏱ *1 hr. Campo San Beneto.* ☎ *041-5200995. 8€. Wed–Mon 10am–6pm. Vaporetto: San Angelo.*

3 ★ Museo della Fondazione Querini Stampalia. Giovanni Querini, a 19th-century scientist, bequeathed his family palazzo and fabulous art to the city of Venice, with the proviso that the premises remain open in the evening. The recently renovated galleries are still the late-night place to see enticing scenes of Venetian life by Pietro Longhi and Giovanni Bellini, as well as contemporary works. ⏱ *45 min. Campo Santa Maria Formosa.* ☎ *041-2711411. www.querinistampalia.it. Museum: 8€. Tues–Sat 10am–8pm; Sun 10am–7pm. Library: Free admission. Tues–Sat 10pm–midnight; Sun 10–7pm. Vaporetto: Rialto.*

4 ★★★ Palazzo Ducale. Doges ruled the Venetian republic from this suitably grandiose palace, built and rebuilt many times from the 7th to the 18th centuries. It's a testament to the stability of the state that the palace was not a castle or fortress but an elegant assemblage of pink and white marble. The facade is punctuated with sculpted figures representing wisdom and other virtues, and the 18 pointed archways are not just decorative: The doges witnessed public executions from the central arch.

The dungeon is part of the medieval fairy tale of the Palazzo Ducale.

Palazzo Ducale

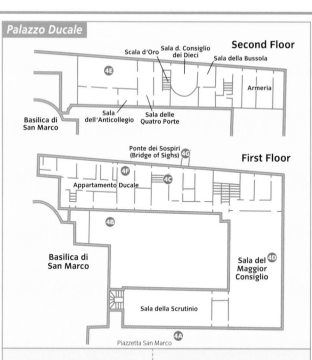

Second Floor

Scala d'Oro
Sala d. Consiglio dei Dieci
Sala della Bussola
Armeria
4E
Basilica di San Marco
Sala dell'Anticollegio
Sala delle Quatro Porte

First Floor

Ponte dei Sospiri (Bridge of Sighs) **4G**
4F
4C
Appartamento Ducale
4B
Basilica di San Marco
Sala del Maggior Consiglio **4D**
Sala della Scrutinio
4A
Piazzetta San Marco

The **4A Porta della Carta** of the Palazzo Ducale, an elaborate archway of pink marble, is named for the edicts once posted here and graced with the two ubiquitous symbols of Venice: Saint Mark and the winged lion. In the courtyard beyond, the **4B Giant's Staircase** is flanked by statues of Mars and Neptune; doges were sworn in at the top. **4C Scala d'Oro,** the Golden Staircase, was designed by 16th-century classicist Sansovino to impress visiting dignitaries. It ascends beneath a 24-carat gold leaf ceiling. The Venetian Grand Council met in the vast **4D Sala del Maggior Consiglio** to appoint holders of public office and to elect new doges. Portraits of 76 of these officials line the walls beneath a ceiling painting of *Paradise* by Jacopo and Domenico Tintoretto; a likeness of doge Marino Faller, beheaded in the 14th century for betraying the senate, is painted over. In the **4E Sala dei Senato,** nobles debated state affairs as the doge looked on from his throne. The **4F Sala dello Scudo** houses the globes and maps that enabled officials to keep track of trade routes and the discoveries of Marco Polo and other explorers. Much-romanticized but quite utilitarian, the **4G Ponte dei Sospiri,** the Bridge of Sighs, links the palace with a 17th-century prison (see p 48, **1**). ⏱ *1 hr. Piazzetta San Marco.* 📞 *041-5224951. Single ticket not available; 12€ for entry to all civic museums. Easter–Nov daily 9am–7pm; Nov–Easter daily 9am–5pm. Vaporetto: San Marco/Vallaresso.*

The white marble facade of the Venetian Baroque Ca' Rezzonico.

5 **Pizzeria Accademia.** It's hard to cross the Accademia Bridge without stopping to take a seat on the waterside terrace here to watch traffic chug up and down the Grand Canal. The pizza, panini, and tramezzi are satisfying as well. *Rio Terra Foscarini.* ☎ *041-5227281.*

6 ★★ **Ca' Rezzonico.** In the one-time home of poets Robert Browning and Elizabeth Barrett Browning, sweeping staircases and flamboyant salons are the backdrop for the **Museo del Settecento Veneziano's** 18th-century artworks, including views of the Grand Canal by Canaletto and Pietro Longhi's scenes of everyday Venetian life. ⏱ *1 hr. Fondamenta Rezzonico.* ☎ *041-2410100. 6.50€. Apr–Oct Wed–Mon 10am–6pm; Nov–Mar Wed–Mon 10am–5pm Vaporetto: Ca' Rezzonico.*

7 ★ **Ca' Pesaro.** In 1628, the illustrious Pesaro family (who appear with so little humility next to the Madonna in Titian's *Madonna di Ca' Pesaro in the Frari;* see p 33, **D**) commissioned architect Baldassare Longhena to combine three Gothic houses to create one of Venice's largest palaces. The elaborate surroundings now house the **Museo d'Arte Orientale**

and the **Galleria Internazionale di Arte Moderna.** Swords, puppets, and other paraphernalia from Japan in the Oriental galleries were the passion of a 19th-century Venetian count-collector. Many of the works in the modern galleries are by De Chirico, Morandi, and other Italians. Chagall, Klimt, Klee, Miró, and the rest of the international Modernist crowd are well represented, too. ⏱ *1 hr.* ☎ *041-5240662. 5.50€. Apr–Oct Tues–Sun 10am–6pm; Nov–Mar Tues–Sun 10am–5pm. Vaporetto: San Stae.*

8 ★ **Ca' d'Oro.** The golden facade that gave this palace its name has faded, but a mosaic-paved entryway, a marble wellhead in the courtyard, and a second-floor balcony overlooking the Grand Canal provide a glimpse of the lifestyle of Renaissance nobility. And plenty of treasures remain within at the **Galleria Franchetti.** *Saint Sebastian,* by Andrea Mantegna, is the artist's last painting and often considered his best. A transcendent *Annunciation* by Carpaccio and works by other masters such as Tintoretto, Signorelli, Titian, and Guardi make a good showing, too. ⏱ *1 hr. Calle Ca' d'Oro.* ☎ *041-5200345. 5€. Mon 8:15am–2pm; Tues–Sun 8:15am–7:15pm. Vaporetto: Ca d'Oro.*

Portrait of a Priest, *by Carena, in the Galleria Internazionale d'Arte Moderna, in Ca' Pesaro.*

Venice's **Best Squares**

1 Piazza San Marco
2 Campo Santi Giovanni e
   San Paolo (San Zanipòlo)
3 Campo della Maddalena
4 Campiello dei Remer
5 Campo Santa Margherita
6 Campo San Barnaba
7 Tonolo
8 Campo San Polo
9 All'Arco
10 The Rialto

0 _____ 1/4 Mi
0 _____ 1/2Km

Laguna
Veneta

Monastero
Carmelitane
Scalze

† La Cappucine
Campo Ghetto
Nuovo
CANNAREGIO

GHETTO

Scuola dei
Mercanti

Madonna
dell'Orto

Casa di
Tintoretto

Casino
d. Spiriti

Sacca della
Misericordia

Isola di S. Michele

S. Maria d.
Misericordia

Pal. Labià
S. Marcuola
La Maddalena
Pal.
Vendramin Pal.
Papafava

Gesuiti
Pal. Donà

S. Marziale †
S. Geremia
Pal.
Erizzo

Ca'
Tron
Ca' Pesaro
Palazzo
Brandolin

Pal.
Boldù
Ca'
d'Oro

S. Felice

S. Sofia

Ss. Apóstoli Pal.
Widman

S. Maria
d. Pianto

Pal. Lezze †
S. Fosca

S. Zan
Degolà
S. Stae

S. Giacomo
dell'Orio †

S. Maria †
Máter
Domini

S. Cassiano

Pescaria
Ca' da
Mosto

Teatro
Málibran

Ospedale
Civile

Ss. Giovanni e
Paolo (S. Zanipolo)

SANTA
CROCE

Fábbriche
Nuove

Fóndaco
D. Tedeschi

Pal. Donà
CASTELLO

Ex Convento
dei Frari

Palazzo
Morolin

SAN POLO
S. Silvestro
Ponte
di Rialto
S. Bartolomeo

S. Maria
Formosa

S. Lorenzo
Pal.
Gritti

S. Rocco †
S. Maria G.
dei Frari
S. Polo

S. Salvador

S. Tomà
Palazzo
Grimani
Ca' Farsetti

Pal. Querini
Stampalia

S. Giovanni Novo

Questura

S. Pantalòn
Ca'
Fóscari
Palazzo
Mocenigo
Cinema
Rossini
SAN MARCO
Pal. Contarini
del Bovolo

Basílica di
San Marco

S. Zaccaria

Pal. Nani
Pal. Grassi
Ateneo Véneto
Teatro
La Fenice
S. Fantin
S. Moisè

La Pietà

Ca' Rezzonico
S. Stefano

Ca' del Duca
Pal. Falièr
Palazzo
Morosini
S. Maria
d. Giglio

S. Bárnaba
Gallerie
dell'Accademia
Palazzo
Pisani
Pal.
Gritti
Palazzo
Tiépolo

S. Trovaso
Pal. Venièr
dei Leoni
(Guggenheim)

S. Maria
d. Salute
Dogana
da Mar

Pal.
Clary
S. Agnese
Gesuati
Spirito
Santo

Palazzo
Ducale

Giardini
ex Reali

S. Maria
d. Visitaz.

Bacino di
San Marco

San Giorgio
Maggiore

Canale di S. Marco

Canale della Giudecca

Fondàm. S. Giácomo

Isola della
Giudecca
Zitelle

Isola di
San Giorgio
Maggiore

Il Redentore †

Ex Chiesa
della Croce

Canàl Grande

Strada Nuova

Outdoor life in Venice is a social enterprise, often transpiring in a lively *campo* (square). A church or two, a few palazzi, a cafe, a row of market stalls, a nearby canal are the backdrops for these outdoor stages, and scenes of Venetian life are the show. START: **Piazza San Marco.**

1 ★★★ Piazza San Marco. The only square in Venice to be known as a *piazza* rather than a *campo* is referred to simply as "the Piazza." Napoleon called the square the "finest drawing room in Europe," evoking San Marco's air of civility and sophistication as well as its raison d'être: It's a place for Venetians and their visitors to rub shoulders, drink coffee, and gawk for the first or the thousandth time at the exotic arches and domes. ⏱ *30 min. See p 7,* **5**.

2 ★★★ Campo Santi Giovanni e San Paolo. Also known as **San Zanipòlo,** there's an amiable bustle of activity around the massive basilica, the medieval Scuola Grande di San Marco, and Verrocchio's equestrian statue of Bartolomeo Colleoni here. *See p 15,* **4**.

3 ★ Campo della Maddalena. Small houses topped with fantastically shaped chimney pots and a

The Piazza San Marco hosts an open-air orchestra.

round, canal-side church lend an exotic air to this backwater corner where little has changed since the Middle Ages. ⏱ *15 min. Cannaregio. Vaporetto: Ca' d'Oro.*

4 ★ Campiello dei Remer. No small part of this little square's charm is the Grand Canal, lapping up against one side of the pavement. Byzantine arches gracing an adjoining palazzo and an ornately decorated well supply a picturesque backdrop for the colorful flotilla ever-present on the canal. ⏱ *15 min. Castello. Vaporetto: Rialto.*

5 ★★★ Campo Santa Margherita. Two churches and two *scuoli* share this welcoming square with cafes, market stalls, and, on a fine day, what seems to be most of the population of Venice stealing a few moments in the sun. The eponymous saint, patron of expectant mothers, is remembered twice: A dragon, her symbol, embellishes a

Verrocchio's equestrian statue in the Campo Santi Giovanni e San Paolo.

niche on the north end, and another decorates the base of the truncated campanile of her namesake church. ◷ *30 min. Dorsoduro. Vaporetto: Ca' Rezzonico.*

6 ★★ **Campo San Barnaba.** Nothing about this little square is what might be termed spectacular, but even a brief walk across its old paving stones is likely to be memorable. The 14th-century campanile of the namesake church rises above the small houses; a boat moored alongside a quay serves as the neighborhood greengrocer; and just downstream is the picturesquely arched Ponte dei Pugni (Bridge of the Punches), where rival clans once slugged out their differences. ◷ *15 min. Dorsoduro. Vaporetto: Ca' Rezzonico.*

7 **Tonolo.** Venetians go out of their way to find themselves in Campo San Pantalon—for the chance to step into the city's legendary pastry shop for a buttery croissant and what many claim is the best cappuccino in all of Venice. *Calle San Pantalon.* ☎ *041-5224410.*

8 ★★ **Campo San Polo.** *Bull Baiting in the Campo San Polo,* a 17th-century painting by German artist Joseph Heintz hanging in the Museo Correr (see p 31, **1**), provides a telling glimpse of the colorful past of this large square, still the lively heart of its namesake neighborhood. These days, the top crowd-drawing spectacle is a summertime outdoor cinema, though the neighborhood comings and goings provide an amusing show at any time. ◷ *15 min. San Polo. Vaporetto: San Tomà.*

9 **All'Arco.** Almost as much a part of the Rialto as the markets, this old-fashion *bacaro* (wine bar) serves tasty *cicheti* (bar snacks). *Calle dell'Ochialer, San Polo.* ☎ *041-5205666.*

10 ★★ **The Rialto.** A series of campos along the Grand Canal accommodate the hustle, bustle, and everyday business around the Ponte di Rialto. Fishmongers, businesspeople, housewives, and, of course, the ubiquitous sightseers congregate in the markets and along narrow alleys of this area. The scene may not be that different today as it was in the 5th century.

A floating greengrocer moored along the quay near the Campo San Barnaba.

The Rialto

Palazzo
Mangilli

Pescaria

10G

Campo della
Pescaria

Rio della Beccarie

Calle Beccarie

Ca' da
Mosto

10F

Campo
Beccarie

Ruga d. Speziale

C. d. Donzella

Fabbriche
Nuove

Canal

Grande

Calle San Mattio

Ruga due Mori

Ruga Vecchia San Giovanni

Campo
della
Cordaria

10D

Palazzo
Civran

10E

San Giovanni
Elemosinario

10B

10A

10C

Fabbriche
Vecchie

San Giacomo
di Rialto

Palazzo
Dieci Savi

Campo
di Rialto
Nuovo

Calle Toscana

Calle d. Madonna

Ruga d. Orefici

Pal. dei
Camerlenghi

Ruga Ravano

C. d. Storione

Dogana di Terra

Calle dei Cinque

Fóndaco
dei Tedeschi

Fondam. del Vin

Ponte di
Rialto

Riva del Ferro

Salizz. Pio X

0   50 yards

0   50 meters

N

The Rialto is centered around the
**A Campo San Giacomo di
Rialto,** a sea of fruit and vegetable
stalls above which rise the facade and
campanile of the oldest church in
Venice, founded the same year as the
city, 421. The present structure dates
to the 11th century. The **B Gobbo
di Rialto,** the "Hunchback of the
Rialto," crouches on one side of the
campo beneath a rostrum from which
proclamations were read. For some
Venetians, the humble figure was a
welcome sight—he marked the end
of a "walk of shame" that those found
guilty of petty crimes were forced to
make naked from San Marco.
C Calle de Banco Giro is a covered passageway that may have been
the world's first banking premises:
Merchants and moneylenders once
gathered here to take advantage of
the city's "giro" system, a paperless
transfer of funds from one party to

another. In **D Campo Erberia,**
stalls piled high with fresh fruit and
vegetables stand in the shadow of
the Fabbriche Nuove and the Fabbriche Vecchie, 16th-century warehouses. **E Ruga degli Orefici,**
the "Passageway of the Goldsmiths,"
still houses a few shops selling gold
and silver, as it has since the 14th
century. In **F Campo Beccarie,**
market stalls selling meat maintain
a long-standing tradition—the
city's abattoir once stood here. In
G Campo della Pescaria, the
porticos of a neo-Gothic hall shelter a
daily fish market. Alleyways leading
off the square likewise bear the telltale names of the tradesmen who
once set up shop in the environs
(Casaria, "Cheese") and of the taverns
that served them (Due Mori, the "Two
Moors"). ⏱ *30 min. San Polo. Daily
7am–1pm. Vaporetto: Rialto.*

Venice's Most Memorable Views

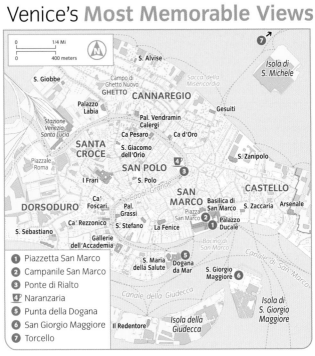

1. Piazzetta San Marco
2. Campanile San Marco
3. Ponte di Rialto
4. Naranzaria
5. Punta della Dogana
6. San Giorgio Maggiore
7. Torcello

Venice is the most whimsical of places, and the play of sky, water, and marble is all the more transporting from any of the city's viewpoints. START: **Piazza San Marco.**

1 ★ Piazzetta San Marco.
No other Venetian view imparts a greater sense of the city as a maritime republic. Two columns (one dedicated to San Marco, one to San Teodoro, the city's other patron saint) frame a flotilla of gondolas and the shimmering waters of the lagoon. Rising out of a sea mist are the domes and towers of Salute, San Giorgio, Redentore, and many other great monuments of Venice. ◷ 15 min. San Marco. Vaporetto: San Marco/Vallaresso.

2 ★★ Campanile San Marco.
A bell tower has risen above the

Piazza San Marco since the 10th century—with the exception of a decade in the early 20th century, when the brick structure by Renaissance master Bertola Bon collapsed without warning on July 14, 1902. The expansive outlook over the city, the sea, and the countryside all the way north to the Alps was restored with the completion of a new tower in 1912. ◷ 1 hr. (or longer, depending on wait). Piazza San Marco. ☎ 041-5224064. 6€. Apr–June, Oct–Nov daily 9am–7pm; July–Sept daily 9am–9pm; Dec–April daily 9:30am–3:45pm. Vaporetto: San Marco/Vallaresso.

3 ★★ **Ponte di Rialto.** A non-stop water show takes place beneath the most monumental of the spans across the Grand Canal: Gondolas, garbage scows, police launches, and all manner of other craft ply the crowded waterway. Also in close view: the centuries-old commercial heart of the city, the Fondaco dei Tedeschi, built in 1508 as a warehouse and now the city's main post office; the Palazzo dei Camerlenghi, built in 1525 and the world's first-known office building; and two of the city's first palaces, the Palazzo Loredan and Palazzo Farsetti, which now jointly house city hall. ⏰ *30 min. San Polo. Vaporetto: Rialto.*

4 **Naranzaria.** Set your sights on the Grand Canal while enjoying a glass of wine and a sandwich at a table on the *fondamenta* (walkway) just beneath the Rialto bridge. *Ruga d'Orifici, San Polo.* ☎ *041-7241035.*

5 ★★ **Punta della Dogana.** From the Customs house at the tip of the Dorsoduro, San Marco glimmers across the basin. Straight ahead are the sea lanes that seduced so many traders and explorers. ⏰ *15 min. Dorsoduro. Vaporetto: Salute.*

6 ★★★ **San Giorgio Maggiore.** The view from the island's campanile is even more expansive than that from the campanile in San Marco, and there's no wait to ascend. ⏰ *30 min. See p 46,* **2**.

7 ★★ **Torcello.** The highest point on the island of the "little tower" is the 12th-century campanile of the cathedral. A ramp twists to the top, and from here, Venice appears as a phantom city across the waters of the lagoon. ⏰ *30 min.* ☎ *041-2702464. 2€. Mar–Oct daily 10:30am–5:30pm; Nov–Mar daily 10am–4:30pm. Vaporetto: Torcello.*

The spectacular view from the Campanile in Piazza San Marco.

Places to **Escape the Crowds**

1 Giudecca
2 San Giorgio Maggiore
3 Bar San Giorgio
4 San Michele

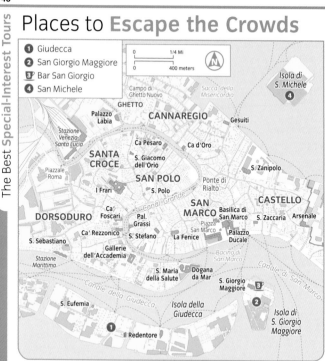

In Venice, an island escape is only a short vaporetto ride away, and the retreat usually comes with a nice smattering of art and architecture. START: **Vaporetto 41, 42, or 82 to Zitelle.**

1 ★★ **Giudecca.** Once a bucolic getaway for wealthy Venetians, this string of eight connected islands still seems far removed from the bustle of the city. Walks through quiet neighborhoods and visits to three famous churches are the pastimes here. **Il Redentore,** the grandest, was begun as an offering to the Redeemer in the midst of a plague outbreak, in 1576. More than a third of the city succumbed to the disease, but work on the church continued for two decades, and it's now an elegant showcase for the restrained classicism of architect Andrea Palladio. **La Zitelle,** the "church of the spinsters," is so

named because young women whose families could not afford a dowry were once sent to the adjoining convent to learn lace making; exile here is a privilege now that the premises house an outpost of the posh Hotel Bauer. The church of **Santa Eufemia** is much older than its Palladian neighbors. It was founded in the 9th century and rebuilt in the 11th century to a Byzantine design. 🕐 *2 hr. Il Redentore: 3€.* ☎ *041-2750642. Mon–Sat 10am–5pm. Vaporetto: Redentore.*

2 ★★★ **San Giorgio Maggiore.** Benedictine monks have inhabited this island directly across the lagoon

from San Marco for more than 1,000 years. They still impose a veil of tranquillity on a stunning complex that includes a church by Andrea Palladio, two cloisters, and a bell tower that affords heart-stopping views over the city and its surroundings (see p 45, ⑥). The **Fondazione Cini,** founded by industrialist Vittorio Cini to support cultural causes, shares the premises with a small community of monks and occasionally hosts conferences and art exhibitions. ⏱ *2 hr.* ☎ *041-5227827. Campanile: 3€. Campanile and church: May–Sept Mon–Sat 9am–12:30pm, 2:30–6:30pm; Sun 9:30–10:30am, 2:30–6pm; Oct–Apr daily 9:30am–12:30pm, 2:30–4:30pm. Guided tours of the foundation, including the art collection, baroque staircase by Baldassare Longhena, and cloisters: 12€; Sat–Sun 10am–4:30pm. Vaporetto: San Giorgio.*

A gondola floats across the Venice lagoon, with San Giorgio Maggiore in the background.

3 **Bar San Giorgio.** The view from this waterside terrace, with San Marco across the basin and the lagoon shimmering before you, is almost as captivating as the outlook from the campanile. *Isola di San Giorgio Maggiore.* ☎ *041-5227827.*

④ ★★ San Michele. The last stop for many Venetians is the cypress-studded island that has served as the city cemetery since the late 18th century, when the city imposed a ban on burying the dead in the water-soaked earth around churches. San Michele is the resting place of many distinguished expatriates—among them Ezra Pound, Igor Stravinsky, and Serge Diaghilev, whose grave is usually strewn with dance slippers. Gondoliers are as lively a presence in death as they were in life, and lie beneath elaborately carved models of the crafts they so deftly maneuvered. Venice's first Renaissance church, **San Michele in Isola,** stands alongside the lagoon at the entrance to this enchanting island of the dead. ⏱ *1 hr. Apr–Sept daily 7:30am–6pm; Oct–Mar daily 7:30am–4pm. Vaporetto: Cimitero.*

Dancer Serge Diaghilev's grave, strewn with flowers and ballet slippers, in the San Michele Cemetery.

Venice's **Most Photogenic Ponti**

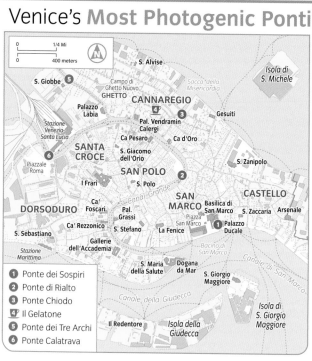

1. Ponte dei Sospiri
2. Ponte di Rialto
3. Ponte Chiodo
4. Il Gelatone
5. Ponte dei Tre Archi
6. Ponte Calatrava

The humorist Robert Benchley once sent a telegram to his editor from Venice: "Streets full of water. Please advise." The response may well have been to make use of the 400 bridges that cross Venice's waterways. That number has increased with the much-anticipated opening of a fourth span across the Grand Canal, designed by the acclaimed Spanish architect Santiago Calatrava. START: **Riva degli Schiavoni.**

1 ★★ **Ponte dei Sospiri.** Legend has it that the **Bridge of Sighs,** Venice's second-most famous bridge, takes its name from the sighs of prisoners stealing their last glimpses of freedom as they made their way to dank cells or the executioner's block. Travelers as savvy as Mark Twain have fallen for the story (he said the bridge led to "the dungeon which none entered and hoped to see the sun again"), but it's bunk. The handsome

span, nicely viewed from the Riva degli Schiavoni, connects the Palazzo Ducale with a prison constructed in the late 16th century to house petty criminals, just about all of whom saw the light of day again. ⏲ *15 min. San Marco. Vaporetto: San Zaccaria.*

2 ★★★ **Ponte di Rialto.** This famous shop-lined marble span, designed by the aptly named A. Ponte, dates from 1590. For a long time, it was the only bridge across the Grand Canal. Today, it's a favorite of souvenir hawkers and tourists. A bridge of boats crossed this narrow stretch of the Grand Canal until the 13th century, when a succession of wooden bridges went up—an especially scenic one appears in Carpaccio's *Miracle of the Relic of the True Cross* in the Accademia (see p 35, ⑥). ⏱ *15 min. San Polo. Vaporetto: Rialto.*

❸ ★ **Ponte Chiodo.** One of Venice's two remaining bridges with no parapets crosses a canal that is literally a quiet backwater at the edge of Cannaregio. The other one, the **Ponte del Diavolo**, is on the island of Torcello (see p 45, ❼). ⏱ *15 min. Cannaregio. Vaporetto: Ca' d'Oro.*

❹ **Il Gelatone.** The reward for a trek into the far reaches of the Cannaregio is a scoop of gelato from this much-admired provider. *Rio Terrà Maddalena, Cannaregio.* ☎ *041-720631.*

The Ponte dei Sospiri (Bridge of Sighs) in the morning mist, looking much as it did to 16th-century prisoners.

The Ponte di Rialto is known for its ornate stone sculptures.

❺ ★ **Ponte dei Tre Archi.** Venice's only three-arched bridge crosses the Cannaregio Canal in a series of steps. Engineer Andrea Tirali, known by his work crew as "Il Tiranno" (The Tyrant), completed the elegant span in 1688. The view from the bridge is rewarding; a parade of boats plies the busy waterway. ⏱ *15 min. Cannaregio. Vaporetto: Ponte Tre Archi.*

❻ ★★★ **Ponte Calatrava.** Spanish architect Santiago Calatrava's graceful arc of steel and glass is the fourth bridge to span the Grand Canal, providing a convenient pathway from the **Piazzale Roma** bus terminal to the trains at the **Stazione Venezia–Santa Lucia** (see p 167). Venetians are still arguing about the bridge's aggressive modernity, but all agree that the structure's arrival in the city in early 2008, when it was floated up the Grand Canal and barely squeaked under the Ponte di Rialto, was a memorable spectacle. ⏱ *15 min. Santa Croce. Vaporetto: Piazzale Roma.*

Craftsmanship in Venice

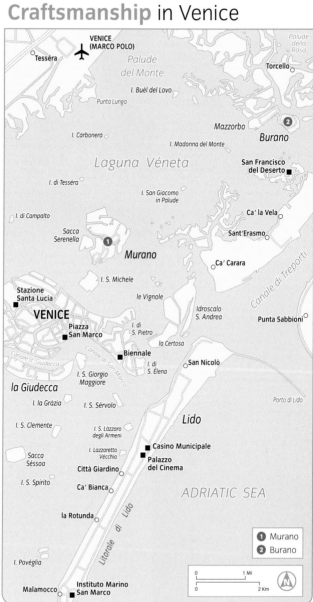

VENICE
(MARCO POLO)

Palude
del Monte

Tesséra

Palude
della
Rosa

Torcello

I. Buèl del Lovo

Punta Lunga

I. Carbonera

Mazzorbo

Burano

2

I. Madonna del Monte

San Francisco
del Deserto

Laguna Véneta

I. di Tesséra

I. San Giacomo
in Palude

Ca' la Vela

I. di Campalto

Sant'Erasmo

Sacca
Serenella

Murano

1

Ca' Carara

I. S. Michele

Canale di Treporti

le Vignole

Stazione
Santa Lucia

Idroscalo
S. Andrea

VENICE

I. di
S. Pietro

Punta Sabbioni

Piazza
San Marco

la Certosa

Canale di San Marco

Biennale

Canale di Giudecca

I. di
S. Élena

San Nicolò

I. S. Giorgio
Maggiore

la Giudecca

I. la Grázia

I. S. Sérvolo

Porto di Lido

I. S. Clemente

I. S. Lázzaro
degli Armeni

Lido

Sacca
Séssoa

I. Lazzaretto
Vécchio

Casino Municipale

I. S. Spirito

Città Giardino

Palazzo
del Cinema

Ca' Bianca

ADRIATIC SEA

la Rotunda

Litorale di Lido

I. Povéglia

Malamocco

Instituto Marino
San Marco

1 Murano
2 Burano

| 0 | | 1 Mi |
| 0 | | 2 Km |

Glassmakers emigrated to Venice in great numbers after the fall of Constantinople in 1292. By the 16th century, glassworks had been relegated to the island of Murano as a measure to prevent fire from raging through the city. Since then, Murano has become synonymous with glass. Meanwhile, lace-making has occupied many of the inhabitants of Burano for centuries. A visit to both islands is an introduction to ages-old Venetian craftsmanship. START: **Vaporetto no. 12 from Fondamenta Nuove to Murano (Colonna stop), continuing to Burano.**

1 ★ **Murano.** The glassmakers' island is not always mellow, especially when shills swoop upon passengers disembarking from the vaporetto like pigeons on bread crumbs in San Marco and try to whisk them off to studios and shops along the Fondamenta dei Vetrai. Even so, many of the glass pieces fashioned in the island furnaces are temptingly attractive. For those who seek a respite from shopping, two beautiful churches provide welcome refuge. *See p 52.*

2 ★★ **Burano.** The most cheerful patch of land in the lagoon is home to lace makers and fishermen. Houses are painted in bright colors, allegedly so they can be spotted from boats at sea. A pleasant scene unfolds on almost any street on the island, where women fashion pieces

Glass-blowing in Murano factories has been an enterprise for 500 years.

The island of Murano is home to the 12th-century Santa Maria e San Donato church.

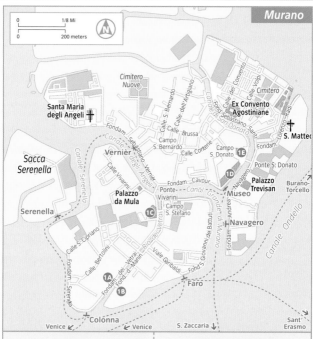

Murano

Many of the establishments offering the best of Murano glass are strung out along the ★★ **Fondamenta dei Vetrai and Fondamenta Manin,** running along both sides of a canal through the center of the island's business quarter. Many of these concerns also show interested buyers their wholesale showrooms, workshops, and furnaces. Some of the island's best-known glass houses—Barovier and Toso, Carlo Moretti, and Venini—show their wares in the **1B Murano Collezione** (Fondamenta Manin; ☎ 041-737272), a handsome contemporary showroom that provides an excellent introduction to the highest-quality Murano glass work. In the church of **1C ★ San Pietro Martire** (Fondamenta dei Vetrai; ☎ 041-739704), chandeliers fashioned in Murano's glass furnaces illuminate paintings of Saint Jerome and Saint Agatha by Veronese, as well as

works by such masters as Tintoretto, Bellini, and Titian. The **1D ★★ Museo dell'Arte Vetraria** (Piazza Galuppi 181; ☎ 041-739586; 5.50€; Thurs–Tues 10am–5pm, until 4pm Nov–Mar), in an old palazzo, displays pieces from ancient Rome and those made on Murano during the Middle Ages and Renaissance, as well as some stunning modern Murano glass. Dating to the 7th century and rebuilt in the 12th century, **1E ★★ Santa Maria e San Donato** (see p 25, **8**) is one of the most splendid Byzantine structures on the lagoon, its floor glittering with mosaics. Look for the mosaic figure of the Virgin, who looks over the apse from a field of gold. The eerie-looking objects behind the altar are bones, said to be those of the dragon slain by Saint Donato. ⏱ *3–4 hr. Venetian lagoon. Vaporetto: Fondamenta Nuove to Murano (Colonna stop).*

of lace in the doorways and men mend fishing nets. The island's lively gathering spots are the Piazza Galuppi and the fish market along Fondamenta Pescheria. Burano has been known for its lace making since the 15th century, when young women in Venice and the islands on the lagoon were encouraged to learn the craft—a genteel pastime, and a lucrative export business. By the 18th century, lace manufacture, and many Venetian lace makers along with it, had shifted to France. Burano is credited with reinvigorating the art with its lace-making school, Scuola di Merletti, founded in 1872 to train new generations in such distinctive stitches as Burano point. *See p 54.*

The colorful fishing village of Burano, easy to spot from sea.

3️ Palmisano Franceso Eredi.
The terrace of this busy bar provides a perch from which to watch the comings and goings on Piazza Galuppi in Burano, and the view is accompanied by sandwiches and a tasty *frizzante* house red wine. *Piazza Galuppi. No phone.*

Intricate Burano lacework can take years to craft.

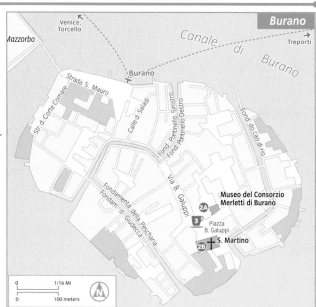

Burano's lace-making Scuola di Merletti has few followers these days, but the museum, **2A** ★★ **Museo del Consorzio Merletti di Burano** (Piazza B. Galuppi 181; closed for renovation), houses a collection of handkerchiefs, collars, napkins, altar cloths, and other items made in intricate lace patterns. The romantically leaning campanile and simple brick facade of **2B** ★ **San Martino** (Piazza B. Galuppi; daily 8am–noon, 3–7pm) face Piazza Baldassarre Galuppi, named for the island-born composer of *opera buffa*. A *Crucifixion* by Tiepolo hangs in the left aisle, near a large stone sarcophagus that legend says was dragged ashore by saints Alban, Dominic, and Orso and island children; a charming painting depicts the event. The presence of the three saints, who are interred in the altar, allegedly saved the island

from the devastating plague outbreak of 1630. ⏱ *2 hr. Venetian lagoon. Vaporetto: Fondamenta Nuove to Burano.* ●

Lacemakers on Burano train at the 19th-century Scuola di Merletti.

3 The Best
Neighborhood Walks

Castello & Sant'Elena

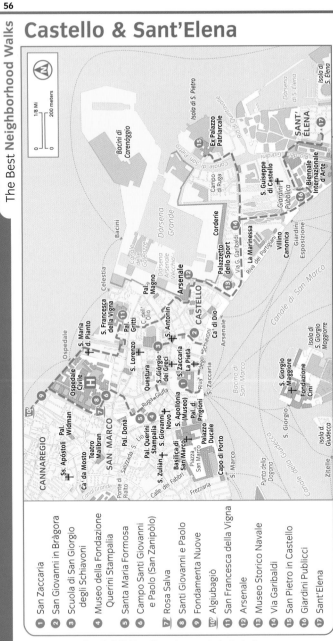

Previous page: The colorful fishing village of Burano, in the Venice lagoon.

Coming upon colorful scenes of everyday Venetian life is one of the great pleasures of wandering though this large area, which stretches from the Rialto east to the island enclave of Sant' Elena. This is Venice, remember, so don't be surprised to find an ornate palazzo or treasure-filled church around nearly every corner.
START: **Riva degli Schiavoni. Take vaporettos 1, 6, 14, 41, or 42 to the San Zaccaria stop. The church of San Zaccaria is just north along Calle San Zaccaria.**

Clotheslines hang over a canal in a quiet neighborhood of Sant'Elena.

① ★★ **San Zaccaria.** This Renaissance/Gothic church dedicated to the father of John the Baptist actually looks like an elaborate picture gallery—the walls are plastered with works by Tiepolo, Tintoretto, Van Dyck, Bellini, and other masters. The location just behind San Marco accounts for the souvenir stands outside and the tombs of several doges inside. ⏱ *30 min. Campo San Zaccaria.* ☎ *041-5221257. Mon–Sat 10am–noon, 4–6pm; Sun 4–6pm. Vaporetto: San Zaccaria.*

② ★ **San Giovanni in Bràgora.** Composer Antonio Vivaldi was baptized here in 1678; the register marking the event is prominently on display. Take time to admire the *Baptism of Christ* by Cima da Conegliano, behind the altar; the detailed backdrop of rolling hills was inspired by the artist's namesake birthplace north of Venice. ⏱ *15 min. Campo Bandiera e Moro.* ☎ *041-2702464. Mon–Sat 9am–noon, 3:30–5:30pm. Vaporetto: Arsenale.*

③ ★★★ **Scuola di San Giorgio degli Schiavoni.** *Schiavoni,* or Slavs from Dalmatia, prospered in Venice; by the 15th century, they had acquired the riches to build this *scuola* (guild house or fraternity) and commission Vittore Carpaccio to paint a sumptuous *Cycle of Saint George* in it. The master's depictions of decomposing bodies, ferocious dragons, and out-of-body experiences are luminous. ⏱ *30 min. Calle dei Furlani.* ☎ *041-2750642. 3€. Mon 2:45–6pm; Tues–Sat 9:15am–1pm, 2:45–6pm; Sun 9:15am–1pm. Vaporetto: San Zaccaria.*

④ ★ **Museo della Fondazione Querini Stampalia.** This Renaissance palazzo with modern embellishments houses a small but stunning collection of works by such masters as Pietro Longhi and Giovanni Bellini. The library is a haven for night owls, who are allowed to linger until midnight. *See p 37,* ③.

⑤ ★ **Santa Maria Formosa.** *Formosa* means "buxom," and this charming 15th-century church honors the image of the Virgin as the fulsome mother of Christ. Fittingly, near the altar is one of the few Venetian masterpieces by a woman, *Allegory of the Foundation*

The popular and beautiful Via Garibaldi, named for Giuseppe Garibaldi.

of the Church, an 18th-century work by Guilia Lama. A grotesquely contorted face (one of many startling details you'll encounter in Venice) overlooks the square from the campanile. ⏲ *15 min.*

⑥ ★★★ Campo Santi Giovanni e Paolo. Pride of place belongs to Bartolomeo Colleoni, a 15th-century mercenary who requested that a statue be erected in his honor in front of San Marco. The doges obliged with an impressive equestrian monument by Verrocchio, but they deceived the old soldier for all eternity—behind him is the Scuola Grande di San Marco, not the San Marco he had in mind. ⏲ *15 min. See p 15,* **④**.

⑦ Rosa Salva. Linger over a pastry and cappuccino while admiring San Zanipòlo at this venerable old cafe. *Campo Santi Giovanni e Paolo.* ☎ *041-5227949. See p 111.*

⑧ ★★ Santi Giovanni e Paolo. One of the largest churches in Venice holds the remains of numerous doges, whose marble tombs line the lofty nave in a show of dusty pomp. The church's great treasures include ceiling paintings by Giovanni Piazzetta in the Chapel of Saint Dominic and those by Paolo Veronese in the Rosary Chapel. ⏲ *30 min. Campo Santi Giovanni e*

Paolo. ☎ *041-5235913. 2.50€. Mon–Sat 9:30am–6pm; Sun 1–6pm. Vaporetto: Fondamente Nuove.*

⑨ ★ Fondamenta Nuove. After your slog through dim churches and picture galleries, you'll welcome the chance to take in some sea air on this long quay-side promenade, the departure point for boats to the outlying islands. Across the water is a vision of trees and marble: San Michele, the cemetery of Venice. For a boat trip to the cemetery island, see p 47, **④**. ⏲ *15 min. Cannaregio. Vaporetto: Fondamente Nuove.*

⑩ Algiubagiò. Take a seat on the terrace and enjoy a pizza or panino as boats come and go. *Fondamenta Nuove.* ☎ *041-5236084.*

⑪ ★ San Francesco della Vigna. Once surrounded by *vigna* (vineyards), this stately edifice now rises above a workaday neighborhood of quiet alleyways and smelly canals. The 15th-century facade is by Andrea Palladio (p 29); Pietro Lombardo sculptures and paintings by Veronese, Giovanni Bellini, and Antonio de Negroponte grace the simple interior. To clear your head of these depictions of saints and sinners, spend a few minutes in the cloisters. ⏲ *30 min. Campo San Francesco della Vigna.* ☎ *041-5206102. Mon–Sat 8am–12:30pm,*

3–6:30pm; Sun 3–6:30pm. Vaporetto: Celestia.

⑫ ★ Arsenale. Experience the glory days of the shipyards that once equipped the republic's navy, first by admiring the elaborate marble land entrance, modeled after a Roman arch and flanked by lions. Then, stand on the bridge across the water entrance for a look at the **Corderia** (rope factory). These and other vast structures at one time employed some 16,000 shipbuilders who, in production-line style, could assemble a galley in a few hours. 🕐 *15 min. Campo dell'Arsenale. Vaporetto: Arsenale.*

⑬ ★ Museo Storico Navale. Here are elaborate centuries-old models of Venetian ships and doges' barges, crafted by ship-builders to show off their final designs. Full-scale craft on display include art collector Peggy Guggenheim's private gondola. 🕐 *1 hr. Campo San Biago.* ☎ *041-5200276. 1.55€. Mon–Fri 8:45am–1:30pm; Sat 8:45am–1pm. Vaporetto: Arsenale.*

⑭ Via Garibaldi. Head inland again past shops and outdoor cafes on this broad avenue (a real rarity in Venice), named for the hero of Italian unification. You'll encounter scenes more typical of the working city as you continue on to the **Fondamenta Sant'Ana,** where, on weekday mornings and evenings, a boisterous floating market supplies the neighborhood with local produce. Look for mounds of purple *carciofi* (artichokes) from the island of Sant'Erasmo and radicchio from the fertile Treviso farmlands. 🕐 *15 min. Castello. Vaporetto: Arsenale.*

⑮ ★ San Pietro in Castello. Some of the earliest Venetians settled in this area, and their fortification, Castello, gave the neighborhood its name. The neglected-looking basilica here was the official cathedral of Venice until 1807, when the privilege was transferred to San Marco. Inside are 2nd-century mosaics on the front of the altar in the Lando Chapel. In the last week of June, the waterside lawns beneath the leaning campanile are filled with revelers celebrating the Feast of San Pietro. 🕐 *45 min. Campo San Pietro.* ☎ *041-2750642. 2.50€. Mon–Sat 10am–5pm. Vaporetto: San Pietro.*

⑯ ★ Giardini Publicci. Crowds descend upon these garden pavilions once a year to attend Venice's acclaimed **Biennale D'Arte Contemporanea e Architettura** (p 125), an exhibition of contemporary art in odd years and architecture in even years. At other times, only birdsong intrudes on the tranquillity, so find a bench and enjoy stunning views over the lagoon. 🕐 *15 min. Sant'Elena. Vaporetto: Giardini Esposizione.*

⑰ ★ Sant'Elena. Monuments and fine art are not what will draw you to the quietest precinct of Venice. Instead, as you wander the narrow streets for glimpses of everyday life, you'll discover that in Venice, what passes for ordinary is pretty extraordinary. 🕐 *1 hr. Vaporetto: Sant'Elena.*

The Arsenale was one of the largest ship-yards in Europe during the Venetian republic's heyday.

Santa Croce & Dorsoduro

0 ... 1/8 Mi
0 ... 200 meters

1. Giardino Papadopoli
2. San Nicolò da Tolentino
3. Santa Maria Gloriosa dei Frari
4. Scuola Grande di San Rocco
5. San Pantalon
6. Gelateria il Doge and Gelateria Causin
7. Campo Santa Margherita
8. Scuola Grande dei Carmini
9. Rio San Barnaba
10. Calle Lunga San Barnaba
11. San Sebastiano
12. Angelo Raffaele
13. San Nicolò Mendicoli
14. Zattere
15. Squero San Trovaso
16. San Trovaso
17. Santa Maria del Rosario ai Gesuati
18. Rio Terrà Foscarini
19. Gallerie dell'Accademia
20. Santa Maria della Salute and Dogana da Mar

These neighborhoods surround some of the city's greatest treasure houses, including Carmini, the Galleria dell'Accademia, and the Peggy Guggenheim Collection—all reason enough for a visit, of course. But you'll also be enchanted by the area's pleasant squares and little alleyways. START: **Piazzale Roma. Take vaporettos 1, 41, 42, 51, 52, 61, 62, or 82 to the Piazzale Roma stop. Follow the Fondamenta Santa Chiara east to Giardini Papadopoli.**

① ★ **Giardino Papadopoli.** Many Venetians only know this garden atop the remains of a convent as a quick route to Piazzale Roma. You might want to linger a bit, though, especially on the Esplanade at the edge of the Grand Canal—it's one of the few public spaces on the banks of this scenic waterway. You will not be able to resist the urge to walk to the middle of the canal on the new bridge by Spanish architect Santiago Calatrava, a graceful arc of steel and glass (see p 49, **⑥**). ⏱ *30 min. Santa Croce. Vaporetto: Piazzale Roma.*

② ★ **San Nicolò da Tolentino.** Immerse yourself in the baroque: Behind the unfinished facade and portico of this church are frescoes and paintings awash in a swirl of *putti* (pink-cheeked cherubs) and saints, including an ecstatic Saint Francis. Frescoes in the third chapel provide a vivid and gory lesson in the lives of Saint Celia and other saints. ⏱ *20 min. Campo dei Tolentini.* ☎ *041-710806. Mon–Sat 8:30am–noon, 4:30–6:30pm; Sun 4:30–6:30pm. Vaporetto: Piazzale Roma.*

③ ★★ **Santa Maria Gloriosa dei Frari.** The saints and sinners of Titian and Bellini inhabit this solid Italian Gothic edifice. ⏱ *30 min. See p 33, **⑩**.*

④ ★★ **Scuola Grande di San Rocco.** Tintoretto was entrusted with decorating this school dedicated to the patron saint of the sick, and some of his greatest works are here. *See p 32, **⑨**.*

⑤ ★★ **San Pantalon.** More than 60 ceiling paintings by Gian Antonio Fumiani illustrate *The Martyrdom and Glory of Saint Pantaleon,* the court physician to the Emperor Galerius who was beheaded under Diocletian. Fumiani's story is no less fervent than the saint's—the artist lay on his back for 24 years to execute these dark-hued masterpieces, then fell from a scaffold to his death as he applied the last brush strokes. The church's other treasure is a nail said to be from the true cross, enshrined in a lavish altar. ⏱ *20 min. Campo San Pantalon.* ☎ *041-5235893. 2€. Mon–Sat 8–10am, 4–6pm. Vaporetto: San Tomà.*

⑥ ★★ **Campo Santa Margherita.** One of the most appealing squares in Venice is a stage set for market stalls, shops, cafes, and the comings and goings of the neighborhood. ⏱ *15 min. Dorsoduro. Vaporetto: Ca' Rezzonico.*

Veronese's Martyrdom of Saint Sebastian, in the San Sebastiano church (p 62).

7⃞ Gelateria il Doge and Gelateria Causin. Campo Santa Margherita is Venice's ground zero for gelato. Many Venetians argue that Il Doge serves the best in town, while others cast their votes with Causin. Why not try a scoop at each and see which you prefer? *Campo Santa Margherita.* Doge: ☎ 041-5234607; Causin: ☎ 041-5236091.

8⃞ ★★★ Scuola Grande dei Carmini. In this perfectly preserved 17th-century bastion of the Carmelite order, the artist Tiepolo steals the show with magnificent ceiling paintings. ⏱ *30 min. See p 32,* **8⃞**.

9⃞ ★ Rio San Barnaba. Follow this canal past lovely houses and a floating market to the **Punti dei Pugni** (Bridge of the Punches), so-called because rival neighborhood factions were allowed to brawl publicly on the span until the practice was banned around 1700. Just beyond, the canal laps against one side of Campo Santa Barnaba, shaded by its namesake church. ⏱ *15 min. Dorsoduro. Vaporetto: San Basilio.*

10⃞ ★ Calle Lunga San Barnaba. The many enticing antiques and crafts for sale along this shopping street and surrounding alleys are upstaged by a floating produce market that ties up near the Ponte dei Pugni. ⏱ *15 min. Dorsoduro. Vaporetto: San Basilio.*

11⃞ ★★ San Sebastiano. The artist Paolo Veronese left his mark on this 16th-century church, where he spent most of his career painting a luridly colorful fresco cycle and huge canvases. Queen Esther is opulently clad and bejeweled, and Sebastian is theatrically pierced with arrows. The artist is buried here amid his creations. ⏱ *20 min. See p 32,* **7⃞**.

People strolling along the Zattere, which runs along the Giudecca in the Dorsoduro sestiere.

12⃞ ★ Angelo Raffaele. A gripping story unfolds in the organ loft, where Antonio Guardi's sumptuous paintings relate the archangel's adventure-filled travels, in human form, with Tobias, an early Christian. The elaborately carved well behind the church in Campo Sant'Angelo was the gift of a plague-stricken 14th-century merchant who mistakenly believed that contaminated water was the cause of his demise and wished to spare others his fate. ⏱ *15 min. Campo Angelo dell'Raffaele.* ☎ *041-5228548. 2€. Mon–Sat 8am–noon, 3–5pm; Sun 9am–noon. Vaporetto: San Basilio.*

13⃞ ★ San Nicolò Mendicoli. *Mendicoli* are beggars, and the poor once took shelter under the portico of this church. The second-oldest church in Venice (after San Giacomo di Rialto) dates from the 7th century. Rebuilt in the 12th century, it has a massive bell tower and other telltale Byzantine features. Of more recent note, the church appeared in the engagingly creepy 1973 cult film *Don't Look Now.* ⏱ *20 min. San Nicolò Mendicoli.* ☎ *041-2750382. Mon–Sat 10am–noon, 4–6pm; Sun 4–6pm. Vaporetto: San Basilio.*

14⃞ ★ Zattere. This busy quay is named for the rafts that arrived here laden with wood to build ships and palaces during the days of the republic. Across the canal, a deep-water channel that is often choked with boat traffic, is the island of Giudecca (see p 46, ❶) and Il Redentore, the impressive dome-topped church designed by Palladio. ⏱ *15 min. Dorsoduro. Vaporetto: Zattere.*

⓯ ★ **Squero San Trovaso.** This shipyard builds and repairs gondolas—a uniquely Venetian operation. The yard's wooden buildings, bedecked with balconies and window boxes, are quite picturesque. A stroll along Fondamenta Nani (a *fondamenta* is a street or quay along a canal) affords an excellent view of the goings-on. ⏱ *15 min. Dorsoduro. Vaporetto: Zattere.*

⓰ ★ **San Trovaso.** Dedicated to two saints, Gervasius and Protasius, this elegant 17th-century church has two similar facades, one at each end, an arrangement allegedly made so that the members of the two warring factions who worshipped here could enter and leave the church without bloodshed. Inside are paintings by two Tintorettos: a *Temptation of Saint Anthony* and the *Last Supper* by Jacopo, known as Il Tintoretto. ⏱ *20 min. Campo San Trovaso.* ☎ *041-2702464. Mon–Sat 2:30–5:30pm. Vaporetto: Zattere.*

⓱ ★ **Santa Maria del Rosario ai Gesuati.** When the Dominican order took over this waterfront church in the 18th century, they commissioned paintings and frescoes of Saint Dominic and other saints. Giambattista Tiepolo had the honor of depicting Dominic's life in a series of colorful ceiling panels. ⏱ *20 min. Fondamenta Zattere ai Gesuati.* ☎ *041-2750642. 3€. Mon–Sat 10am–5pm. Vaporetto: Zattere.*

⓲ ★ **Rio Terrá Foscarini.** This shop-lined street leads north from the Zattere to the Grand Canal and the Accademia Bridge. Wander off the Rio into some of the adjoining alleys to get a sense of the quiet neighborhood. ⏱ *15 min. Dorsoduro. Vaporetto: Zattere or Accademia.*

⓳ ★★★ **Gallerie dell'Accademia.** Viewing Carpaccio's *Ursula* cycle in room 21 and Gentile Bellini's *Procession in Saint Mark's Square* cycle is like gazing up at the Milky Way: Another splendid detail emerges with every blink of the eye. *See p 34.*

⓴ ★★ **Santa Maria della Salute/Dogana da Mar.** The prospect of seeing the Grand Canal, San Marco, and the lagoon from this remarkable church and Customs house supplies a dramatic ending to your walk. *See p 11, ❶ and ❷.*

A gondola being raised in the Squero San Trovaso shipyard, just north of the Zattere.

Cannaregio & The Ghetto

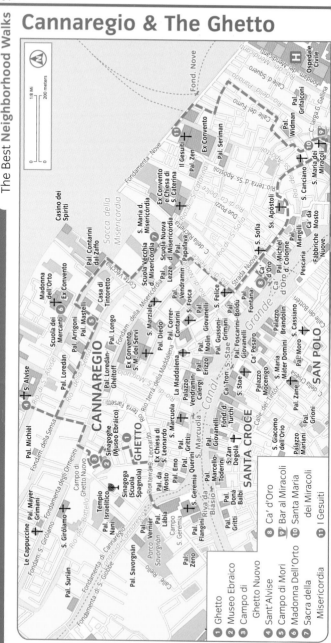

1 Ghetto
2 Museo Ebraico
3 Campo di Ghetto Nuovo
4 Sant'Alvise
5 Campo di Mori
6 Madonna Dell'Orto
7 Sacra della Misericordia
8 Ca' d'Oro
9 Bar al Miracoli
10 Santa Maria dei Miracoli
11 I Gesuiti

The sprawling Cannaregio stretches north from the Grand Canal to the lagoon. Here you'll discover quiet squares, shops, and one splendid art-filled church after another. START: **Campo Ghetto Nuevo. Take vaporettos 41, 42, 51, or 52 to the Ponte Guglie stop. From there, the Sottoportego di Ghetto Vecchio leads northeast through the Campo delle Scuole to the Campo di Ghetto Nuovo.**

The Casa Israelitica di Riposo in the Ghetto is a Jewish home for the aged.

❶ ★ Ghetto. The term "geto" originated in Venice and referred to a medieval foundry where metals for cannons were cast. Until Napoleon conquered Venice in 1797, Jews were allowed to live only in the Ghetto. A few synagogues and kosher restaurants and food shops remain, and the neighborhood still feels cut off from the rest of the city. 🕐 *15 min. Cannaregio. Vaporetto: Ponte de Guglie.*

❷ ★ Museo Ebraico. The most memorable part of a visit to this small museum celebrating Venetian Judaism is the guided tour of three synagogues that occupy the top floors of nearby houses and are easily recognized from the street by their five distinctive windows. 🕐 *1 hr. Campo Ghetto Nuovo.* ☎ *041-715359. www.museoebraico.it. 3€ museum, 8€ museum and synagogue tour. June–Sept Sun–Fri 10–7pm; Oct–May*

Sun 10am–6pm, Mon–Fri 10am–5:30pm. Vaporetto: Ponte de Guglie.

❸ ★★ Campo di Ghetto Nuovo. The extraordinary height of the houses around this square testifies to the overcrowded conditions in the Ghetto: Prevented from expanding into other parts of the city, residents could only build up. A monument of bas-relief panels commemorates Venetian Jews deported by the Nazis. 🕐 *15 min. Cannaregio. Vaporetto: Ponte de Guglie.*

❹ ★ Sant'Alvise. Lurid canvases of the *Flagellation* and the *Road to Calvary* by Gianbattista Tiepolo are the masterpieces here, but they are not as enchanting as the eight almost-primitive tempura paintings of biblical scenes by an unknown 15th-century artist from the school of Lazzaro Bastiani. 🕐 *30 min. Campo Sant'Alvise.* ☎ *041-2750462. 3€. Mon–Sat 10am–5pm. Vaporetto: Sant'Alvise.*

❺ ★ Campo di Mori. Three 13th-century statues are the de facto guardians of this quiet square. The figures are allegedly three Moorish brothers who made their fortunes trading with the Near East and built a palazzo nearby. Tintoretto also lived in a canal-side house just around the corner from the square on Fondamenta dei Mori until his death in 1594. 🕐 *15 min. Cannaregio. Vaporetto: Madonna dell'Orto.*

❻ ★★ Madonna Dell'Orto. Tintoretto is buried in this neighborhood church, surrounded by several of his works, including his *Beheading of Saint Christopher.* 🕐 *30 min.*

The Jews of Venice

Jews began settling in Venice in great numbers in the 16th century, and the republic soon came to value their services as moneylenders, physicians, and traders. For centuries, the Jewish population was forced to live on an island that now encompasses the Campo Ghetto Nuovo, and drawbridges were raised to enforce a nighttime curfew. By the end of the 17th century, as many as 5,000 Jews lived in the Ghetto's cramped confines. Today, the city's Jewish population is comprised of only about 500 people, few of whom live in the Ghetto.

Campo Madonna Dell'Orto. ☎ *041-2750642. 3 €. Mon–Sat 10am–5pm. Vaporetto: Madonna dell'Orto.*

⑦ ★ **Sacra della Misericordia.** The Fondamenta di Gasparo Contarini provides a perfect perch from which to take in the view over the Sacra, a protected cove in the lagoon where all manner of colorful craft can be seen. Just to the south, everyday business transpires on the *fondamenti* along two canals that cut broad swaths through the neighborhood, the Rio della Sensa and Rio della Misericordia. ⏱ *15 min. Cannaregio. Vaporetto: Madonna dell'Orto.*

⑧ ★★★ **Ca' d'Oro.** An alley leads off busy Strada Nuova, an atypically straight avenue laid out in the 1860s to facilitate foot traffic to and from the railway station, to a far more pleasing setting: this ornate Gothic palazzo, home to the **Galleria Franchetti.** *See p 39,* ⑧.

⑨ **Bar al Miracoli.** Panini and other snacks are served at outdoor tables alongside a canal in a pretty campo. *Campo Santa Maria Nova.* ☎ *041-5231515.*

⑩ ★★★ **Santa Maria dei Miracoli.** A top contender for the most beautiful church in Venice is sheathed in gleaming white marble; the effect is especially stunning when the exterior is lit at night. Inside, painted panels in the barrel-vaulted ceiling depict the prophets. ⏱ *30 min. Campo Santa Maria dei Miracoli.* ☎ *041-2750462. 3€. Mon–Sat 10am–5pm. Vaporetto: Rialto.*

⑪ ★ **I Gesuiti.** The Venetian outpost of the Jesuit order is tucked away in a quiet neighborhood of narrow alleys and simple houses. These humble surroundings belie the extravagant baroque fantasy inside: The apse and side chapels are festooned with *trompe l'oeil* drapery swags, unfurling carpets, and brocaded ropes, all fashioned from green and white marble. ⏱ *20 min. Campo dei Gesuiti.* ☎ *041-5286579. Daily 10am–noon, 4–6pm. Vaporetto: Fondamenta Nuove.* ●

The church of Santa Maria dei Miracoli is a model of early Renaissance style.

Shopping **Best Bets**

Best **Silk Ties That Look Like Paper**
★★ Alberto Valese-Ebrû, *Campo Santo Stefano, San Marco (p 87)*

Best Place for **Charming Glass Creatures**
★★ Amadi, *Calle Saoneri, San Polo (p 81)*

Best **Goblets with a Pedigree**
★★★ Barovier and Taso, *Fondamenta dei Vetrai 28, Murano (p 81)*

Most **Beautiful Glass Jewelry**
★★★ Davide Penso, *Fondamenta Riva Longa 48, Murano (p 84)*

Best **Chance to Shod Yourself in Stylish Comfort**
★★★ Fratelli Rossetti, *Salizzada San Moisé, San Marco (p 79)*

Best **Views of the Grand Canal from a Shop**
★★★ Genninger Studio, *Calle del Traghetto, Dorsoduro (p 82)*

Best Place to **Have a Personalized Bookplate Made**
★★ Gianni Basso, *Calle dei Fumo, Cannaregio (p 87)*

Best Place to **Pretend to Be a Gondolier**
★★★ Gilberto Penzo, *Calle Saoneri, San Polo (p 77)*

Best **Gloves in Town**
★★★ J. B. Guanti, *Calle II Aprile, San Marco (p 85)*

Best **Stop for Exquisite Lace**
★★★ Jesurum Outlet, *Fondamenta della Sensa, Cannaregio (p 85)*

Best Place to **Buy Paper with a Pedigree**
★★★ Legatoria Piazzesi, *Campiello Feltrina, San Marco (p 88)*

Best Place to **Hide Behind a Mask**
★★★ MondoNovo Mashchere, *Rio Terrà Canal, Dorsoduro (p 87)*

Best Place for **Creative Jewelry with a Twist**
★★★ Papuniart, *Ponte del Pugni, Dorsoduro (p 85)*

Best Place to **String a Necklace**
★★ Perle e Dintorni, *Calle della Mandola, San Marco (p 84)*

Best Place to **Come Face to Face with an Adriatic Sea Creature**
★★★ Pescaria Market, *between Campo delle Beccarie and the Grand Canal (p 86)*

Best Place to **Pamper Yourself in Medieval Scents**
★★ Santa Maria Novella, *Salizzada San Samuele, San Marco (p 88)*

Best **Paperweights**
★★ Sergio Tiozzo, *Fondamenta Manin, Murano (p 83)*

Best Place to **Dip Your Oar in the Water**
★★★ Spazio Legno, *Fondamenta San Giacomo, Giudecca (p 78)*

Best **Recordings of Baroque Music**
★★ Vivaldi Store, *Salizzada del Fontego dei Tedeschi, San Marco (p 76)*

Previous page: A vintage Venetian commedia dell'arte Carnevale mask.

San Marco & Castello Shopping

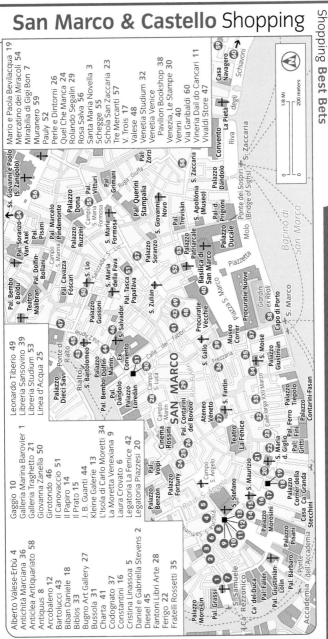

Alberto Valese-Ebrù 4
Antichità Marciana 36
Anticlea Antiquariato 58
Antiquus 3
Arcobaleno 12
Bartolucci 43
Biban Daniele 18
Biblos 33
Bugno Art Gallery 27
Bussola 31
Charta 41
Codognato 37
Constantini 16
Cristina Linassoa 5
Daniel e Gabriella Stevens 2
Diesel 45
Fantoni Libri Arte 28
Fergo 22
Fratelli Rossetti 35

Gaggio 10
Galleria Marina Barovier 1
Galleria Traghetto 21
Giovanna Zanella 50
Girotondo 46
Il Canovaccio 51
Il Papiro 14
Il Prato 15
J. B. Guanti 44
Kleine Galerie 13
L'Isola di Carlo Moretti 34
La Moretta Venexiana 9
Laura Crovato 6
Legatoria La Fenice 42
Legatoria Piazzesi 20

Leonardo Tiberio 49
Libreria Sansovino 39
Libreria Studium 53
Linea d'Acqua 25

Mario e Paola Bevilacqua 19
Mercatino dei Miracoli 54
Mirabilia di Gigi Bon 7
Muranero 59
Pauly 52
Perle e Dintorni 26
Quel Che Manca 24
Rolando Segalin 29
Rosa Salva 56
Santa Maria Novella 3
Schegge 55
Schola San Zaccaria 23
Tre Mercanti 57
V. Trois 17
Valese 48
Venetia Studium 32
Venetia Venice
Pavilion Bookshop 38
Venezia, Le Stampe 30
Venini 40
Via Garibaldi 60
Vineria Dall do Cancari 11
Vivaldi Store 47

Cannaregio Shopping

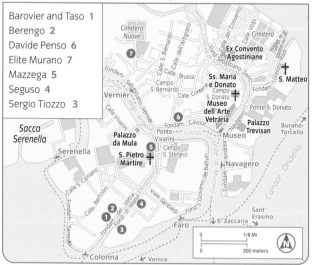

Antichità 9
COIN 5
Giacomo Rizzo 6
Giani Basso 8
Jesurum Outlet 3
Lili e Paolo Darin 1
Mercatino dei
  Miracoli 7
San Leonardo
  (market) 2
Standa 4

Murano Shopping

Barovier and Taso 1
Berengo 2
Davide Penso 6
Elite Murano 7
Mazzega 5
Seguso 4
Sergio Tiozzo 3

Dorsoduro & Giudecca Shopping

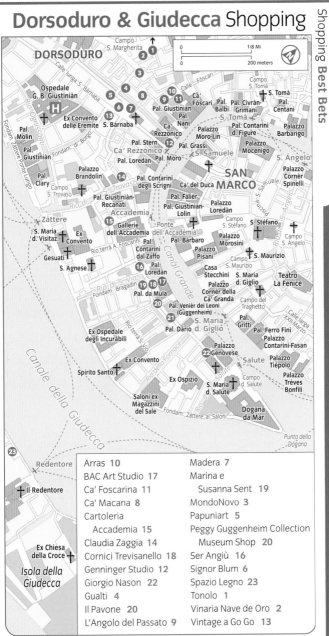

San Polo & Santa Croce Shopping

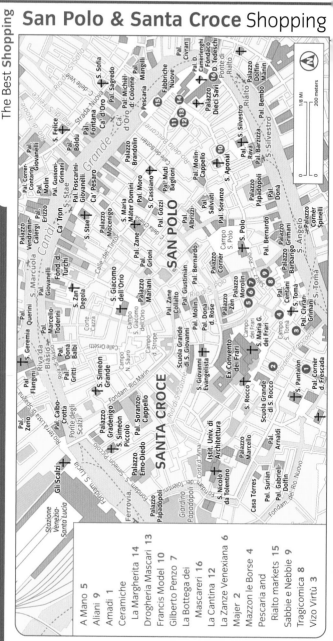

A Mano 5
Aliani 9
Amadi 1
Ceramiche
  La Margherita 14
Drogheria Mascari 13
Francis Model 10
Gilberto Penzo 7
La Bottega dei
  Mascareri 16
La Cantina 12
La Zanze Venexiana 6
Majer 2
Mazzon le Borse 4
Pescaria and
  Rialto markets 15
Sabbie e Nebbie 9
Tragicomica 8
Vizo Virtù 3

Shopping A to Z

Antiques

★★ Antichità CANNAREGIO Vintage Murano glass pieces, including tableware and beads, are among the finds in this intriguing collection. *Calle del Fumo.* ☎ *0389-6795785. Cash only. Vaporetto: Fondamente Nuove. Map p 70.*

★★ Antiquus SAN MARCO What holds this wide-ranging collection of old paintings, silver, china, and jewelry together is an eye for the highest quality. *Calle delle Botteghe.* ☎ *041-5206395. AE, DC, MC, V. Vaporetto: San Samuele. Map p 69.*

★★ Biban Daniele SAN MARCO The small but exquisite selection of paintings, tableware, and etchings is an enchanting treasure trove of old Venice. *Campo Santa Maria del Giglio.* ☎ *041-5222082. MC, V. Vaporetto: Santa Maria del Giglio. Map p 69.*

★★ Kleine Galerie SAN MARCO This appealingly crowded shop is the best place in town to find an old print of Venice. *Calle delle Botteghe.* ☎ *041-5222177. No credit cards. Vaporetto: Sant' Angelo. Map p 69.*

★★ Quel Che Manca SAN MARCO Your reward for finding this out-of-the-way shop on a narrow *calle* near the Museo Fortuny is a treasure trove of old bric-a-brac, from Cynar ashtrays

to gilded *putti* to glassware. *Salizzada de la Chiesa o de Teatro.* ☎ *0348-3729717. No credit cards. Vaporetto: San Samuele. Map p 69.*

Art

★★ Arcobaleno SAN MARCO Painters swoon over the lustrous pigments on offer for mix-your-own Venetian shades; offerings also include all manner of supplies, as well as papers and artful objects such as glass wine stoppers. *Calle delle Botteghe.* ☎ *041-5236818. MC, V. Vaporetti: San Samuele. Map p 69.*

★ BAC Art Studio DORSODURO Prints by local artists are quite affordable, and a wide range of photographic reproductions of Venetian scenes are also available. *Campo San Vio.* ☎ *041-5228171. MC, V. Vaporetto: Accademia. Map p 71.*

★★ Bugno Art Gallery SAN MARCO Venetians and other contemporary Italian artists are represented in this large, airy space, where the small, museum-like permanent collection includes works by DeChirico and other Italian greats. *Campo San Fantin.* ☎ *041-5231305. www.bugnoart gallery.it. AE, DC, MC, V. Vaporetto: Santa Maria del Giglio. Map p 69.*

A handmade antique Venetian character marionette.

Opening Times

In the old days, Venetian shopkeepers took Sundays and Monday mornings or Wednesday afternoons off, but in these modern times, only neighborhood grocers and other local services tend to keep traditional hours. Many Venice shops are now open 7 days a week, especially during the busy summer season and Carnevale. Shopping hours are from around 9am to 1pm and 3 or 4pm to 7:30 or 8pm, though many shops that cater to tourists forgo the long lunch and keep the doors open throughout the day.

★ **Cartoleria Accademia** DOR-SODURO   Has Venice inspired you to pick up a brush? This well-stocked shop has been supplying artists for almost 200 years. *Campiello Calbo.* ☎ *041-5207086. AE, MC, V. Vaporetto: Accademia. Map p 71.*

★★ **Galleria Traghetto** SAN MARCO   One of Venice's most respected galleries is well known for showing works by the city's sizable community of painters and sculptors, with an emphasis on abstract painting. *Calle di Piovan.* ☎ *041-5221188.*

Bound writing notebooks on display at Legatoria La Fenice.

AE, DC, MC, V. Vaporetto: Santa Maria del Giglio. Map p 69.

★★★ **Legatoria La Fenice** SAN MARCO   What stands out at this purveyor of fine papers is a stunning collection of old prints of Venice, as well as handsomely framed reproductions. *Calle Fiubera.* ☎ *041-5209331. AE, MC, V. Vaporetto: San Marco/Vallaresso. Map p 69.*

★★ **Schola San Zaccaria** SAN MARCO   Venice-born architect and artist Gianfranco Missiaja fills his small gallery with his delightful variations of traditional themes—harlequins here morph into a swirl of sinuous lines. *Gallery: Campo San Maurizio.* ☎ *041-5221209. MC, V. Vaporetto: Santa Maria del Guglio. Studio: Salizzada dei Greci, Castello.* ☎ *041-5234343. Vaporetto: Arsenale. Map p 69.*

★★ **Studio d'Arte "Mirabilia"** SAN MARCO   A "room of amazement" is how this workshop-cum-gallery has been described, filled as it is with rare carpets, antiques, and the whimsical creatures Ms. Gigi Bon sculpts, as well as her surrealistic paintings. Call to arrange a visit if the shop is closed. *Calle Malipiero (off Calle degli Zotli).* ☎ *041-5239570. www.gigibonvenezia.it. MC, V. Vaporetto: San Samuele. Map p 69.*

Charta's leather-bound volumes are kept carefully under guard.

★★ **Venezia, Le Stampe** SAN MARCO   Venice has been captivating printmakers for centuries, and one of the city's best sources for antique prints is filled with a beautiful sampling of their output. *Calle Teatro Goldoni.* ☎ *041-5234318. AE, MC, V. Vaporetto: Rialto. Map p 69.*

Books & Music

★ **Ca' Foscarina** DORSODURO The bookstore of the University of Venice carries the city's largest selection of books in English, on a wide variety of subjects, spread out over several small shops. *Campiello degli Squellini.* ☎ *041-5229602. AE, DC, MC, V. Vaporetto: San Tomà. Map p 71.*

★★★ **Charta** SAN MARCO   Beautiful leather-bound volumes, from old classics to journals, revive the art of Venetian bookbinding. *Calle dei Fabbri.* ☎ *041-5229801. AE, MC, V. Vaporetto: Rialto. Map p 69.*

★★ **Fantoni Libri Arte** SAN MARCO   Lavishly illustrated volumes on art, photography, and design fill the tables, making this the perfect stop to find a coffee-table book to take home. *Salizzada San Luca.* ☎ *041-5220700. AE, DC, MC, V. Vaporetto: Rialto. Map p 69.*

★★★ **Libreria Sansovino** SAN MARCO   One of Venice's most venerable bookstores carries antiquarian books as well as lavish volumes on Venetian art; the stock also includes a good selection of English-language titles. *Bacino Orseolo.* ☎ *041-5222623. AE, DC, MC, V. Vaporetto: San Marco/Vallaresso. Map p 69.*

★ **Libreria Studium** SAN MARCO A good stop for English-language travel guides, as well as some vacation reading—the selection of fiction and nonfiction from England and the U.S. is fairly extensive. *Calle Canonica.* ☎ *041-5222382. AE, DC, MC, V. Vaporetto: San Zaccaria. Map p 69.*

★★★ **Linea d'Acqua** SAN MARCO   Beautifully bound rare volumes and antique prints of Venice are among the offerings. *Calle della Mandola.* ☎ *041-5224030. www. lineadacqua.it. AE, DC, MC, V. Vaporetto: Sant'Angelo. Map p 69.*

★★ Peggy Guggenheim Collection Museum Shop

DORSODURO   Among the lavishly illustrated volumes on modern art, photography, and Venice are many fine European editions. *Fondamenta Venier dal Leoni.* ☎ *041-2405424. AE, DC, MC, V. Vaporetto: Accademia. Map p 71.*

★★ Venice Pavilion Bookshop

SAN MARCO   The bookshop of the Venice tourism office is amply stocked with English-language guidebooks and maps, as well as handsome volumes on Venetian art and architecture. *Giardinetti Reali.* ☎ *041-5226356. AE, DC, MC, V. Vaporetto: San Zaccaria. Map p 69.*

★★ Vivaldi Store

SAN MARCO   Works by the eponymous composer and other masters line the shelves. *Salizzada del Fontego dei Tedeschi.* ☎ *041-5221343. MC, V. Vaporetto: Rialto. Map p 69.*

Crafts

★ **A Mano** SANTA CROCE   True to the name, everything—mirrors, picture frames, lamps, and other decorative items—is handmade and one of a kind. *Rio Terrà.* ☎ *041-715742. MC, V. Vaporetto: San Tomà. Map p 72.*

★★ **Antichità Marciana** SAN MARCO   Hand-painted velvets, sold by the meter, make unique coverings for cushions and are works of art in themselves, ideal as wall hangings. *Frezzeria.* ☎ *041-5235666. AE, DC, MC, V. Vaporetto: San Marco/Vallaresso. Map p 69.*

★ **Arras** DORSODURO   Woolens and silks, sold by the yard and fashioned into scarves and garments, are woven by a cooperative that employs the disabled. *Campiello della Squellini.* ☎ *041-5226460. AE, DC, MC, V. Map p 71.*

★ **Bartolucci** SAN MARCO   The tiny shop itself is a Venetian sight— filled with clocks, key chains, models of cars, gaudy paintings of cartoon-like animals, and so on, all made from wood. *Foot of Ponte de Rialto.* ☎ *041-5221960. www.bartolucci. com. AE, MC, V. Map p 69.*

★★★ Ceramiche La Margherita

SANTA CROCE   Margherita Rossetto is a master ceramics craftsperson, producing teapots, cups, and other items that she then hand-paints in charming designs. Prices in her little shop near the Ponte di Rialto are remarkably reasonable. *Sottoportico della Siora Bettina.* ☎ *041-723120.*

The ceramic work at Ceramiche La Margherita, near the Ponte di Rialto.

An example of Gaggio's textile work, on display in the showroom.

www.lamargheritavenezia.com. AE, MC, V. Vaporetto: San Stae. Map p 72.

★★ **Cornici Trevisanello** DORSODURO This studio specializes in picture frames adorned with gold leaf, ceramic, and glass inlays and other tasteful touches. *Campo San Vio.* ☎ *041-5207779. MC, V. Vaporetto: Accademia. Map p 71.*

★★★ **Gaggio** SAN MARCO Sumptuous, hand-blocked textiles based on old Venetian designs are fashioned into cushions, scarves, and other elegant goods, or sold by the meter. *Calle delle Botteghe.* ☎ *041-5228574. Vaporetto: San Samuele. Map p 69.*

★★★ **Gilberto Penzo** SAN POLO If you marveled over the models of doges' craft in the **Museo Storico Navale** (see p 59, ⑬), you'll be charmed by these wooden replicas of gondolas and other boats. Signori Penzo's replicas may not fit your budget, but you will be able to take home a build-your-own kit. *Calle Saoneri.* ☎ *041-719372. MC, V. Vaporetto: San Tomà. Map p 72.*

★★ **La Zanze Venexiana** SAN POLO A sense of whimsy

permeates this delightful workroom, filled with puppets and wooden re-creations of Venetian landmarks. *Rio Terrà.* ☎ *041-5327983. Vaporetto: San Tomà. Map p 72.*

★★ **Madera** DORSODURO Wooden bowls, vases, and other household items are boldly designed, as are the ceramics and other pieces on display. *Campo San Barnaba.* ☎ *041-5224181. www.madera venezia.it. AE, MC, V. Vaporetto: Ca' Rezzonico. Map p 71.*

★★★ **Mario e Paola Bevilacqua** SAN MARCO Fine weaving is a time-honored Venetian tradition, and some of the highest-quality work emanates from this distinguished shop founded in 1700, which sells brocade and braid work as well as lush fabrics. *Campo Santa Maria del Giglio.* ☎ *041-2415133. AE, MC, V. Vaporetto: Santa Maria del Giglio. Map p 69.*

★★ **Sabbie e Nebbie** SAN POLO The beautiful pottery and ceramics are from Japan and Italy. *Calle dei Nomboli.* ☎ *041-719073. MC, V. Vaporetto: San Tomà. Map p 72.*

★★ **Signor Blum** DORSODURO A group of local women fashion

Fortuny-fabric lampshades at Venetia Studium.

San Maurizio. ☎ 041-5222905. AE, DC, MC, V. Vaporetto: Santa Maria del Giglio. Map p 69.

★★ **Valese** SAN MARCO   Stop in to see the art of bronze casting; the output includes small statuary, door knockers, paper weights, and other decorative items. *Calle Fiubera.* ☎ 041-5227282. AE, MC, V. Vaporetto: San Marco/Vallaresso. Map p 69.

★★ **Venetia Studium** SAN MARCO   Fortuny-style designs are the distinctive hallmarks of the stunning silk and glass lamps here; they also find their way onto everything from scarves to pillows. *Calle Larga XXII (other branches around the city).* ☎ 041-5229281. *www.venetiastudium.com.* AE, DC, MC, V. Vaporetto: Santa Maria del Giglio. Map p 69.

wonderful wood models and painted panels of Venetian monuments and scenes, as well as fairy-tale castles and palaces. *Campo San Barnaba.* ☎ 041-5211399. *www.signorblum.com.* MC, V. Vaporetto: Ca' Rezzonico. Map p 71.

★★★ **Spazio Legno** GIUDECCA   The serious business at hand here is making oars, *forcoli* (oar rests), and other wooden components for gondolas. Visitors can watch work in progress and walk away with wooden bookmarks shaped like *forcoli* or other small objects made from leftover materials. *Fondamenta San Giacomo.* ☎ 041-2775505. AE, DC, MC, V. Vaporetto: Redentore. Map p 71.

★★ **V. Trois** SAN MARCO   Become inspired by the creations of Spanish designer Mariano Fortuny, on display in his home, **Museo Fortuny** (see p 37, ②), then come here to shop for fabrics based on vintage Fortuny designs. *Campo*

Department Stores

★ **Coin** CANNAREGIO   High fashion, designer housewares, cosmetics, and other appealing items are on offer in this branch of one of Italy's higher-end chains. *San Giovanni Crisostomo.* ☎ 041-520358. AE, DC, MC, V. Vaporetto: Rialto. Map p 70.

★★ **Standa** CANNAREGIO   Sensible, run-of-the-mill clothing and household goods fill the shelves; the supermarket is a gourmand's paradise and a good place to stock up on Italian delicacies. *Strada Nuova.* ☎ 041-5238046. AE, DC, MC, V. Vaporetto: Ca' d'Oro. Map p 70.

Fashion

Bruno Magli, Giorgio Armani, Prada, and many other Italian or European designers have shops around Piazza San Marco.

★★ **Cristina Linassoa** SAN MARCO   Intimate apparel for women, along with other clothing

Sandwiches for sale in a takeout food shop.

and fine table linens, are fashioned from sumptuous silks and cottons. *Tra Campo Sant'Angelo e Campo Santo Stefano.* ☎ *041-5230578. AE, MC, V. Vaporetto: San Samuele. Map p 69.*

★ **Diesel** SAN MARCO   The hip firm that's made a fortune clothing fashionable youth in extravagantly priced jeans is based here in the Veneto. *Salizzada Pio X.* ☎ *041-2411937. AE, DC, MC, V. Vaporetto: Rialto. Map p 69.*

★★★ **Fratelli Rossetti** SAN MARCO   This family-run concern is dedicated to making what must be some of the world's most comfortable shoes. *Salizzada San Moisé.* ☎ *041-5220819. AE, DC, MC, V. Vaporetto: San Marco/Vallaresso. Map p 69.*

★★ **Giovanna Zanella** SAN MARCO   Giovanna, who's quickly becoming known as one of Italy's more innovative designers, sells her fine line of stylish women's clothing and accessories from this delightful shop. *Campo San Lio.* ☎ *041-5235500. AE, DC, MC, V. Vaporetto: Rialto. Map p 69.*

★ **Laura Crovato** SAN MARCO A good selection of secondhand women's clothing and jewelry often

yields some remarkable buys. *Calle delle Botteghe.* ☎ *041-5204170. MC, V. Vaporetto: Sant'Angelo. Map p 69.*

★ **Ser Angiù** DORSODURO Designer labels at discounted prices—a winning formula that draws crowds of local shoppers. *Piscina del Forner.* ☎ *041-5231149. MC, V. Vaporetto: Accademia. Map p 71.*

★★ **Vintage a Go Go** DORSO-DURO   If you have the yen to look like an Italian film star of days gone by, this is the place to adorn yourself in gently used high fashions. *Calle Lunga San Barnaba.* ☎ *041-2777895. Vaporetto: Ca' Rezzonico. Map p 71.*

Food

★ **Aliani** SAN POLO   The perfect place to stock up on hotel-room provisions—wine, cheese, and meats from all over Italy fill the busy, aromatic shop. *Ruga Rialto.* ☎ *041-5224913. No credit cards. Vaporetto: San Silvestro. Map p 72.*

★★★ **Drogheria Mascari** SAN POLO   Step in to savor the aromas of spices, coffees, and teas. Huge jars are filled with dried fruits, nuts, and sweets. The selection of olive oil, vinegar, and wine from throughout

Italy is probably the best in the city. *Ruga degli Speziali.* ☎ *041-5229762. No credit cards. Vaporetto: San Silvestro. Map p 72.*

★★ **Giacomo Rizzo** CANNAREGIO Basic foodstuffs fill the shelves, but the draw is the pasta—in dozens of shapes and colors. Many, such as those shaped like Carnevale masks, are too beautiful to eat. *Calle San Giovanni Crisostomo.* ☎ *041-5222824. AE, DC, MC, V. Vaporetto: Rialto. Map p 70.*

★★ **I Tre Mercanti** CASTELLO A huge selection of many of Italy's best wines is complemented with shelves of fine oils, decadent chocolate spreads, and other gourmet Italian fare. *Casselleria.* ☎ *041-2774166. AE, MC, V. Vaporetto: San Marco/Vallaresso. Map p 69.*

★ **La Cantina** SAN POLO Bring your own bottle and take your choice: Wines from throughout the Veneto are dispensed from huge vats. *Ruga Rialto.* ☎ *041-5235042. Vaporetto: Rialto. Map p 72.*

★★ **Majer** SAN POLO A well-established vendor of fine wines dispenses offerings from the Veneto and other regions in high-tech surroundings. *Calle de Scaleter.*

☎ *041-722873. Vaporetto: San Tomà. Map p 72.*

★★★ **Rosa Salva** CASTELLO One of the city's most renowned pastry shops is a popular place to sit and linger over a sweet treat and a cappuccino, but you can also take home the tempting baked goods. *Campo Santi Giovanni e Paolo.* ☎ *041-5227949. No credit cards. Vaporetto: Fondamenta Nuove. Map p 69.*

★★★ **Tonolo** DORSODURO A fine selection of cakes makes this elegant little place a popular stop in the Campo San Pantalon neighborhood. *Calle San Pantalon.* ☎ *041-5237209. No credit cards. Vaporetto: San Tomà. Map p 71.*

★★ **Vineria Dail do Cancari** SAN MARCO A welcoming shop just off Campo Santo Stefano sells the output of many small vintners and dispenses some excellent local wines from large vats. *Calle delle Botteghe.* ☎ *041-2410634. MC, V. Vaporetto: San Samuele. Map p 69.*

★★ **Vineria Nave de Oro** DORSODURO Locals bring their own containers for a fill-up from huge vats of regional wines, also available by the bottle. *Campo Santa*

Customers waiting for some of the city's best pastries at Rosa Salva.

A floating vegetable market, a common sight on the Grand Canal.

Margherita. ☎ 041-5222693. No credit cards. Vaporetto: Ca' Rezzonico. Map p 71.

★★★ VizioVirtù SAN POLO Hand-crafted chocolates, made from traditional recipes, are downright decadent. *Calle del Campaniel.* ☎ 041-2750149. MC, V. Vaporetto: San Tomà. Map p 72.

Glass
★★ Amadi SAN POLO Glass becomes whimsical as it is fashioned into tiny, enchanting animals and sea creatures—the perfect, easy-to-carry memento. *Calle Saoneri.* ☎ 041-5238089. MC, V. Vaporetto: San Silvestro. Map p 72.

★★★ Barovier and Taso MURANO The most prestigious glass shop in Venice traces its roots to the 13th century. With a lineage like that, and with such creations to

its credit as the Bouvier Wedding Cup, a Renaissance masterpiece, the shop's creations are regarded as museum pieces by all but a fortunate few. *Fondamenta dei Vetrai 28.* ☎ 041-739049. www.barovier.com. AE, DC, MC, V. Vaporetto: Colonna. Map p 70.

★★★ Berengo MURANO One of Murano's best-known glassworks specializes in glass sculpture and platters, vases, and other items that are more decorative than functional. *Fondamenta dei Vetrai 109.* ☎ 041-5276364. www.berengo.com. AE, DC, MC, V. Vaporetto: Colonna. Map p 70.

★★ Elite Murano MURANO This house specializes in exquisite and often colorful reproductions of traditional Venetian goblets and other glassware. *Calle del Cimitero 6.* ☎ 041-736168. AE, MC, V. Vaporetto: Venier. Map p 70.

★★ Galleria Marina Barovier SAN MARCO One of the city's top showplaces for contemporary designers, run by a member of a distinguished line of glass crafters, also specializes in classic 20th-century

Vintage Venetian vases and glasses, pictured in a salted paper print from 1855.

pieces by Venetian artisans. *Salizzada San Samuele.* ☎ *041-5226102. www.barovier.it. No credit cards. Vaporetto: San Samuele. Map p 69.*

★★★ Genninger Studio DORSODURO
A salon overlooking the Grand Canal is a showcase for Byzantine-style oil lamps, goblets, jewelry embellished with silver and gold, and other glass creations by American Leslie Ann Genninger. *Calle del Traghetto.* ☎ *041-5225565. www.genningerstudio.com. AE, DC, MC, V. Vaporetto: Ca' Rezzonico. Map p 71.*

★★ L'Angolo del Passato DORSODURO
The superb collections of vintage glass include 19th- and 20th-century Murano pieces rarely on offer; contemporary artisans are represented as well. *Calle del Capeller.* ☎ *041-5287896. AE, DC, MC, V. Vaporetto: Ca' Rezzonico. Map p 71.*

★★ Leonardo Tiberio SAN MARCO
Many of the sophisticated designs are family creations, though works by other local artisans are represented, alongside vintage pieces. *Calle Fubiero.* ☎ *041-5232250. AE, DC, MC, V. Vaporetto: San Marco/Vallaresso. Map p 69.*

★★ L'Isola di Carlo Moretti
SAN MARCO One of Venice's top glass designers is known internationally for his colorful, often functional wares, making his shop especially alluring. *Campo San Moisè.* ☎ *041-5231973. AE, DC, MC, V. Vaporetto: San Marco/Vallaresso. Map p 69.*

★★★ Marina e Susanna Sent
DORSODURO The daughters of the well-known Murano glass clan present bowls, vases, and sculptural pieces by contemporary designers that are elegant and light. *Calle San Vio.* ☎ *041-52008138. AE, MC, V. Vaporetto: Accademia. Map p 71.*

★ Mazzega MURANO
Chandeliers and glass sculptures are specialties of the house. Visitors are invited in to see pieces being made. *Fondamenta da Mula.* ☎ *041-736888. www.mazzega.it. AE, DC, MC, V. Vaporetto: Venier. Map p 70.*

★ Pauly SAN MARCO
The output of several Murano glass factories is sold here at prices that aren't discounted but are quite reasonable, especially given the prestigious San Marco location. *Calle Larga San Marco.* ☎ *041-5209899. www.pauly glassfactory.it. AE, DC, MC, V.*

A detail of glasswork from the Berengo collection, on the island of Murano.

The stark, modern store window of the famed Venini glass shop.

Vaporetto: San Marco/Vallaresso. Map p 69.

★★★ **Seguso** MURANO You might find some pieces by this elite glass house, in business since 1397, in Murano's Museo dell'Arte Vetraria; for sale in the boutique and showroom are sculpturelike vases, bowls, and other work that would be the pride of any collection. *Fondamenta Marin.* ☎ *041-5274785. AE, MC, V. Vaporetto: Colonna. Map p 70.*

★★ **Sergio Tiozzo** MURANO The specialty of the house is *murrine*, a technique in which glass flowers are melted together to form colorful mosaic patterns. The designs are well suited to decorative pieces, not to mention plates, glassware, and vases. *Fondamenta Manin.* ☎ *041-5274155. AE, MC, V. Vaporetto: Faro. Map p 70.*

★★★ **Venini** SAN MARCO The standard-bearer of all Venetian glass shops, a fixture on the Piazza San Marco since the 1920s, has been bought by a foreign corporation but remains an essential stop. Top designers from around the world still create exquisite contemporary designs for the shop. *Piazetta*

Leoncini, Piazza San Marco. ☎ *041-5224045. www.venini.com. AE, DC, MC, V. Vaporetto: San Marco/Vallaresso. Map p 69. Also: Fondamenta Vetrai, Murano.* ☎ *041-2737204.*

Glass Beads

★ **Anticlea Antiquariato** CASTELLO Many of the beads here are antique and rare treasures, but the new creations are also exquisite. Antique music boxes and other treasures also fill the crammed premises. *Campo San Provolo.* ☎ *041-5286946. AE, DC, MC, V. Vaporetto: San Zaccaria. Map p 69.*

★ **Claudia Zaggia** DORSODURO Glass beads are made into jewelry, ornaments, and other decorative items. *Calle de la Toletta.* ☎ *041-5223159. AE, MC, V. Vaporetto: Accademia. Map p 71.*

★ **Constantini** SAN MARCO Readymade bracelets as well as hundreds of variations of colorful beads are very well priced. *Campo San Maurizio.* ☎ *041-5210789. MC, V. Vaporetto: Santa Maria del Giglio. Map p 69.*

★★ **Lili e Paolo Darin** CANNAREGIO Beads in this enticing shop are

An abstract glass jewelry design from Gualti.

one-of-a-kind creations, strung together into beautiful and affordable bracelets and necklaces. *Salizzada Santa Geremia.* ☎ *041-7175770. MC, V. Vaporetto: San Marcuola. Map p 70.*

★★ Perle e Dintorni SAN MARCO The exotic beads here recall Venice at the height of its maritime powers—based on age-old designs, they show Byzantine, Asian, and African influences. Buy them by the piece and the shop will help you string together a bracelet or necklace. *Calle della Mandola.* ☎ *041-5205068. www.perle-e-dintorni.it. AE, DC, MC, V. Vaporetto: Sant'Angelo. Map p 69. Also: Salizzada San Polo 2102A, San Polo.* ☎ *041-710031. Vaporetto: San Tomà.*

Jewelry

★★ Codognato SAN MARCO One of Italy's better-known jewelers caters to an international clientele. *Calle Seconda dell'Ascensione.* ☎ *041-5225042. AE, DC, MC, V. Vaporetto: San Marco/Vallaresso. Map p 69.*

★★ Daniel e Gabriella Stevens SAN MARCO Daniel fashions colorful glass and Gabriella creates beautiful traditional and contemporary designs for necklaces and other

pieces. *Calle dell Carrozze.* ☎ *041-5227563. MC, V. Vaporetto: San Samuele. Map p 69.*

★★★ Davide Penso MURANO A top contender for some of Murano's most beautiful jewelry creates stunning contemporary pieces. *Fondamenta Riva Longa 48.* ☎ *041-5274634. AE, MC, V. Vaporetto: Colonna. Map p 70.*

★★★ Giorgio Nason DORSODURO Each of the hand-blown pieces are works of art, handmade in contemporary designs and fashioned into stunning necklaces, bracelets, and earrings. *Campo San Gregorio.* ☎ *041-5239426. AE, MC, V. Vaporetto: Salute. Map p 71.*

★★★ Gualti DORSODURO The distinctive contemporary jewelry, each piece a work of art in bursts of colorful glass, is made on the premises by one of the city's stellar artisans. *Rio Terà Canal.* ☎ *041-5201731. www.gualti.it. AE, DC, MC, V. Vaporetto: Ca' Rezzonico. Map p 71.*

★★★ Muranero CASTELLO Niang Moulaye combines the art of his native Senegal with Venetian traditions to create exotic pieces in glass. *Calle Crosera.* ☎ *041-277829. http://muranero.blogspot.com. Vaporetto: San Zaccaria. Map p 69.*

★★★ Papuniart DORSODURO
Ninfa Salerno decided to break away from traditional Venetian glass designs and turned to stones and even PVC for her whimsical and beautiful creations. *Ponte del Pugni.* ☎ 041-2410434. MC, V. Vaporetto: Ca' Rezzonico. Map p 71.

Lace
★★★ Jesurum Outlet CANNARE-
GIO Venice's most renowned purveyor of lace traces its origins to Burano almost 150 years ago and still produces exquisitely embroidered linens and towels. Don't let the prices put you off: Affordable items on offer include linen coasters and napkins. *Fondamenta della Sensa.* ☎ 041-5242540. www.jesurum.it. AE, DC, MC, V. Vaporetto: San' Alvise. Map p 70.

Leather
★★ Bussola SAN MARCO The
selection of beautifully crafted bags, wallets, and diaries is enormous and enticing. *Calle delle Teatro.*

An example of intricate Burano lacework.

☎ 041-5229846. AE, MC, V. Vaporetto: Sant'Angelo. Map p 69.

★★★ Francis Model SAN POLO
A family business fashions briefcases, bags, and other goods in beautiful leather at work tables on the premises. *Ruga del Ravano.* ☎ 041-5212889. AE, DC, MC, V. Vaporetto: San Silvestro. Map p 72.

★★ Girotondo SAN MARCO
The collection of handsome purses extends to large bags and suitcases. *Campo San Bartolomeo.* ☎ 041-2777982. AE, DC, MC, V. Vaporetto: Rialto. Map p 69.

★★★ J. B. Guanti SAN MARCO
Gloves have never looked as appealing as they do here—embellished with sequins, trimmed with fur, and just plain, in sumptuous leather of every shade imaginable. *Calle II Aprile.* ☎ 041-5228633. AE, MC, V. Vaporetto: Rialto. Map p 69.

★★ Mazzon le Borse SAN POLO
Any Venetian can lead you to this store, a well-known local favorite for high-quality, handmade leather goods. *Campiello San Tomà.* ☎ 041-5203421. AE, DC, MC, V. Vaporetto: San Tomà. Map p 72.

★★ Rolando Segalin SAN
MARCO If a pair of handmade Italian shoes in fine leather is on your wish list, here's the place to fulfill it. *Calle dei Fuseri.* ☎ 041-5222115. AE, DC, MC, V. Vaporetto: Rialto. Map p 69.

Markets
★ Mercatino dei Miracoli
CASTELLO Venice's flea market is a monthly affair, and a satisfying place to browse for prints, old jewelry, and other bric-a-brac. *Campo San Canciano & Campo Santa Maria Nova. 2nd or 3rd weekend of the month. Vaportetto: Ca' d'Oro.* Map p 70.

★★★ Pescaria/Rialto markets

SAN POLO Venice's *pescaria* (fish market) transpires under the arcades of a neo-Gothic hall on the banks of the Grand Canal, and produce markets enliven the adjoining squares. Adding to the general fray are stalls selling souvenirs. Even if you're not in the market for eel, the goings on, the mix of locals and tourists, and the centuries-old ambience provide one of the best shows in town. *See p 43,* ⑩. *Map p 72.*

★ San Leonardo CANNAREGIO

Produce vendors set up shop on the banks of a canal, providing a perfect setup shot for shutterbugs looking for everyday Venetian scenes. *Rio Terra San Leonardo. Mon–Sat about 8am–7:30pm. Map p 72.*

★ Via Giribaldi CASTELLO Stalls

serving the large residential Castello neighborhood sell everything from produce to carving knives. *Via Giribaldi. Sept–May Mon–Sat 8am–5pm. Vaporetto: Arsenale. Map p 69.*

Masks

★★ Ca' Macana DORSODURO

See masks being made at one of Venice's most popular stops for Carnevale wear, and take home a fairly standard one or a marvelous one-of-a-kind creation. *Calle delle Botteghe.* ☎ *041-5203229. AE, DC, MC, V. Vaporetto: Ca' Rezzonico. Map p 71.*

★ Il Canovaccio CASTELLO

Named for a common plot device in *commedia dell'arte,* this shop near San Marco veers from tradition to produce stunning original designs. *Calle delle Bande.* ☎ *041-5210393. AE, MC, V. Vaporetto: San Zaccaria. Map p 69.*

★★ La Bottega dei Mascareri

SAN POLO The Boldrin brothers sell an amazing variety of masks from their crowded shop at the end of the Rialto bridge next to the church of San Giacomo. *Calle de Cristo.* ☎ *041-5223857. AE, MC, V. Vaporetto: Rialto. Map p 72.*

★★★ La Moretta Venexiana

SAN MARCO In case you didn't know just how tasteful a Carnevale mask can be, step into this lovely little store to see glorious creations that are crafted in nearby workshops. *Calle delle Botteghe.* ☎ *041-5228244. MC, V. Vaporetto: San Samuele. Map p 69.*

A customer buying produce at the Rialto market.

A craftswoman creates Carnevale masks from papier-mâché at MondeNovo Mashchere.

★★★ MondoNovo Mashchere
DORSODURO   Venice's most noted provider of Carnevale masks offers creations in papier-mâché that transform the wearer into just about any conceivable persona, from Renaissance dandy to mythological beast. *Rio Terrà Canal.* ☎ *041-5287344. www.mondonovomaschere.it. AE, DC, MC, V. Vaporetto: Ca' Rezzonico. Map p 71.*

★★ Schegge SAN MARCO   Nontraditional masks made by traditional methods are the stock in trade, and many of the elaborate papier-mâché pieces easily pass as works of modern art. *Calle Lunga Santa Maria Formosa.* ☎ *041-5225789. AE, DC, MC, V. Vaporetto: San Zaccharia. Map p 69.*

★★ Tragicomica SAN POLO
Mask-making is serious business here, and the handmade creations in papier-mâché and leather are gorgeous. *Calle dei Nomboli.* ☎ *041-721102. www.tragicomica.it. AE, DC, MC, V. Vaporetto: San Toma. Map p 72.*

Paper
★★ Alberto Valese-Ebrû SAN
MARCO   Aficionados of marbled papers will be delighted to see the technique creatively applied to silk scarves and ties, and to a wide range of paper products. *Campo Santo Stefano.* ☎ *041-5238830. AE, DC, MC, V. Vaporetto: San Samuele. Map p 69.*

★ Biblos SAN MARCO   The several Biblos outlets around Venice sell a nice selection of well-priced picture frames, boxes, and other items made from marbled papers. *Calle Larga XXII Marzo.* ☎ *041-5210714. AE, MC, V. Vaporetto: Santa Maria del Giglio. Map p 69.*

★★ Gianni Basso CANNAREGIO
Beautiful papers are personalized with your choice of name and illustration and presented as bookplates, note cards, and stationery. *Calle dei Fumo.* ☎ *041-5234681. MC, V. Vaporetto: Fondamenta Nuove. Map p 70.*

★ Il Papiro SAN MARCO   The Venice outpost of one Italy's most renowned stationers provides well-designed desk accessories to accompany its lines of fine papers. *Calle del Spezier.* ☎ *041-5221202. AE, DC, MC, V. Vaporetto: Santa Maria del Giglio. Map p 69.*

★ Il Pavone DORSODURO   Items are adorned with the shop's distinctive floral motifs in rich hues and

★★★ Legatoria Piazzesi SAN
MARCO At this 150-year-old shop, frequented by the likes of Ernest Hemingway and Prince Charles, handmade papers are sold by the piece and fashioned into boxes, address books, and other enticing items. *Campiello Feltrina.* ☎ 041-5221202. www.legatoriapiazzesi.it. *AE, MC, V. Vaporetto: Santa Maria del Giglio. Map p 69.*

★ Paolo Olbi SAN MARCO
Address books and notepads covered in marbled papers are works of art. *Calle della Mandola.* ☎ 041-5285025. *MC. Vaporetto: Sant'Angelo. Map p 69.*

Personal Care

★★ Ferigo SAN MARCO Gentlemen are pampered with a refined collection of razors, shaving lotions, soaps, and other necessities for good grooming. *Off Calle de le Ostrighe. AE, MC, V. Vaporetto: Santa Maria del Giglio. Map p 69.*

Bath powders and soaps at the Santa Maria Novella pharmacy.

include beautiful picture frames. *Fondamenta Venier dei Leoni.* ☎ 041-5234517. *AE, DC, MC, V. Vaporetto: Accademia. Map p 71.*

★★ Il Prato SAN MARCO Never mind that this purveyor of fine papers, leather knickknacks, and fine glassware has outposts as far afield as Las Vegas: the goods are luxuriously Venetian. *Calle delle Ostreghe.* ☎ 041-5231148. *AE, MC, V. Vaporetto: Santa Maria del Giglio. Map p 69.*

★★ Santa Maria Novella SAN
MARCO The medieval Florentine pharmacy has opened shop in Venice, dispensing its enchanting array of herbal soaps, scents, and other magical elixirs. *Salizzada San Samuele.* ☎ 041-5220814. *MC, V. Vaporetto: San Samuele. Map p 69.* ●

Rolls of colorful handmade paper at the Legatoria Piazzesi paper shop.

A **Waterside Walk**

S. Giacomo
dell'Orio
Palazzo
Brandolin Pescaria
Ss. Apóstoli
Pal.
Widman

S. Maria
Máter
Domini
S. Cássiano
Ca' da
Mosto
Teatro
Málibran

Fábbriche
Nuove

Palazzo
Dieci Savi
Fóndaco
D. Tedeschi

Palazzo
Morolin
SAN POLO
Ponte
di Rialto
S. Bartolomeo
Pal. Donà
CASTELLO
Pal.
Gritti

S. Polo
S. Silvestro
S. Salvador
S. Maria
Formosa
S. Lorenzo

Palazzo
Grimani
Ca' Farsetti
Pal. Querini-
Stampalia
S. Giovanni Novo

S. Tomà
Palazzo
Palazzo
Mocenigo
Palazzo
Fortuny
Cinema
Rossini
SAN MARCO
Pal. Contarini
del Bovolo
Basílica di
San Marco
S. Zaccaria
Questura
Arsenale

Pal. Grassi
Ateneo Véneto
Teatro
La Fenice
S. Fantin
Piazza
San Marco
La Pietà

S. Stefano
S. Moisè
Palazzo
Ducale
Ca'
di Dio

Pal. Falièr
Palazzo
Morosini
S. Maria
d. Giglio
Giardini
ex Reali

Palazzo
Pisáni
Pal.
Gritti
Palazzo
Tiépolo

Gallerie
dell'Accademia
S. Maria
d. Salute
Dogana
da Mar

Pal. Venier
dei Leoni
(Guggenheim)
Bacino di
San Marco
Canale di San Marco

Spirito
Santo **2**
San Giorgio
Maggiore

Canale della Giudecca
Isola di
San Giorgio
Maggiore

Isola della
Giudecca
Zitelle

3
Il Redentore
Ex Chiesa
della Croce

0 ——— 1/4 Mi
0 ——— 1/2Km

1 Giardini Pubblici
to San Marco
2 Zattere
3 Giudecca

If you're looking for long, unbroken stretches of pavement
that are well suited for a fast walk or even a jog, do as the Venetians do: Head to the *fondamenti* (quays or streets) that trace the
city's major waterways. Studded with landmarks and abuzz with
activity, the following three such locales provide much more than a
chance simply to stretch your legs. START: **Take vaporetto 1, 41, or 42
to the Giardini stop.**

**1 Giardini Pubblici to San
Marco.** Start with a stroll in the
public gardens, then follow the busy
riva (promenade) that skirts the
Bacino di San Marco, changing its
name every so often—from Riva dei
Sette Martiri (for seven slain World
War II partisans) to the Riva degli
Schiavoni, named for the Slavic

*Previous page: Sunset at San Giorgio
Maggiore, just east of the Giudecca.*

community that founded the nearby
Scuola di San Giorgio degli Schiavoni
(see p 31, **2**). End the walk with
a flourish, with a saunter through
Piazza San Marco. *If you want to
keep walking, board a vaporetto
no. 1 for Salute at the San Marco/
Vallaresso stop.*

2 Zattere. Begin at the eastern
end of this broad quay, named for
the rafts that once unloaded timber
here for the construction of Venetian

Islands in the Lagoon

You'll find a Venetian version of country living on two adjacent islands, **Sant'Erasmo** and **Vignole,** where the main business is growing vegetables for the city markets. Sant'Erasmo is especially famous for its purple artichokes, *carciofi violetto.* Indeed, the thing to do on both islands is to simply stroll along the few roads and admire fields of these and other produce, along with some pleasing views over the lagoon. Take vaporetto 13 to both islands; disembark at the Chiesa stop on Sant'Erasmo.

palazzi. Just beyond the Salute vaporetto stop is the Punta della Dogana—a tip of land adjacent to the Customs house (see p 45, **5**) that affords breathtaking views of the lagoon, the Grand Canal, and San Marco. As you follow the walk west, your entertainment will be the spectacle of traffic in the Giudecca Canal. The deep-water channel is often jammed with freighters and cruise ships coming and going from the busy port, Stazione Maritima, at the western end of the promenade. *See p 62, **14**. If you want to keep walking, from the San Basilio vaporetto stop at the western end of the Zattere, board a no. 82 boat and*

cross the canal to the Sant'Eufemia stop on Giudecca.

3 **Giudecca.** The *fondamenta* on the northern side of the Giudecca Canal provides a long stretch of pavement well suited for an uninterrupted session of physical exertion— a convenience not lost on the strollers and joggers who make the trip over to the island in good weather. The scenery includes two Palladian churches, Le Zitelle and Il Redentore (see p 46, **1**), but the eye-filling views are those toward the shimmering city on the other side of the canal. *From the Zitelle stop, return to San Marco (San Zaccaria stop) on a no. 82 boat.*

A bird's-eye view of the Riva degli Schiavoni, which faces San Giorgio Maggiore.

The **Lido**

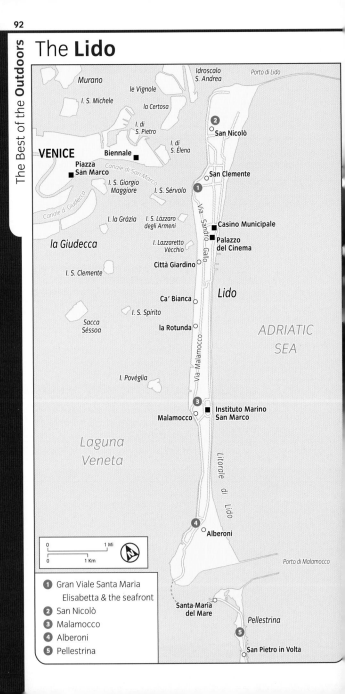

Murano
le Vignole
I. S. Michele
la Certosa
Idroscalo S. Andrea
Porto di Lido
I. di S. Pietro
I. di S. Élena
VENICE
Biennale ■
Piazza San Marco ■
Canale di San Marco
I. S. Giorgio Maggiore
I. S. Sérvolo
Canale di Giudecca
I. la Grázia
I. S. Lázzaro degli Armeni
I. Lazzaretto Vécchio
la Giudecca
I. S. Clemente
San Nicolò ②
San Clemente
Casino Municipale ■
Palazzo del Cinema ■
Città Giardino
Via Sandro Gallo
Lido
Ca' Bianca
I. S. Spírito
la Rotunda
Sacca Séssoa
ADRIATIC SEA
I. Povéglia
Via Malamocco
Malamocco ③
Instituto Marino San Marco ■
Laguna Veneta
Litorale di Lido
Alberoni ④
Porto di Malamocco
0 — 1 Mi
0 — 1 Km
Santa Maria del Mare
Pellestrina
San Pietro in Volta ⑤

① Gran Viale Santa Maria Elisabetta & the seafront
② San Nicolò
③ Malamocco
④ Alberoni
⑤ Pellestrina

This stretch of sand, 12km (7½ miles) long and barely 1km (½ mile) wide, separates the Adriatic from the lagoon and is where Venetians come to play—along the lines of swimming, golfing, riding bikes, and playing tennis. The Lido is also a pleasant place to walk on attractive, shady streets or along the miles of sand beaches. As you explore, you can try to conjure up a bit of belle-epoque decadence, a la Thomas Mann's novella *Death in Venice,* but these days the Lido is more bourgeois suburb than elite playground.

START: **Take vaporetto 1, 41, 42, 51, 52, or 53 to Lido.**

❶ Gran Viale Santa Maria Elisabetta & the seafront. The Lido's main street runs between the Lido vaporetto stop at Piazzale Maria Elisabetta to Piazzale Bucontoro on the seafront. *Fin de siècle* luxury is in evidence, especially around the extravagant Hotel des Bains and Excelsior Palace on the Lungomare Marconi, just south of Piazzale Bucontoro, as is plenty of idleness: The private cabana-backed beaches are packed with hotel guests and Venetians who pay a handsome price to pass a summer day relaxing in the sun. *To reach Piazzale Bucontoro and the seafront from Piazzale Maria Elisabetta, walk down Gran Viale (about 15 min.); or take bus no. 11, B, or V.*

❷ San Nicolò. This town at the northern tip of the Lido has a long history, with a church founded in the 11th century, a 14th-century Jewish cemetery, and the offshore 16th-century Fortezza di Sant'Andrea, built to defend the Porto di Lido, the main sea entrance to the lagoon. Of more interest to many visitors are the miles of public beaches that surround the town. *Guided tours of cemetery Sun 2:30pm.* ☎ *041-715359. Bus nos. A and B run from Piazzale Maria Elisabetta to San Nicolò, about 1.5km (1 mile).*

❸ Malamocco. The most attractive community on the Lido is a quaint fishing village surrounding a pretty campo. Once a bustling port for the inland city of Padua, Malamocco was swept away in a tidal wave in 1106 and rebuilt in its present guise in the 15th century. *Bus nos. 11, B, and V run from Piazzale Maria Elisabetta to Malamocco, about 5km (3 miles).*

Cabanas on a Lido beach, evocative of the Venice Thomas Mann captured.

The Jewish cemetery at St. Nicolò, dating to the 14th century.

4 Alberoni. At the edge of the southernmost settlement on the Lido are the greens of the only golf course in Venice (see "Getting Active on the Lido," below). The town's attractive beaches are backed by dunes and pine forests. *Bus no. 11 runs from Piazzale Maria Elisabetta to Alberoni, about 12km (7½ miles).*

5 Pellistrina. This island, separated from the Lido by a narrow channel, is where many Venetians prefer to spend a day at the beach. The 10km-long (6-mile) strip of scrubby vegetation is no more than a sand bar, with two attractive fishing communities, San Pietro in Volta and Pellistrina. *Bus no. 11 runs from Piazzale Maria Elisabetta to Pellistrina, about 13km (8 miles).* ●

Getting Active on the Lido

The terrain of the Lido lends itself to outdoor activities. In addition to swimming and relaxing at the beach, you can golf, bike, play tennis, jog, and so on. The 18-hole, par-72 **golf course,** Strada Vecchia 1, Alberoni (☎ 041-7313333; www.circologolfvenezia.it), is the only place to play golf in Venice, and is one of Italy's top courses. It's open April to September Tuesday to Sunday 8am to 8pm; October to March Tuesday to Sunday 8:30am to 6pm. It costs 55€ Monday to Friday, 70€ Saturday and Sunday; cart rental is 35€ for 18 holes.

For **bicycle rentals,** try Giardin Anna Valli, Piazzale Santa Maria Elisabetta (☎ 041-2760005), open May to October 8am to 8pm. Bikes are 2.60€ an hour, 8€ a day.

One of the Lido's best public **tennis** facilities, the Tennis Club Ca' del Moro, Via Ferrucio Parri 6 (☎ 041-770965), is open Monday to Saturday 8:30am to 8:30pm, and Sunday 8:30am to 8pm, and costs 8.50€ per hour.

Dining **Best Bets**

Best **Deep-Dish Pizza**
★★ Acqua Pazza $$–$$$ *Campo Sant'Angelo, San Marco* (p 101)

Best **Panino with a View**
★★ Algiubagiò $ *Fondamenta Nuove, Cannaregio* (p 102)

Best Place for a **Meal on an Out-of-the-Way Square**
★★ Alla Frasca $ *Campeillo della Caritá, Castello* (p 102)

Best **Vegetarian Meal**
★★ Alla Zucca $ *Ponte del Megio, Santa Croce* (p 102)

Best **Hot Chocolate**
★★★ Antica Pasticceria Inguan-otto $ *Ponte del Lovo, San Marco* (p 103)

Best **Value for an Excellent Meal**
★★★ Bea Vita $$ *Fondamenta delle Cappuccine* (p 104)

Best Place to **Get a Whiff of Student Life**
★★ Caffè dei Frari $ *Fondamenta dei Frari, San Polo* (p 105)

Best **Panini and Crostini in Town**
★★★ Cantinone già Schiavi $ *Ponte San Travaso* (p 105)

A classic carpaccio (thinly sliced raw beef), an original Venice creation.

Best **Affordable Seafood Meal**
★★★ Corte Sconta $$ *Calle del Pestrin, Castello* (p 105)

Best **Stop for Carnivores**
★★★ Dalla Marisa $ *Fondamenta San Giobbe, Cannaregio* (p 105)

Best **Atmosphere for a Quick Bite**
★★ Do Mori $ *Calle dei Do Mori, San Polo* (p 107)

Best **Gelato**
★★★ Gelateria Nico $ *Fondamenta Zattere, Dorsoduro* (p 107)

Best Place to **See the Rich & Famous, and the Rich & Not So Famous**
★★ Harry's Bar $$$$ *Calle Valla-resso, San Marco* (p 107)

Best **Thin-Crust Pizza**
★★★ Il Refolo $$–$$$ *Campeillo del Piovan, Santa Croce* (p 107)

Best Place to **Enjoy Renais-sance Recipes and Rare Wines**
★★★ Le Bistrot de Venise $$$ *Calle dei Fabbri, San Marco* (p 108)

Best Place to **Propose Marriage**
★★★ Locanda Cipriani $$$$ *Piazza Santa Fosca, Torcello* (p 108)

Best Place to **Take a Break from Italian Cooking**
★★ Mirai $$ *Lista di Spagna, Cannaregio* (p 108)

Best **Meal in Town**
★★★ Osteria da Fiore $$$$ *Calle delle Scaleter, San Polo* (p 110)

Best Place to **Have a Pastry & a Cappuccino**
★★★ Rosa Salva $ *Campo Santi Giovanni e Paolo, Castello* (p 111)

Previous page: An outdoor dinner for two off a Venice canal.

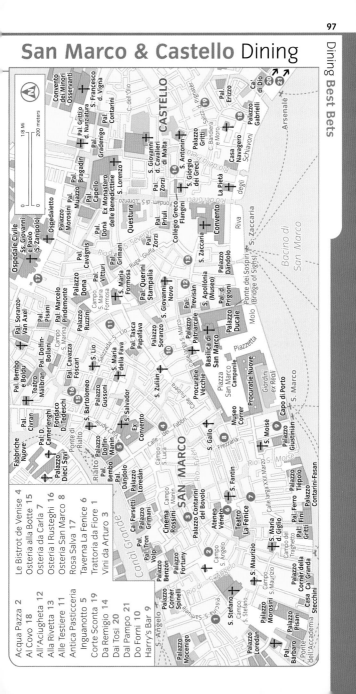

Acqua Pazza 2
Al Covo 18
All'Aciugheta 12
Alla Rivetta 13
Alle Testiere 11
Antica Pasticceria
Inguanotto 5
Corte Sconta 19
Da Remigio 14
Dai Tosi 20
Dal Pampo 21
Do Forni 10
Harry's Bar 9
Le Bistrot de Venise 4
Osteria alla Botte 15
Osteria da Carla 7
Osteria I Rusteghi 16
Osteria San Marco 8
Rosa Salva 17
Taverna La Fenice 6
Trattoria da Fiore 1
Vini da Arturo 3

Cannaregio Dining

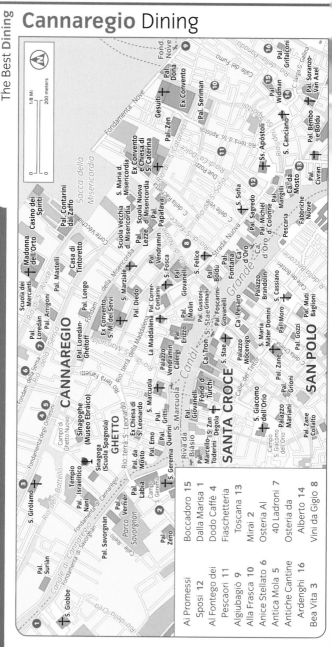

Ai Promessi Sposi 12
Al Fontego dei Pescaori 11
Algiubagiò 9
Alla Frasca 10
Anice Stellato 6
Antica Mola 5
Antiche Cantine Ardenghi 16
Bea Vita 3
Boccadoro 15
Dalla Marisa 1
Dodo Caffè 4
Fiaschetteria Toscana 13
Mirai 2
Osteria Al 40 Ladroni 7
Osteria da Alberto 14
Vini da Gigio 8

Dorsoduro Dining

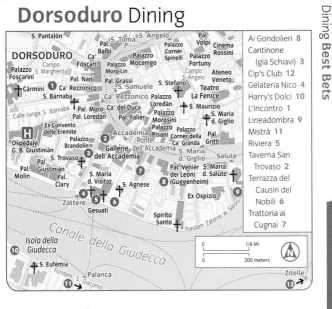

Ai Gondolieri **8**

Cantinone
(già Schiavi) **3**

Cip's Club **12**

Gelateria Nico **4**

Harry's Dolci **10**

L'Incontro **1**

Lineadombra **9**

Mistrà **11**

Riviera **5**

Taverna San
Trovaso **2**

Terrazza del
Causin del
Nobili **6**

Trattoria ai
Cugnai **7**

San Polo & Santa Croce Dining

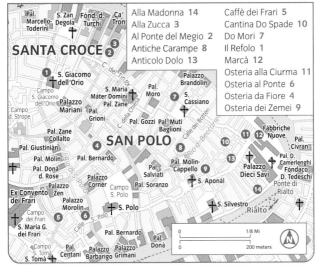

Alla Madonna **14**

Alla Zucca **3**

Al Ponte del Megio **2**

Antiche Carampe **8**

Anticolo Dolo **13**

Caffè dei Frari **5**

Cantina Do Spade **10**

Do Mori **7**

Il Refolo **1**

Marcà **12**

Osteria alla Ciurma **11**

Osteria al Ponte **6**

Osteria da Fiore **4**

Osteria dei Zemei **9**

The Islands Dining

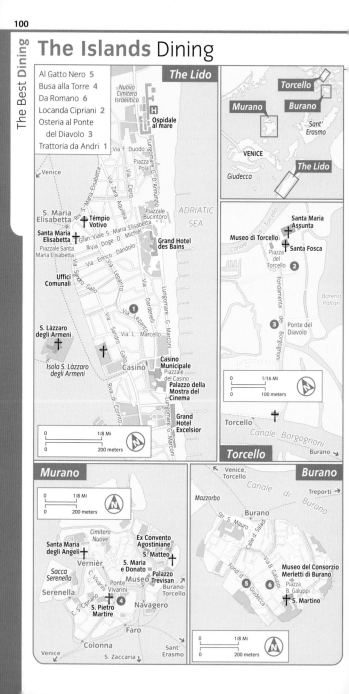

Al Gatto Nero 5
Busa alla Torre 4
Da Romano 6
Locanda Cipriani 2
Osteria al Ponte
  del Diavolo 3
Trattoria da Andri 1

The Lido

Nuovo
Cimitero
Israelitico

Ospidale
al mare

Via F. Duodo

Venice

Via S. Maria Elisabetta

Riv. S. Maria Elisabetta

Via. Zara

Via. Cipro

Aquileia

Piazza
Pola

Lungomare. G. D'Annunzio

S. Maria
Elisabetta

Témpio
Votivo

Santa Maria
Elisabetta

Gran Viale S. Maria Elisabetta

Via Doge D. Michiel

Piazzale
Bucintoro

ADRIATIC
SEA

Piazzale Santa
Maria Elisabetta

Via. Enrico. Dándolo

Grand Hotel
des Bains

Uffici
Comunali

Via. Sandro. Gallo

Via. Lepanto

Via. Dardenelli

S. Lázzaro
degli Armeni

Via. L. Marcello

Lungomare. G. Marconi

Isola S. Lázzaro
degli Armeni

Via. Sandro. Gallo

Casinò

Casino
Municipale

Piazzale
del Casino

Palazzo della
Mostra del
Cinema

Riva. di. Corinto

Lungomare. G. Marconi

Grand
Hotel
Excelsior

0   1/8 Mi
0   200 meters

Torcello

Torcello

Murano

Burano

Sant'
Erasmo

VENICE

The Lido

Giudecca

Canale di Torcello

Santa Maria
Assunta

Museo di Torcello

Santa Fosca

Canale

Piazza
del
Torcello

Fondamenta

Barena
Paltan

Ponte del
Diavolo

Fondamenta del Borgognoni

0   1/16 Mi
0   100 meters

Torcello

Canale Borgognoni

Burano →

Torcello

Murano

0   1/8 Mi
0   200 meters

Cimitero
Nuove

Ex Convento
Agostiniane

Santa Maria
degli Angeli

S. Matteo

Verniér

S. Maria
e Donato

Sacca
Serenella

C. Vivarini

Ponte
Vivarini

Palazzo
Trevisan

Museo

Burano-
Torcello

Serenella

C. S. Cipriano

S. Pietro
Martire

Navagero

Colonna

Faro

Sant'
Erasmo

Venice

S. Zaccaria ↓

Burano

Venice,
Torcello

Canale   di   Burano

Treporti →

Mazzorbo

Burano

Str. S. Mauro

Calle d. Sabalí

Via B. Galuppi

Museo del Consorzio
Merletti di Burano

Fond. di

Giudecca

Piazza
B. Galuppi

S. Martino

0   1/8 Mi
0   200 meters

Dining A to Z

★★ Acqua Pazza SAN MARCO *NEAPOLITAN* This perennially busy indoor-outdoor pizzeria-ristorante is a good place to come with companions with varying appetites and bankrolls: You can dine simply and moderately on the delicious, deep-dish Neapolitan pies or sample one of the many fish and seafood dishes inspired by the southern city. *Campo Sant'Angelo.* ☎ *041-2770688. Entrees 9€–25€. AE, DC, MC, V. Tues–Sun noon–3pm, 7–11pm. Vaporetto: Sant'Angelo. Map p 97.*

★★★ Ai Gondolieri DORSODURO *ITALIAN* In this charming old inn alongside a canal, the freshest vegetables from the farmland surrounding the lagoon augment a rare offering in Venice—a wide selection of meat dishes, concentrating on such seasonal favorites as duck and venison. *Ponte del Formager.* ☎ *041-5286396. Entrees 25€–35€. MC, V. Wed–Mon noon–2:30pm, 7–9:30pm. Vaporetto: Accademia. Map p 99.*

★★ Ai Promessi Sposi CANNAREGIO *ITALIAN* This is a great place to sample *cicheti,* the Venetian version of tapas—rice balls, fried olives, marinated seafood, grilled vegetables, and on and on. The simple pasta and meat dishes are excellent and well priced, too. *Calle dell'Oca.* ☎ *041-5228609. Entrees 7€–10€. No credit cards. Thurs–Tues 10am–10pm. Vaporetto: Fondamente Nuove. Map p 98.*

★★★ Al Covo CASTELLO *VENETIAN/SEAFOOD* Only the freshest fish and seafood are used in the delightful preparations that include a memorable pasta with scallops. The appealing contemporary surroundings extend onto a pretty terrace. *Campiello della Pescaria.* ☎ *041-5223812. Entrees 14€–28€.*

Patrons enjoying the cafe scene on a Venice piazza.

No credit cards. Fri–Tues 12:45–3:30pm, 7:30pm–midnight. Vaporetto: Arsenale. Map p 97.

★★★ Al Fontego dei Pescaori CANNAREGIO *VENETIAN/SEAFOOD* Not too far from the Rialto fish markets, this chic eatery puts a new spin on Venetian seafood classics with the addition of fresh seasonal produce and creative spices. Meat dishes are approached with the same refreshing touch. *Sottoportego del Tagliapietra.* ☎ *041-5200538. Entrees 15€–30€. AE, DC, MC, V. Mon, Wed–Sun noon–2:30pm, 7–10pm. Vaporetto: Ca d'Oro. Map p 98.*

★★★ Al Gatto Nero BURANO *VENETIAN/SEAFOOD* A delicious meal of fresh fish or seafood pasta comes with a view of Burano's fish market across the canal by day and quiet island life in the evening. *Fondamenta della Giudecca.* ☎ *041-730120. Entrees 19€–35€. AE, DC, MC, V. Tues–Sun noon–2:30pm, 7–10pm. Vaporetto: Burano. Map p 100.*

The Best Dining

★★ **Algiubagiò** CANNAREGIO *CAFE* The terrace provides a view of the busy comings and goings at the vaporetto stop, the departure point for the islands. Before boarding, fortify yourself with a sandwich or grab a slice of pizza from the adjoining counter to take with you; by night, a dining room is the setting for excellent pastas and seafood. *Fondamenta Nuove.* ☎ *041-5227949. Entrees 3€–8€; at night, 14€–22€. AE, DC, MC, V. Daily 6:30am–11:30. Vaporetto: Fondamenta Nuove. Map p 98.*

★★ **All'Aciugheta** CASTELLO *VENETIAN/ITALIAN Cicheti—* Venetian snacks, such as small meatballs and stuffed peppers—are the specialty here, served with a vast selection of wine. Some excellent pasta dishes, such as black tagliatelle with squid and cuttlefish, are also available. *Campo Santi Filippo e Giacomo.* ☎ *041-5224292. Entrees 9€–15€. MC, V. Daily noon–11pm. Vaporetto: San Zaccaria. Map p 97.*

★★ **Alla Frasca** CANNAREGIO *VENETIAN* You'll feel you've been transported to a village square at this simple, out-of-the-way little place that dispenses deliciously fresh seafood and hearty pastas on a

vine-covered terrace and in an unfussy room. *Campeillo della Carità.* ☎ *041-5285433. Entrees 10€–15€. No credit cards. Mon–Sat, noon–2:30pm, 6:30–10pm. Closed 1 week in Aug and 2 weeks in Dec–Jan. Vaporetto: Fondamenta Nuove. Map p 98.*

★★★ **Alla Madonna** SAN POLO *VENETIAN/SEAFOOD* As befits a location near the Rialto fish market, this clamorous, charming trattoria serves the freshest fish and seafood available, which arrives at the table in such classic Venetian preparations as a rich *zuppa di pesce* (fish soup) and *vermicelli al nero di seppia* (vermicelli with a sauce of cuttlefish ink). *Calle della Madonna.* ☎ *041-5223824. Entrees 9€–15€. AE, MC, V. Thurs–Tues noon–3pm, 7–10pm. Closed Jan, 2 weeks in Aug. Vaporetto: Rialto. Map p 99.*

★★ **Alla Rivetta** CASTELLO *VENETIAN/ITALIAN* The proximity of San Marco doesn't deter from a casual neighborhood atmosphere— or the good value of one of the best-prepared *fritto misto* (mixed fry) in town. *Ponte San Provolo.* ☎ *041-5287302. Entrees 9€–19€. AE, MC, V. Tues–Sun 8am–11pm. Vaporetto: San Zaccaria. Map p 97.*

★★ **Alla Zucca** SANTA CROCE *ITALIAN/VEGETARIAN* The emphasis here is on vegetarian cooking, which, given the bounty of the Veneto, is not to be overlooked; even so, deftly prepared fish and lamb dishes also appear on the menu. *Ponte del Megio.* ☎ *041-5241570. Entrees 9€–17€. AE, DC, MC, V. Mon–Sat 12:30–2:30pm, 7–10:30pm. Vaporetto: San Stae. Map p 99.*

★★★ **Alle Testiere** CASTELLO *VENETIAN/SEAFOOD* One of Venice's trendiest and most hyped restaurants well deserves its fame, serving aromatic seafood dishes,

The wood-beamed trattoria Alla Madonna.

A typical Venetian lunch scene: Gondolas glide past canal-side diners.

fine wines, and excellent cheeses in causal-chic surroundings. *Calle del Mondo Novo.* ☎ *041-5227220. Entrees 19€–30€. MC, V. Tues–Sun noon–2pm, 7–10:30pm. Vaporetto: Rialto. Map p 97.*

★★ **Al Ponte del Megio** SANTA CROCE *VENETIAN/SEAFOOD* With tables in a rustic room and set out next to a small canal in warm weather, this neighborhood favorite is a friendly spot for a meal of excellent seafood pastas and fresh fish. *Calle Larga.* ☎ *041-719777. Entrees 12€–24€. MC, V. Mon–Sat 12:30–2:30pm, 6:30pm–12:30am. Vaporetto: San Stae. Map p 99.*

★★★ **Anice Stellato** CANNAREGIO *VENETIAN* The simple, laid-back decor in the small beamed rooms and the reasonable prices might not prepare you for what's coming your way here: exceptionally good preparations of fish and such classics as *fegato all veneziana* (calf's liver, Venetian style, sautéed with onions). *Fondamenta della Sensa.* ☎ *041-5238153. Entrees 14€–24€. MC, V. Wed–Sun 12:30–2pm, 7:30–10pm. Closed 3 weeks in Aug. Vaporetto: Fondamente Nuove. Map p 98.*

★ **Antica Mola** CANNAREGIO *VENETIAN* The homey garden

dining room and canal-side tables are usually packed with neighborhood families, and it's easy to understand why once you enjoy the simply prepared seafood dishes and pastas—and see the prices. *Fondamenta Ormesini.* ☎ *041-717492. Entrees 7€–19€. MC, V. Thurs–Tues 12:30–2:30pm, 7–10pm. Vaporetto: San Marcuola. Map p 98.*

★★★ **Antica Pasticceria Inguanotto** SAN MARCO *CAFE* This Venetian institution—founded in 1750 and also known as **Caffè al Ponte del Lovo**—accompanies its fine pastries with delicious hot chocolate and excellent coffee. *Ponte del Lovo.* ☎ *041-5208439. 2€–4€. MC, V. June–Sept Mon–Sat 8am–8:30pm; Oct–May Mon–Sat 8am–8:30pm, Sun noon–8pm. Vaporetto: Rialto. Map p 97.*

★★ **Antiche Cantine Ardenghi** CANNAREGIO *VENETIAN/SEAFOOD* The food is typically Venetian, with a small but flavorful selection of seafood dishes made fresh daily; but the experience—from the unmarked location to the quirky patrons to the bottomless carafes of house wine—may be unlike any you've had before. *Calle della Testa.* ☎ *041-5237691. Entrees 50€ prix fixe. No credit cards. Tues–Sat 8pm*

(1 seating). Vaporetto: Fondamente Nuove. Map p 98.

★★★ Antiche Carampane SAN POLO

VENETIAN/SEAFOOD The place is almost impossible to find, and a sign announcing "NO PIZZA. NO LASAGNA. NO TELEPHONE. NO TOURIST MENU" is less than welcoming—but persevere: The excellent and exotic seafood pastas and sophisticated fish preparations will win you over. *Rio Terra della Carampe.* ☎ 041-5240165. Entrees 19€–26€. MC, V. Tues–Sat 12:30–2:30pm, 7:30–10:30pm. Vaporetto: San Silvestro. Map p 99.

★★★ Anticolo Dolo SAN POLO

VENETIAN/SEAFOOD The nearby fruit and vegetable markets supply the freshest ingredients for homemade pastas with seafood and perfectly prepared fish, served in a cramped narrow room hung with brass pots and old photographs. *Ruga Vecchia San Giovanni (Ruga Rialto).* ☎ 041-5226546. Entrees 19€–26€. AE, DC, V. Tues–Sun 12:30–2:30pm, 7–11pm. Vaporetto: Rialto. Map p 99.

★★★ Bea Vita CANNAREGIO

VENETIAN A complimentary glass

The cozy and quaint red decor of Anticolo Dolo.

A seafood-medley appetizer canal-side at Bea Vita.

of Prosecco sets the tone for an amiable meal that features homemade pastas and fresh fish and meat in innovative preparations. A meal here is a great value, especially the prix fixe lunch. *Fondamenta delle Cappuccine.* ☎ 041-2759347. Entrees 18€–23€. AE, MC, V. Mon–Sat noon–2:30pm, 7:30–10:30pm. Vaporetto: Fondamente Nuove. Map p 98.

★★★ Boccadoro CANNAREGIO

VENETIAN/SEAFOOD The relaxed dining room and quiet, out-of-the-way campo are for many Venetians the best place in town to enjoy fresh, inventive seafood dishes. *Pesce crudo* (raw fish) selections feature the freshest sashimi of perfectly spiced Adriatic fish, and mussels, clams, and shrimp appear in elegant pasta and risotto dishes. *Campiello Widman.* ☎ 041-5211021. Entrees 15€–30€. AE, DC, MC, V. Tues–Sun 12:30–2:30pm, 8–11:30pm. Vaporetto: Fondamente Nuove. Map p 98.

★★★ Busa alla Torre MURANO

VENETIAN/SEAFOOD Escape the island's glass-shop craze and take a seat in the pleasant dining room or on the terrace beneath the bell tower—the welcome respite includes an excellent meal of such specialties as *ravioli di pesce.* *Campo Santo Stefano.* ☎ 041-739662. Entrees 13.50€–20€. AE, MC, V. Mon–Sat noon–3:30pm, 6:30–11:30pm. Vaporetto: Colonna. Map p 100.

★★ Caffè dei Frari SAN POLO
CAFE This cozy nook is popular with students from the university and provides a nice refuge for weary visitors to the nearby Frari and Scuola Grande di San Rocco (see p 32, **9**). *Fondamenta dei Frari.* ☎ *041-5241877. Entrees 3€–6€. No credit cards. Mon–Fri 8am–midnight; Sat 5pm–midnight; Sun 5–9pm. Vaporetto: San Tomà. Map p 99.*

★★★ Cantina Do Spade SAN
POLO *VENETIAN/WINE BAR* Dating from the 15th century and serving a clientele that has included Casanova, this atmosphere-soaked wine bar can indeed call itself a Venice institution. You can dine well on the *cicheti*—snacks of fried calamari and other morsels—and the fixed-price menus served at the few tables offer tasty and affordable full meals. *Sottoportego do Spade.* ☎ *041-5210574. Entrees 7€–10€. AE, MC, V. Daily 9am–3pm, 5–11pm. Vaporetto: Rialto. Map p 99.*

★★★ Cantinone già Schiavi
DORSODURO *WINE BAR* This neighborhood institution draws large crowds for its delicious panini that, along with a tempting array of crostini topped with cheeses, vegetables, smoked fish, and other morsels, can easily suffice for lunch or a light evening meal and should be accompanied by a glass of one of the many house wines. *Ponte San Trovaso.* ☎ *041-5230034. Entrees 4€–7€. No credit cards. Mon–Sat 8:30am–8:30pm; Sun 9am–1pm. Vaporetto: Accademia. Map p 99.*

★★ Cip's Club GIUDECCA *VENETIAN/SEAFOOD* Is the view worth the price? Sitting on the wooden terrace overlooking the Giudecca Canal and San Marco is certainly a treat. If the hefty tab for such house specialties as *mazzancolle* (prawns) with capers is going to break the bank, settle for just a first course, such as the delicious risotto with scallops and baby artichokes—or, for that matter, a cocktail at sunset. *Hotel Cipriani.* ☎ *041-5207744. Entrees 30€–45€. AE, DC, MC, V. Daily noon–3:30pm, 7–11pm. Vaporetto: Zitelle. Map p 99.*

★★★ Corte Sconta CASTELLO
VENETIAN/SEAFOOD One of the top choices in town for fresh, deftly prepared seafood, much of which comes to the table in delectable pasta dishes and risottos. Reserve well in advance, and request a table in the namesake courtyard. *Calle del Pestrin.* ☎ *041-5227024. Entrees 14€–22€. MC, V. Tues–Sat 12:30–2pm, 7–10pm. Vaporetto: Giardini. Map p 97.*

★ Dai Tosi CASTELLO *ITALIAN*
This is something Venice has all too few of—a friendly neighborhood pizzeria, complete with a rear garden. Handy for the Biennale (p 125), which is held in the adjacent public gardens. *Secco Marina.* ☎ *041-5237102. Entrees 8€–16€. MC, V. Mon–Tues, Thurs noon–2pm; Fri–Sun noon–2pm, 7–9:30pm. Vaporetto: Giardini. Map p 97.*

★★★ Dalla Marisa CANNAREGIO
ITALIAN No serious carnivore will

The bar at Cantina Do Spade has been serving wine for 600 years.

to leave Venice without enjoy-
...g at least one meal at this simple
and inexpensive osteria near the
Ponte di Tre Archi. (In fact, you can
see this landmark from the tables
out front alongside the canal.) Old-
fashioned ways still hold sway in the
kitchen, which sends out traditional
preparations of *osso buco* (braised
veal shanks), *tripa* (tripe), and other
classics. *Fondamenta San Giobbe.*
☎ *041-720211. Entrees 9€–14€.
No credit cards. Tues, Thurs–Fri
noon–2:30pm, 8–9:15pm; Sat–Mon
noon–2:30pm. Closed Aug.
Vaporetto: Tre Archi. Map p 98.*

★★ **Dal Pampo** SANT'ELENA
VENETIAN/ITALIAN   The official
name is **Osteria Sant'Elena,** but
everyone knows this busy trattoria in
the out-of-the-way Sant'Elena neighborhood as "Pampo's Place." Pasta
dishes, *fritto misto* (mixed fry, here
of seafood), and other traditional
favorites, along with bar snacks,
satisfy a crowd of regulars. *Calle
Generale Chinotto.* ☎ *041-5208419.
Entrees 7€–15€. AE, MC, V.
Mon–Wed, Fri–Sun noon–2:30pm,
7:30–9pm. Vaporetto: Sant'Elena.
Map p 97.*

★★ **Da Remigio** CASTELLO
VENETIAN/SEAFOOD   What the
busy premises lack in charm is more
than compensated by the mostly

seafood menu, expertly prepared
and featuring such Adriatic staples
as *fritto misto* and fish caught that
day and simply grilled. *Salizzada dei
Greci.* ☎ *041-5230089. Entrees
8€–18€. AE, DC, MC, V. Mon,
Wed–Sat 12:30–2:30pm, 7:30–10pm;
Sun 12:30–2:30pm. Vaporetto: Arsenale. Map p 97.*

★★ **Da Romano** BURANO *VENET-
IAN/SEAFOOD*   Such specialties as a
simple risotto flavored with fish broth
are memorable, but Romano banks
on its celebrated clientele—some
famous, others of an artistic bent
whose paintings cover every inch
of the walls. *Via Galuppi.* ☎ *041-
730030. Entrees 15€–30€. AE, DC,
MC, V. Tues–Sat noon–3:30pm,
7–9:30pm; Sun noon–3:30pm.
Vaporetto: Burano. Map p 100.*

★★★ **Do Forni** SAN MARCO
VENETIAN/INTERNATIONAL   The
former bakery of the monastery of
San Zaccaria now serves excellent
Venetian seafood specialties in two
dining rooms, one (the more appeal-
ing) rustic and whitewashed, the
other upholstered and paneled like a
carriage car on the *Orient Express.
Calle dei Specchieri.* ☎ *041-5232148.
Entrees 13€–24€. AE, DC, MC, V.
Daily noon–3pm, 7–11pm. Vaporetto:
San Marco/Vallaresso. Map p 97.*

People flock to Gelateria Nico for the homemade gelato.

Le Bistrot de Venise serves traditional Venetian fare indoors and out.

★★ **Do Mori** SAN POLO *VENET-IAN/WINE BAR* This dark, battered-looking old place situated in the midst of the Rialto markets has been dispensing wine and tidbits of fish, meats, and cheeses for some 6 centuries and still packs in an appreciative crowd of regulars. *Calle dei Do Mori.* ☎ *041-5225401. Entrees 2€–3€. No credit cards. Mon–Sat 8:30am–8:30pm. Vaporetto: Rialto. Map p 99.*

★★ **Fiaschetteria Toscana** CANNAREGIO *VENETIAN/ITALIAN* The name refers to the Tuscan wines and oils once stored and sold from the now-elegant premises. These days the offerings are such Venetian specialties as grilled sardines and *fegato alla veneziana* (calf's liver sautéed in oil and spices). The flawless preparations and excellent service provide a memorable dining experience that may well be worth the splurge. *Salizzada San Giovanni Grisostomo.* ☎ *041-5285281. Entrees 18€–40€. AE, DC, MC, V. Mon 7:30–10:30pm; Wed–Sun 12:30–2:30pm, 7:30–10:30pm. Vaporetto: Rialto. Map p 98.*

★★★ **Gelateria Nico** DORSO-DURO *CAFE* Sandwiches are available on a terrace overlooking the Giudecca Canal, but the draw for most patrons is the terrific gelato

made on the premises. *Fondamenta Zattere.* ☎ *041-5225293. Entrees 3€–8€. No credit cards. June–Sept daily 7:30am–11:30pm; Oct–May daily 9:30am–3pm. Vaporetto: Zattere. Map p 99.*

★★ **Harry's Bar** SAN MARCO *VENETIAN/INTERNATIONAL* A favorite for many, way too over-priced and generic for others. But everyone agrees that Harry's wafer-thin carpaccio (invented here) and scampi are memorable classics. You may be just as happy settling for a Bellini at the bar. (The frothy concoction of peach juice and sparkling wine was also invented here.) Harry's Dolci on Giudecca trades pedigree for views from a canal-side terrace. *Calle Vallaresso.* ☎ *041-5285777. Entrees 36€–45€. AE, DC, MC, V. Daily noon–3pm, 7–11pm. Vaporetto: San Marco/Vallaresso. Map p 97. Dolci: Fondamenta San Biagio.* ☎ *041-5224844. Entrees 30€–55€. AE, DC, MC, V. Apr–Oct Wed–Mon noon–3pm, 7–10:30pm. Vaporetto: Sant'Eufemia.*

★★★ **Il Refolo** SANTA CROCE *PIZZA/MEDITERRANEAN* Venetians arrive at the canal-side tables in droves by boat and foot to partake of excellent pizzas with such exotic toppings as roasted figs. This warm-weather-only hit was established by

The food is as sophisticated as the setting at Lineadombra.

the clan that so ably operates Osteria da Fiore (p 110). *Campiello del Piovan.* ☎ 041-5240016. *Entrees 15€–30€. AE, MC, V. Apr–Oct Wed–Sun noon–3pm, 7–11pm, Tues 7–11pm. Map p 99.*

★★★ Le Bistrot de Venise

SAN MARCO *VENETIAN* Ages-old Venetian recipes and rare, special-production wines are paired for a memorable dining experience in sophisticated surroundings. *Calle dei Fabbri.* ☎ 041-5236651. *Entrees 14€–28€. AE, MC, V. Daily noon–1am. Vaporetto: Rialto. Map p 97.*

★★★ L'Incontro DORSODURO

SARDINIAN A Sardinian chef brings the hearty fare of his island to Venice, serving roast rabbit, suckling pig, and some of the finest steaks in town, accompanied, of course, by Sardinian wines. *Rio Terrà Canal.* ☎ 041-5222404. *Entrees 15€–20€. AE, DC, MC, V. Tues 7:30–10:30pm, Wed–Sun 12:30–2:30pm, 7:30–10:30pm. Closed Jan. Vaporetto: Ca' Rezzonico. Map p 99.*

★★★ Lineadombra DORSODURO

VENETIAN The sleek dining room and sporty waterside terrace seem readymade for patrons of the new contemporary art museum next door, and add zest to such innovative pairings as tuna tartare and sea bass. *Ponte dell'Umilta.* ☎ 041-2411881. *Entrees 15€–25€. AE, DC, MC, V. Daily 12:30–2:30pm,* 7:30–10:30pm. Closed Jan and Feb. Vaporetto: Salute. Map p 99.*

★★★ Locanda Cipriani TOR-

CELLO *VENETIAN/SEAFOOD* For many devotees, the sole purpose of a trip to this enchanting island in the lagoon is a meal on the shady terrace of this elegantly rustic hotel. The atmosphere wins out over the food, however, which stays in the predictable range of *vitello tonnato* (poached veal with a sauce of tuna and capers), seafood pastas, and grilled fish. To add one more ingredient to a romantic evening here, arrange your transport in the hotel's private launch (about 20€ a person). *Piazza Santa Fosca.* ☎ 041-730150. *Entrees 25€–40€. AE, DC, MC, V. Wed–Mon noon–3:30pm, 7–9pm. Closed Jan. Vaporetto: Torcello. Map p 100.*

★★ Mirai CANNAREGIO *JAPANESE*

It stands to reason that Venice's bountiful fresh fish and seafood are ideal for sushi and sashimi creations, and here they are—served in attractive surroundings that fuse Venetian and Asian chic. *Lista di Spagna.* ☎ 041-2206000. *Entrees 10€–25€. AE, DC, MC, V. Tues–Sun 7:30–11:30pm. Vaporetto: Ferrovia. Map p 98.*

★★ Mistrà GIUDECCA *VENETIAN*

A bright and airy dining room above a boatyard offers excellent seafood pastas and fresh fish to those willing to find their way to the backwaters

of the Giudecca. A set-price lunch is a real bargain at 12€. *Off Calle San Giacomo.* ☎ *041-5220743. Entrees 10€–25€. AE, DC, MC, V. Mon noon–3:30pm; Wed–Sun noon–3:30pm, 7:30–10:30pm. Vaporetto: Redentore. Map p 99.*

★★ Osteria al 40 Ladroni

CANNAREGIO *VENETIAN/SEAFOOD* The freshest fish, simply prepared, keeps a crowd of regulars happy—especially when they're lucky enough to snag one of the outdoor tables next to the canal. *Fondamenta della Sensa.* ☎ *041-715736. Entrees 13€–20€. DC, MC, V. Tues–Sun noon–2:30pm, 7–10:30pm. Vaporetto: San Marcuola. Map p 98.*

★★ Osteria alla Botte SAN

MARCO/RIALTO *VENETIAN Sarde in saor* (sardines marinated in vinegar), *frittura mista,* and other Venetian seafood staples top the menu in an ancient timbered room on a narrow alleyway in the shadow of the Ponte Rialto. *Calle della Bissa.* ☎ *041-5209775. Entrees 12€–15€. Cash only. Mon–Sat noon–3pm, 6:30–11pm; Sun noon–3pm. Vaporetto: San Silvestro. Map p 97.*

★★ Osteria alla Ciurma SAN

POLO/RIALTO *ITALIAN/BAR FOOD* Vendors from the surrounding markets and gondoliers know just where to go for a glass of good wine and a snack of *antipasto misti,* as well as a daily pasta dish or two. *Calle Galliazza.* ☎ *041-5239514. Entrees 5€–8€. Cash only. Daily noon–8:30pm. Vaporetto: Rialto. Map p 99.*

★★★ Osteria al Ponte del Diavolo TORCELLO *VENETIAN/ SEAFOOD* The neighbor of Locanda Cipriani on Torcello very capably plays a quieter role, offering excellent fish and seafood specialties served in attractive, rustic rooms, on a patio, and in a garden. *Fondamenta Borgognoni.* ☎ *041-730401. Entrees 15€–30€. AE, DC, MC, V. Thurs–Tues noon–3:30pm, 7–9pm. Vaporetto: Torcello. Map p 100.*

★★ Osteria Al Ponte SAN POLO

VENETIAN/WINE BAR The name **La Patatina,** as this tavern is commonly known, refers to the specialty of the house, fried potatoes served as a quick snack. Many other tasty morsels are also on hand at the bar, and heartier fish and pasta dishes are served at the tables. *Ponte San Polo.* ☎ *041-5237238. Entrees 7€–15€. AE, DC, MC, V. Mon–Sat noon–2:30pm, 6:30–10pm. Vaporetto: San Tomà. Map p 99.*

The patio of Locanda Cipriani, on the island of Torcello.

★★★ Osteria da Alberto

CANNAREGIO *VENETIAN/SEAFOOD*
Little wonder this is a neighborhood favorite: Daily specials often include heavenly pastas and risottos with radicchio and some form of seafood, as well as *granseola* (spider crab) and other local favorites from the Adriatic. For a postprandial treat, walk over to see the spectacle of the marble-clad church of Santa Maria dei Miracoli (p 66, ⑩) bathed in light. *Calle Giacinto Gallina.* ☎ 041-5238153. *Entrees 12€–22€. MC, V. Mon–Sat noon–3pm, 6:30–9:30pm. Vaporetto: Fondamenta Nuove. Map p 98.*

★★★ Osteria da Carla SAN

MARCO *VENETIAN/SEAFOOD* Four or five daily pasta dishes are often made with fresh fish and seafood, accompanied by such traditional Venetian starters as *sarde in saor* (sardines in a vinegar sauce with onions, raisins, and pine nuts), served in a smart room just steps from Piazza San Marco but nicely tucked away off the beaten track. *Off the Frezzeria.* ☎ 041-5237855. *Entrees 15€–25€. AE, MC, V. Mon–Sat 8:30–10:30pm. Vaporetto: San Marco. Map p 97.*

★★★ Osteria da Fiore SAN POLO

VENETIAN/SEAFOOD The Martin family has earned a Michelin star along with a reputation for serving

the best food in Venice, for offerings that include a vast selection of seafood antipasti, elegant pasta dishes, and such flavorful entrees as sea bass in balsamic vinegar. *Calle delle Scaleter.* ☎ 041-721308. *Entrees 20€–40€. AE, DC, MC, V. Tues–Sat 12:30–2:30pm, 7:30–10:30pm. Closed Aug. Vaporetto: San Stae. Map p 99.*

★★ Osteria dei Zemei SAN POLO

ITALIAN/WINE BAR This neighborhood favorite on a delightful little square makes tempting crostini, *paninetti* (single-bite sandwiches), and a few choice pasta dishes. *Rughetta dei Ravanno.* ☎ 041-5208546. *Entrees 10€–15€. MC, V. Daily noon–10pm. Vaporetto: Rialto. Map p 99.*

★★ Osteria I Rusteghi RIALTO/

SAN MARCO *WINE BAR* A secluded courtyard is a quiet setting for a platter of cheese and salami or one of the 28 kinds of bite-size *paninetti* sandwiches on offer. *Corte del Tentor.* ☎ 041-5232205. *Entrees 5€–8€. Mon–Sat 10am–3pm, 6–9:30pm. Vaporetto: Rialto. Map p 97.*

★★★ Osteria San Marco SAN

MARCO *ITALIAN/WINE BAR* This snazzy new wine bar does justice to its upscale San Marco neighborhood, serving a nice selection of *cicheti* (tapas-like snacks) at the bar and deftly prepared fare in the chicly austere dining room, where

A small back balcony overlooks the water at Osteria da Fiore.

the emphasis is on fresh fish and local produce. *Frezzeria.* ☎ 041-5285242. Entrees 13€–28€. AE, MC, V. Mon–Sat 12:30–2:30pm, 7:30–11pm. Vaporetto: San Marco/Vallaresso. Map p 97.

★★ **Riviera** DORSODURO *VENETIAN/SEAFOOD* Accomplished cooking and colorful views of the busy Giudecca Canal are a winning combination in this tiny dining room and its large terrace. This is a perfect retreat for a warm evening and offers a small but well-chosen menu of meat and fish dishes. *Zattere.* ☎ 041-5227621. Entrees 18€–24€. MC, V. Tues–Sun noon–2:30pm, 7:30–10:30pm. Vaporetto: Zattere. Map p 99.

★★★ **Rosa Salva** CASTELLO *CAFE* A delicious cappuccino comes with a view of one of the most beautiful squares in Venice, San Zanipòlo (see p 41, ④), as well as a nice assortment of pastries, sandwiches, and delicious gelato made on the premises. *Campo Santi Giovanni e Paolo.* ☎ 041-5227949. Entrees 2€–4€. No credit cards. Mon–Tues, Thurs–Sat 7:30am–8:30pm; Sun 8:30am–8:30pm. Vaporetto: Fondamenta Nuove. Map p 97.

★★ **Taverna La Fenice** SAN MARCO *VENETIAN* A favorite with theatergoers and performers, this Venice institution prepares delightful risottos and is especially adept at its seafood dishes, including a heaping platter of *frittura mista.* *Campo San Fantin.* ☎ 041-5223856. Entrees 13€–28€. AE, MC, V. Wed–Mon noon–midnight. Vaporetto: Santa Maria del Giglio. Map p 97.

★★ **Taverna San Trovaso** DORSODURO *VENETIAN* A cozy setting of paneled walls and a brick-vaulted ceiling provides just the place to enjoy such heart-warming Venetian classics as *fritto misti* (here, a mix of

Terrazza del Casin del Nobili's strawberry panna cotta is a good way to finish a meal.

fried seafood) or grilled fish. (Don't confuse the taverna for the touristy garden restaurant of the same name around the corner.) *Fondamenta Priuli.* ☎ 041-5203703. Entrees 8€–16€. AE, DC, MC, V. Tues–Sun noon–2:30pm, 7–9:30pm. Vaporetto: Rialto. Map p 99.

★★ **Terrazza del Casin del Nobili** DORSODURO *VENETIAN* An outpost of the popular pizzeria/trattoria of the same name near Campo San Barnaba adds views over the Giudecca canal from an airy dining room and a summertime terrace. Deft preparations of traditional favorites such as *schie* (tiny shrimp) on a bed of polenta, zucchini flowers, and roast rabbit prove that there's more to this place than a great setting. *Zattere.* ☎ 041-5206895. Entrees 12€–22€. AE, MC, V. Tues–Sun 12:30pm–2:30pm, 7–10:30pm. Vaporetto: Zattere. Map p 99. Ristorante-Pizzeria Casin dei Nobili: Calle Casin. ☎ 041-2411841. Entrees 10€–20€. AE, MC, V. Tues–Sun 12:30pm–2:30pm, 7–10:30pm. Vaporetto: Ca' Rezzonico.

★★ **Trattoria ai Cugnai** DORSODURO *VENETIAN* Homemade pastas and soups and nicely prepared

Salute! Drinking Like a Venetian

Vineyards throughout the Veneto region supply many delightful wines that are perfect accompaniments to the seafood and other fare of which the city is justly proud. Whites, such as the Soaves, tend to be dry, and the reds, Valpolicellas and cabernets dei Friuli among them, fairly light and gentle on the palate. Many Venetians begin the evening with a spritz: a mix of white wine, Campari, Aperol, or another sweet, and sparkling water—most refreshing when deftly blended, disastrously bland when not well concocted. Prosecco, the sparkling white wine from the Veneto, is also often served before a meal, and, though some Venetians might raise an eyebrow at the notion, can continue to be poured through a light repast of seafood. After dessert, out comes the grappa, a headily alcoholic digestivo made from fermented skins and seeds left behind when the grapes are pressed for wine.

versions of such Venetian standards as *fegato* (calf's liver) make this informal, family-run eatery a popular stop with visitors to the nearby Accademia (p 34) and Guggenheim (see p 11, **3**) galleries. *Calle Nuova Sant'Agnese.* ☎ *041-5289238. Entrees 6€–18€. MC, V. Tues–Sun 12:30–3pm, 7–10:30pm. Vaporetto: Accademia. Map p 99.*

★★ Trattoria da Andri LIDO *VENETIAN/SEAFOOD* Superbly prepared fish dishes, served on a delightful terrace, ensure a pleasant meal on the Lido. *Via Lepanto.* ☎ *041-5265482. Entrees 15€–30€. AE, DC, MC, V. Wed–Sun noon–3:30pm, 7–9:30pm. Vaporetto: Lido. Map p 100.*

★★★ Trattoria da Fiore SAN MARCO *VENETIAN* Only the freshest fish and seafood make it to the tables in these rustic rooms, and for lighter fare, the adjoining bar serves snack-sized calamari, octopus, and other Adriatic treats, washed down with wines of the Veneto. (Not to be confused with the famous San Polo osteria of the same name; see p 110.) *Calle delle Botteghe.* ☎ *041-5235310.*

Entrees 13€–29€. MC, V. Wed–Mon noon–3pm, 7–10pm. Vaporetto: San Samuele. Map p 97.

★★ Vini da Arturo SAN MARCO *ITALIAN* The offerings in this small, narrow room will delight diners who've had their fill of Venetian seafood staples—the emphasis here is on well-prepared beef and veal dishes and simple pastas. *Calle dei Assassini, San Marco.* ☎ *041-5286974. Entrees 15€–31€. No credit cards. Mon–Sat 12:30–2:30pm, 7:30–11pm. Closed Aug. Vaporetto: Rialto. Map p 97.*

★★★ Vini da Gigio CANNAREGIO *ITALIAN* The noteworthy selection of wines might get the marquee treatment here, but the culinary offerings are by no means overlooked: *Canestrelli all griglia* (grilled razor clams) and *masorini* (roasted duck) are among the innovative choices. *Fondamenta San Felice.* ☎ *041-5285140. Entrees 15€–20€. AE, DC, MC, V. Tues–Sun noon–2:30pm, 7:30–10:30pm. Closed part of Aug–Sept and Jan–Feb. Vaporetto: Ca d'Oro. Map p 98.* ●

Nightlife **Best Bets**

Best Places for a Glass of Wine on a Beautiful Square
★★ Al Prosecco and ★★ Al Bagolo, *Campo San Giacomo dell'Orio, Santa Croce* (p 117)

Best Place for an After-Dinner Drink with a Water View
★★ Bar-Caffè La Piscina, *Zattere, Dorsoduro* (p 117)

Best Pint of Guinness (Arguable)
★★ Café Blue, *Salizzada San Pantalon, Dorsoduro* (p 117)

Best Place to Blow a Wad on a Cup of Coffee
★★★ Caffè Florian, *Piazza San Marco* (p 117)

Best Place to Lose Your Fortune
★★★ Casino Municipale, *Palazzo Vendramin Calergi, Fondamenta Vendramin, Cannaregio* (p 120)

Best Way to Transport Yourself to a London Pub
★ Devil's Forest, *Calle Stagneri, San Marco* (p 118)

Best Pint of Guinness in Town
★★ Fiddler's Elbow, *Corte dei Pali gia Testori, Cannaregio* (p 119)

Best Place to Blow a Wad on a Cup of Coffee If You Can't Get a Table at the Florian
★★★ Gran Caffè Quadri, *Piazza San Marco* (p 119)

Best Bellini in the World
★★★ Harry's Bar, *Calle Vallaresso, San Marco* (p 119)

Best Place to See Young Venetians Peacocking Around in the Wee Hours
★★ Margaret Duchamp, *Campo Santa Margherita, Dorsoduro* (p 119)

Best Stage in Town (a Boat Moored in the Adjacent Canal)
★★ Paradise Perduto, *Fondamenta della Misericordia, Cannaregio* (p 120)

Best Place to Bump into Venetian Youth (Literally)
★ Picolo Mondo, *Calle Contarini Corfù, Dorsoduro* (p 120)

Best Latin Sounds in Town
★ Round Midnight, *Fondamenta dei Pugni, Dorsoduro* (p 120)

Best View of Venice
★★ Skyline Bar, *Hilton Molino Stucky, Giudecca* (p 119)

Best Yuppie-Spotting
★★ Vitae, *Calle Sant'Antonio, San Marco* (p 120)

Previous page: A window into the world-famous Harry's Bar.

San Marco & Dorsoduro
Nightlife

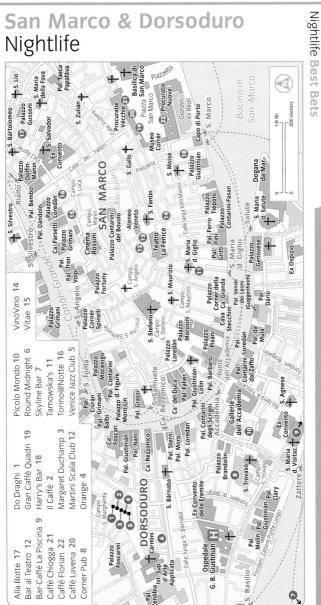

Alla Botte 17
Bar al Teatro 12
Bar-Caffè La Piscina 9
Caffè Chiogga 21
Caffè Florian 22
Caffè Lavena 20
Corner Pub 8

Do Draghi 1
Gran Caffè Quadri 19
Harry's Bar 18
Il Caffè 2
Margaret Duchamp 3
Martini Scala Club 12
Orange 4

Picolo Mondo 10
Round Midnight 6
Skyline Bar 7
Tarnowska's 11
Torino@Notte 16
Venice Jazz Club 5

VinoVino 14
Vitae 15

Santa Croce, San Polo & Cannaregio Nightlife

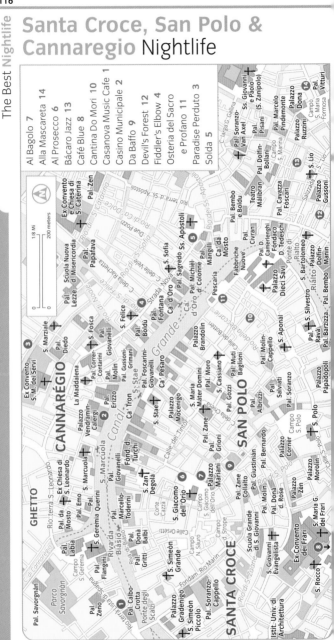

Nightlife A to Z

Bars & Cafes

★★ Al Bagolo SANTA CROCE   Like Café Flor and Les Deux Magots in Paris, Al Bagolo is part of a pair with Al Prosecco, fronting one of Venice's most beautiful squares and serving good wines by the glass. *Campo San Giacomo dell'Orio.* ☎ *041-717584. Vaporetto: Rialto. Map p 116.*

★★ Al Prosecco SANTA CROCE   A seat at this spot on a delightful out-of-the-way square affords a nice selection of wines and a view of a diminishing sight—everyday Venetian life transpiring. The panini provide a nice light meal. *Campo San Giacomo dell'Orio.* ☎ *041-5220222. Vaporetto: Rialto. Map p 116.*

★★ Bar al Teatro SAN MARCO   Venice's favorite hangout for theatergoers is situated next door to La Fenice and comes alive before and after the opera. *Campo San Fantin.* ☎ *041-5221052. Vaporetto: Sant' Angelo. Map p 115.*

★★ Bar-Caffè La Piscina DORSODURO   A view of the Giudecca Canal, stunning by day or night, is the floorshow at this warm-weather perch on the dock in front of the Hotel Calcina. *Zattere.* ☎ *041-2413889. Vaporetto: Zaterre. Map p 115.*

★★ Café Blue DORSODURO   A good pint of Guinness, single-malt whiskeys, and dozens of wines bring in an appreciative crowd of socializers and drinkers. *Salizzada San Pantalon.* ☎ *041-710227. Vaporetto: Rialto. Map p 116.*

★ Caffè Chioggia SAN MARCO   The Piazza San Marco watering hole affords ringside views of the moors striking the hours atop the Torre dell' Orologio (p 8, **5B**). *Piazza San Marco.* ☎ *041-5285011. Vaporetto: San Marco/Vallaresso. Map p 115.*

★★★ Caffè Florian SAN MARCO   What is probably Venice's most famous cafe—the Gran Caffè Quadri, across the square, comes in at a close second—has lost none of its allure since its doors opened in 1720. Goethe and Byron were regulars— and who knows what luminaries might be among today's patrons willing to pay so many hard-earned euros to sip an espresso while being serenaded by an orchestra? *Piazza San Marco.* ☎ *041-5205641. www.caffeflorian.com. Vaporetto: San Marco/Vallaresso. Map p 115.*

★★ Caffè Lavena SAN MARCO   A little less flossy than its neighbors on the Piazza San Marco, this

Patrons enjoying cafe society at Caffè Florian, on the Piazza San Marco.

A quiet moment inside Harry's Bar, a Venetian institution.

250-year-old institution has none-theless been the favorite of Richard Wagner, Gabriele D'Anunzio, and generations of Venetians. *Piazza San Marco.* ☎ *041-5224070. www. venetia.it/lavena. Vaporetto: San Marco/Vallaresso. Map p 115.*

★★★ **Cantina Do Mori** SAN POLO   In what's said to be the old-est wine bar in town, rows of copper pots hang from the ceiling and wine is poured from huge vats. *Calle Dei Do Mori.* ☎ *041-5225401. Vaporetto: San Silvestro. Map p 116.*

★ **Corner Pub** DORSODURO One of the few funky hangouts in this staid part of town is a quiet retreat during the day, a raucous *boîte de nuit* after dark. *Calle de la Chiesa.* ☎ *340-2581448. Vaporetto: Accademia. Map p 115.*

★ **Devil's Forest** SAN MARCO The dartboard, London phone box, and afternoon teas are a hit with Anglophones, but this cozy pub is most popular with locals who linger over beers and games of chess. *Calle Stagneri.* ☎ *041-5200623. Vaporetto: Rialto. Map p 116.*

There's Something About Harry's

The most famous bar in Venice—well, maybe the world—opened on the San Marco waterfront in 1931, and people have been talking about the place ever since. Maria Callas and the Aga Kahn were regulars; Harry's was Ernest Hemingway's favorite watering hole; Woody Allen, who loves Venice, pops in from time to time. Some people wouldn't dare darken the noted doorway because Harry's is so popular with the rich and famous (and the rich and not-so-famous); others go for that very reason. If you do join the legions of travelers who include Harry's on their itinerary, here are some tips. **What to order:** A Bellini, a refreshing concoction of chilled peach juice and Prosecco, and carpaccio, waver-thin slices of beef served with a dollop of mayonnaise and lemon juice. Both were invented at Harry's, and both are named after Venetian painters. **What to bring:** An awful lot of money, because Harry's is ridicu-lously expensive. **What not to bring:** High expectations for friendly service and stunning cuisine, because both are underwhelming. **What to wear:** Something natty. **What not to wear:** Shorts.

★★ Fiddler's Elbow CANNAREGIO Guinness, of course, is on hand and taken seriously at this Irish outpost, as are the soccer matches shown on the large screen out front. *Corte dei Pali gia Testori.* ☎ 041-5239930. *Vaporetto: Ca' d'Oro. Map p 116.*

★★★ Gran Caffè Quadri SAN MARCO Keeping this long-established watering hole neck and neck with the Florian for the title of "most famous" is a similar roster of famous devotees (here including Proust and Stendhal), an equally elegant orchestra, and the same sumptuous views of the domes of the Basilica di San Marco. *Piazza San Marco.* ☎ 041-5222105. www.quadrivenice. com. *Vaporetto: San Marco/Vallaresso. Map p 115.*

★★★ Harry's Bar SAN MARCO Two reasons to make a stop at this Venetian institution: The Bellini (the sparkling wine/peach-juice concoction that's become a brunch-time staple) was invented here, and Hemingway, along with legions of other celebs, drank here. *Calle Vallaresso.* ☎ 041-5285777. www.cipriani.com. *Vaporetto: San Marco/Vallaresso. Map p 115.*

★★ Il Caffè DORSODURO As if in counterpoint to its young neighbor Orange, Il Caffè is known to regulars

The Casino Municipale (p 120), housed in a Renaissance palace.

The elegant entrance of the Martini Scala Club piano bar (p 120).

as **Il Rosso** (a reference to the facade) and is the oldest drinking establishment on the square. Live music and excellent wines draw a loyal clientele. *Campo Santa Margherita.* ☎ 041-5287998. *Vaporetto: Ca' Rezzonico. Map p 115.*

★★ Margaret Duchamp DORSODURO One of Venice's most popular hangouts keeps the campo animated well into the wee hours. *Campo Santa Margherita.* ☎ 041-286255. *Vaportetto: Ca' Rezzonico. Map p 115.*

★★ Orange DORSODURO The crowd is young but the drinks are grown-up: Bartenders mix some of the best cocktails in Venice. *Campo Santa Margherita.* ☎ 041-5234740. *Vaporetto: Ca' Rezzonico. Map p 115.*

★★ Skyline Bar GIUDECCA Venice was endowed with another viewpoint when the old Molino Stucky pasta factory was converted to a Hilton hotel and this bar opened on the top floor. When you tire of the lights of La Serenissima twinkling at your feet, check out the rooftop swimming pool. *Hilton Molino Stucky.* ☎ 041-272331. *Vaporetto: Palanca. Map p 115.*

The waterside cafes and bars around the Ponte di Rialto light up Venice at night.

★★ **VinoVino** SAN MARCO   The emphasis in these rustic rooms is on wine by the glass, accompanied by light dishes that include such homey Venetian favorites as salt cod and fresh sardines. *Ponte delle Veste.* ☎ *041-5237027. Vaporetto: San Marco/Vallaresso. Map p 115.*

★★ **Vitae** SAN MARCO   Chic surroundings and expertly poured cocktails appeal to a well-heeled younger crowd. *Calle Sant'Antonio.* ☎ *041-5205205. Vaporetto: Rialto. Map p 115.*

Clubs

★★ **Bácaro Jazz** SAN MARCO   A boisterous cocktail bar doubles as a late-night jazz venue. *Salizzada del Fontego dei Tedeschi, San Marco.* ☎ *041-5285249. Vaporetto: Rialto. Map p 116.*

★ **Casanova Music Cafe** CANNAREGIO   Venetians and visitors of all ages enjoy the city's largest disco, where Friday is salsa night; if you get bored, just pop into the adjoining Internet cafe and check your e-mail. *Lista di Spoagna.* ☎ *041-2750199. Vaporetto: Ferrovia. Map p 116.*

★★★ **Casino Municipale** CANNAREGIO   The surroundings, a 15th-century palace on the Grand Canal, add a sophisticated spin to the proceedings. *Palazzo Vendramin Calergi, Fondamenta Vendramin.* ☎ *041-5297111. Vaporetto: San Marcuola. No admission without* passport; jacket for men required. *Map p 116.*

★★ **Martini Scala Club** SAN MARCO   The most refined piano lounge (and perhaps the only one) in town is the place for a late-night snack accompanied by easy listening. *Campo San Fantin.* ☎ *041-5237027. Vaporetto: Santa Maria del Giglio. Map p 115.*

★★ **Paradise Perduto** CANNAREGIO   Jazz, blues, and seafood concoctions draw the crowds. Sit on the terrace and listen to an ensemble playing from a boat moored in the canal alongside—you'll think you've found paradise. *Fondamenta della Misericordia.* ☎ *041-720581. Vaporetto: Ferrovia. Map p 116.*

★ **Picolo Mondo** DORSODURO   Students from the nearby university get their local disco fix at this small, intimate club, one of very few places in town where you can dance the night away. *Calle Contarini Corfù.* ☎ *041-5200371. Vaporetto: Accademia. Map p 115.*

★ **Round Midnight** DORSODURO   Latin sounds prevail on a tiny, cramped dance floor near the university. *Fondamenta dei Pugni.* ☎ *041-5232056. Vaporetto: Accademia. Map p 115.*

★★ **Torino@Notte** SAN MARCO   Live jazz some nights and DJ mixes others keep packing in the crowds. *Campo San Luca.* ☎ *041-5223914. Vaporetto: Rialto. Map p 115.* ●

Arts & Entertainment **Best Bets**

Best Place to **Watch a Movie under the Stars**
★★ Arena di Campo San Polo, *Campo San Polo (p 125)*

Best **Time to See Contemporary Art**
★★★ Biennale D'Arte Contemporanea e Architettura, *Giardini Pubblici (p 125)*

Best **Time to Hide Behind a Mask**
★★★ Carnevale, *various locations (p 125)*

Best **Times to Walk across Water**
★★★ Festa della Madonna della Salute, *Campo della Salute (p 125);* and ★★★ Festa del Redentore, *Giudecca (p 125)*

Most **Mellow Setting for a Concert**
★ Festa di San Pietro, *Campo San Pietro (p 125)*

Best Place to **Hear Early Music**
★★ Museo della Fondazione Querini Stampalia, *Campo Santa Maria Formosa (p 125)*

Best Place to **See an Opera**
★★★ La Fenice, *Campo San Fantin (p 128)*

Best **Time to See the Latest International Films**
★★★ Mostra Internazionale d'Arte Cinematografica, *Palazzo del Cinema, Lungomare Marconi 90, Lido (p 125)*

Most **Colorful Time to See the Grand Canal**
★★ Regata Storica, *Grand Canal (p 126)*

Best Places to **Hear Vivaldi Performed by Musicians in Period Costume**
★★ San Giacomo di Rialto, *Campo Santa Maria Formosa (p 127);* and ★★ Scuola Grande di San Teodoro, *Salizzada San Teodoro (p 128)*

Best Place to **See Experimental Theater**
★★ Teatro a l'Avogaria, *Corte Zappa (p 128)*

Best Place to **Hear a Symphony**
★★★ Teatro Malibran, *Calle dei Milion (p 128)*

Best **Weekend for Free Music**
★★ Venezia Suona, *various locations (p 126)*

Getting Tickets

Keep up with cultural happenings around Venice by checking out *Il Gazzettino,* the city's newspaper, and **La Nuova Venezia,** a bimonthly in Italian and English. Tourist offices (p 164) also provide information on concerts and other events. Tickets are usually available at a venue's box office just before a performance. A good one-stop shop for tickets to Venice events is **LaVela,** Calle Fuseri 1810, off the Frezzeria in San Marco (☎ 041-5287886; www.actv.it; Mon–Sat 7:30am–7pm), and in Piazzale Roma (☎ 041-2722249; www.velaspa. com; daily 7:30am–8pm). Book well in advance for performances that are likely to sell out, such as operas at La Fenice.

Santa Croce & San Polo A&E

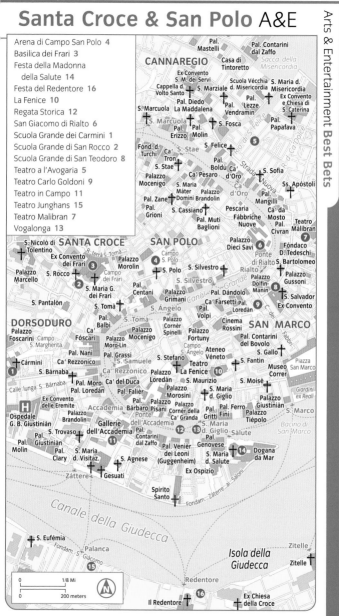

Page 121: A Carnevale performer in costume.

Cannaregio, San Marco & Castello A&E

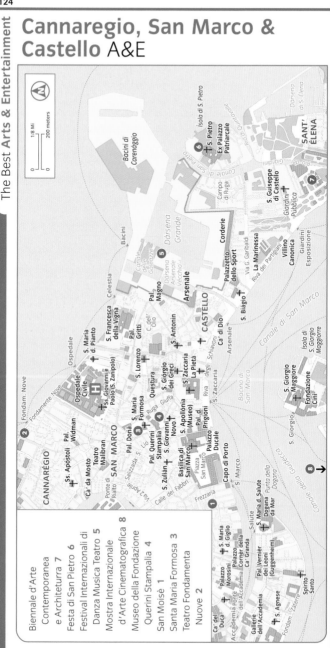

Arts & Entertainment A to Z

Cinema

★★ Arena di Campo San Polo
SAN POLO The square becomes a free outdoor cinema for 6 weeks every summer. Unfortunately, the setting sometimes tops what's on screen, typical Hollywood fare dubbed into Italian. *Campo San Polo. www.venicebanana.com. Late July to early Sept 9:30pm. Vaporetto: San Tomà. Map p 123.*

★★★ Mostra Internazionale d'Arte Cinematografica LIDO
Biennale (see below) events include the Mostra, one of the world's most prestigious film festivals. Seats are hard to come by; tickets are available from outlets in the city (p 122) and the festival box office in the casino, Lungomare Marconi. *Palazzo del Cinema, Lungomare Marconi 90, Lido. ☎ 041-5218711. www.labiennale. org. Tickets 5€–15€. Vaporetto: Lido. Map p 124.*

Festivals & Events

★★★ Biennale D'Arte Contemporanea e Architettura
CASTELLO Venice has been staging its prestigious Biennale since 1895, showing the best in contemporary art. Architecture, dance, music, cinema, and theater have been added to the mix over the years. Art and architecture exhibits take over early-20th-century pavilions in the **Giardini Pubblici:** art in odd years (mid-June to Nov) and architecture in even years (Sept–Oct). *Biennale office: Ca' Giustinian, Calle del Ridotto. ☎ 041-5218846. www.labiennale.org. Ticket office: Giardini Pubblici. Tickets 15€, 8€ students, 34€ families of up to 2 adults and 2 children. Vaporetto: Giardini. Map p 124.*

★★★ Carnevale Pre-Lenten celebrations, revived in 1980 to promote

winter tourism, draw masked revelers to the city. Highlights include a masked ball. Several masked processions, one by gondola, snake through the city during the revelries. *10 days before Ash Wednesday. www.carnevale.venezia.it.*

★★★ Festa della Madonna della Salute DORSODURO Like Il Redentore (below), the cathedral of **Santa Maria della Salute** was built as an offering for relief from a plague epidemic, this one in 1630. On November 21, Venetians give thanks by making the pilgrimage across the Grand Canal on a specially built pontoon bridge to light candles in the church. *See p 11, ❶. Map p 123.*

★★★ Festa del Redentore
GIUDECCA The church of **Il Redentore** was begun in 1576 as an offering of thanks to the Redeemer for delivering Venice from a plague epidemic. Ever since, the city has set aside the third weekend in July as the time to make a pilgrimage to the church and offer thanks anew. Once a

A little boy dressed in costume for Carnevale.

Crossing a pontoon bridge to and from Il Redentore for the Festa del Redentore.

colorful bridge of boats facilitated the trip across the Guidecca canal; these days the Italian army builds a temporary pontoon bridge. On Saturday evening, fireworks light the sky. *See p 46, ❶. Map p 123.*

★ Festa di San Pietro CASTELLO
In the last week of June, the waterside lawns beneath the leaning campanile of the *chiesa* (church) of **San Pietro in Castello** are filled with revelers celebrating the saint's feast and enjoying a series of concerts. *See p 59, ⑮. Map p 124.*

★★ Festival Internazionali di Danza Musica Teatro CASTELLO
The International Festival of Dance, Music, and Theater debuts in newly renovated theaters in the Arsenale, the Fenice, and other venues. The music and theater festivals take place in late September and early October; the dance festival in June. *Biennale office: Ca' Giustinian, Calle del Ridotto. ☎ 041-5218846. www.labiennale.org. Tickets: dance & music 13€–25€; theater 8€–10€ students. Vaporetto: Arsenale. Map p 124.*

★★ Regata Storica GRAND CANAL
The Grand Canal becomes a stage for processions and boat races on the first Sunday in September. *Grand Canal. Map p 123.*

★★ Teatro in Campo DORSODURO
Plays, operas, and dance performances are staged in Campo Pisani, the garden of the Peggy Guggenheim Collection, the cloisters of San Giobbe, and other evocative locales around the city and on the islands. It's organized by Pantakin da Venezia, a cultural organization. *Pantakin: Giudecca 620/622. ☎ 041-5221740. www.pantakin.it. Tickets from 13€. Map p 123.*

★★ Venezia Suona
Musicians take over many *campi* around the city for a day of free concerts, from baroque to hard rock. *Sun closest to June 21. ☎ 041-2750049. www.veneziasuona.it.*

★★ Vogalonga GRAND CANAL
Rowers from around the world converge on Venice to make a circuit around the lagoon and down the

The Regata Storica's colorful procession of boats.

Venice's opera house, La Fenice, rebuilt from the ashes of a 1996 fire.

Grand Canal. *Sun in May.* ☎ 041-5210544. www.vogalonga.it. *Map p 123.*

Music & Dance

★ **Basilica dei Frari** SAN POLO This massive, art-filled church hosts a fall and spring series of church music and recitals on the church's organs. *Campo dei Frari.* ☎ 041-719308. *Vaporetto: San Tomà. Map p 123.*

★★ **Museo della Fondazione Querini Stampalia** CASTELLO Half-hour recitals of Renaissance and baroque music at the museum-palazzo are a nice appetizer for an evening in Venice. *See p 37,* ❸. *Recitals: Fri–Sat 5, 8:30pm. Vaporetto: Rialto. Map p 124.*

★ **San Moisè** SAN MARCO A spring season of organ concerts at this unsightly church features works by Venice's own Antonio Vivaldi. *See p 7,* ❷. *Map p 124.*

★★ **San Giacomo di Rialto** SAN POLO The oldest church in Venice is the setting for concerts by the **Ensemble Antonio Vivaldi,** a chamber-music group whose repertoire ranges from Mozart to Rossini. *Campo di San Giacometto. Church:* ☎ 041-5224745. *Mon–Sat 8am–noon, 3–7pm. Ensemble:*

☎ 041-4266559. www.ensemble antoniovivaldi.com. *Tickets 19€ (on sale at church from 11am on performance days). Wed, Fri, Sun 8:45pm. Vaporetto: Rialto. Map p 123.*

★★ **Santa Maria Formosa** CASTELLO **Collegium Ducale,** a baroque ensemble, performs 3 or 4 nights a week throughout the year in this 15th-century church (for details, see p 57, ❺), which also hosts many visiting choirs. Some concerts, including the Collegium Ducale's jazz series, are held in the former prisons of the Palazzo delle Prigioni in Piazza San Marco. *Campo Santa Maria Formosa. Church:* ☎ 041-2750462. *3€. Mon–Sat 10am–5pm. Collegium:* ☎ 041-984252. www.collegium ducale.com. *Tickets 20€–25€. Box office open from 10:30am on days of performance. Vaporetto: Rialto. Map p 124.*

★★ **Scuola Grande dei Carmini** DORSODURO One of the city's grandest *scuole* (guildhalls) sets an appropriate background for a spring opera series. A ticket includes a guided tour of the works by Tiepolo. *Campo dei Carmini. Scuola:* ☎ 041-5289420. *5€. Daily 10am–4pm. Opera:* ☎ 041-0994371. www.prgroup.it. *Tickets 35€. Vaporetto: Ca' Rezzonico. Map p 123.*

★ **Scuola Grande di San Rocco**
SAN POLO   Giovanni Gabrielli and Claudio Monteverdi are among the composers associated with this *scuola grande,* and the **Accademia di San Rocco** often performs their repertoire in salons painted by Tintoretto. *Campo San Rocco. Scuola:* ☎ *041-5234864. 5.50€. Apr–Oct daily 9am–5:30pm; Nov–Mar daily 10am–5pm. Accademia:* ☎ *041-962999. www.musicinvenice.com. Ticket prices vary. Vaporetto: San Tomà. Map p 123.*

★★ **Scuola Grande di San Teodoro** SAN MARCO   **I Musici Veneziani** don period costumes to perform Vivaldi and other baroque masters 3 evenings a week. Opera arias by Mozart, Rossini, and others are performed 2 evenings a week. *Salizzada San Teodoro.* ☎ *041-5210294. www.imusiciveneziani.com. Tickets 20€–35€. Concert pieces Wed, Fri, Sun 9pm; opera pieces Sat, Tues 9pm. Vaporetto: Rialto. Map p 123.*

★★★ **Teatro Malibran** CANNAREGIO   Built in the 17th century and recently restored, the Malibran is often the venue for concerts by the orchestra of La Fenice. *Calle dei Milion.* ☎ *899-909090. www.teatrolafenice.it. Vaporetto: Rialto. Map p 123.*

A metal carving from the gates of the Teatro Carlo Goldoni.

Opera
★★★ **La Fenice** SAN MARCO   The lights are back on in Venice's grand opera house, rebuilt after a fire in 1996. The November-to-June season includes a roster of classic and contemporary operas performed by some of the world's greatest voices. *Campo San Fantin.* ☎ *041-786575. www.teatrolafenice.it. Tickets 35€–200€. Vaporetto: Santa Maria del Giglio. Map p 123.*

Theater
★★ **Teatro a l'Avogaria** CANNAREGIO   The theater founded by noted 20th-century director Giovanni Poli continues a tradition of experimental works. *Corte Zappa.* ☎ *041-5206130. Ticket prices vary. Vaporetto: San Basilio. Map p 123.*

★★ **Teatro Carlo Goldoni** SAN MARCO   The resident company, **Teatro Stabile del Veneto,** stages classic Italian drama as well as contemporary works. *Calle Goldoni.* ☎ *041-2402011. www.teatro stabileveneto.it. Shows: Mon, Wed, Fri–Sat 8:30pm; Thurs, Sun 4pm. Ticket prices vary. Vaporetto: Rialto. Map p 123.*

★ **Teatro Fondamenta Nuove** CANNAREGIO   The repertoire includes experimental drama, dance, readings, and performance art. The singers of **Musica in Maschera** perform here throughout the year, delivering famous opera arias while attired in 18th-century costumes and masks. *Fondamenta Nuove.* ☎ *041-5224498. www.musicainmaschera.it. Ticket prices vary. Vaporetto: Fondamenta Nuove. Map p 124.*

★ **Teatro Junghans** GIUDECCA   A converted warehouse hosts dance concerts and plays. *Campo Junghans.* ☎ *041-2411971. Ticket prices vary. Vaporetto: Palanca. Map p 123.* ●

Lodging **Best Bets**

Most **Hospitable Innkeepers**
★★★ Al Ponte Mocenigo $$ *Fondamenta Rimpetto Mocenigo (p 135)*

Best Place to **Feel You're Staying in an Elegant Venetian Home**
★★★ Ca' della Corte $$ *Corte Surion, Dorsoduro (p 136)*

Most **Hip**
★★★ Ca' Pisani $$$ *Rio Terrà Antonio Foscarini, Dorsoduro (p 137)*

Best **Bargain Hideaway**
★★ Casa Bocassini $ *Calle del Volto, Cannaregio (p 137)*

Best Place to **Hang Out by the Pool**
★★★ Cipriani $$$$ *Giudecca 10 (p 138)*

Best **Lobby**
★★★ Danieli $$$$ *Riva Degli Schiavoni, Castello (p 138)*

Most **Stylish Small Inn**
★★★ DD.724 $$$ *Rio Terrà Antonio Foscarini, Dorsoduro (p 138)*

Best Place to **Be Pampered in Luxury**
★★★ Gritti Palace $$$$ *Campo Santa Maria del Giglio, San Marco (p 139)*

Best Place to **Stay in Style without Breaking the Bank**
★★★ Hotel Al Piave $$ *Ruga Giuffa, Castello (p 140)*

Best Place to **Be Decadent**
★★★ Hotel des Bains $$$$ *Lungomare Marconi 17, Lido (p 141)*

Best **Bargain View of the Grand Canal**
★★★ Hotel Galleria $–$$ *Rio Terrà Antonio Foscarini (p 141)*

Best **Palace Hotel for the Money**
★★★ La Residenza $–$$ *Campo Bandiera e Moro, Castello (p 143)*

Best **Medieval Garret Experience**
★★ La Villeggiatura $$–$$$ *Calle dei Botteri, San Polo (p 143)*

Best Place to **Get Away from It All**
★★★ Locanda Cipriani $$$–$$$$ *Piazza Santa Fosca 29, Torcello (p 143)*

Best **Value Family Suites**
★★★ Locanda San Barnaba, $$ *Calle del Traghetto, Dorsoduro (p 144)*

Best **Romantic Hideaway**
★★ Oltre il Giardino $$–$$$ *Fondamenta Contarini (p 145)*

Best **Hotel Garden**
★★★ Pensione Accademia/Villa Maravege $$–$$$ *Fondamenta Bollani, Dorsoduro (p 146)*

Best Place to **Savor the Rialto Markets**
★★ Pensione Guerrato $ *Calle Drio la Scimia, San Polo (p 146)*

Best **Old-Fashioned** *Pensione* **Experience**
★★★ Pensione Seguso $$ *Fondamenta Zattere ai Geuati, Dorsoduro (p 146)*

Previous page: The opulent lobby of the Danieli.

San Marco & Castello Lodging

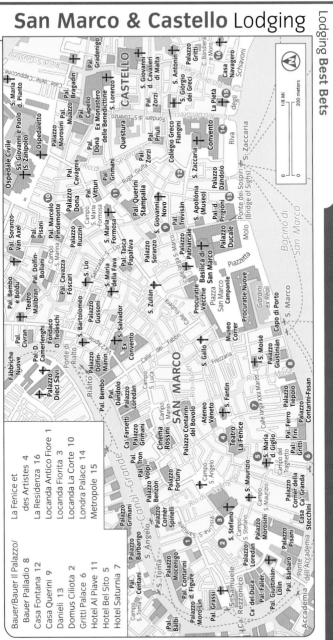

Bauer/Bauer Il Palazzo/
Bauer Palladio **8**

Casa Fontana **12**

Casa Querini **9**

Danieli **13**

Domus Ciliota **2**

Gritti Palace **6**

Hotel Al Piave **11**

Hotel Bel Sito **5**

Hotel Saturnia **7**

La Fenice et
des Artistes **4**

La Residenza **16**

Locanda Antico Fiore **1**

Locanda Fiorita **3**

Locanda La Corte **10**

Londra Palace **14**

Metropole **15**

Cannaregio Lodging

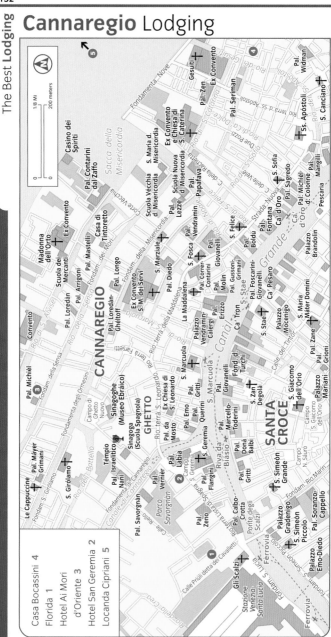

Dorsoduro & Giudecca Lodging

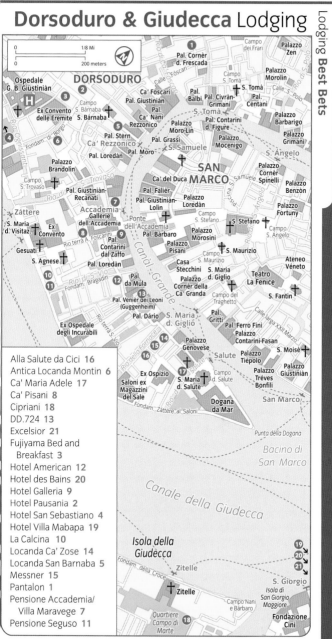

Alla Salute da Cici 16
Antica Locanda Montin 6
Ca' Maria Adele 17
Ca' Pisani 8
Cipriani 18
DD.724 13
Excelsior 21
Fujiyama Bed and
  Breakfast 3
Hotel American 12
Hotel des Bains 20
Hotel Galleria 9
Hotel Pausania 2
Hotel San Sebastiano 4
Hotel Villa Mabapa 19
La Calcina 10
Locanda Ca' Zose 14
Locanda San Barnaba 5
Messner 15
Pantalon 1
Pensione Accademia/
  Villa Maravege 7
Pensione Seguso 11

San Polo & Santa Croce Lodging

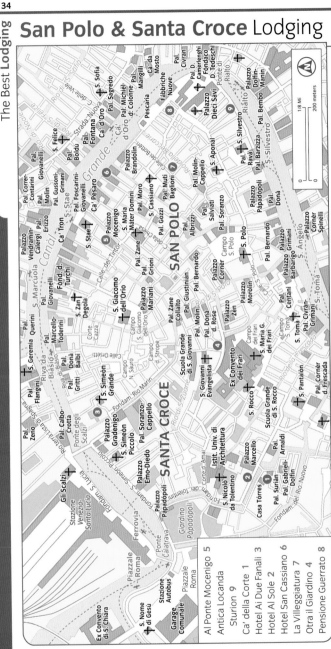

Lodging A to Z

The courtyard entrance to Al Ponte Mocenigo.

★★ **Alla Salute da Cici** DORSO-DURO A 16th-century palazzo in the backwaters of the Dorsoduro offers high-ceilinged guest rooms with Grand Canal or garden views, while quarters in a modern annex trade character for such modern conveniences as air-conditioning and shiny new bathrooms. *Fondamenta Ca' Balà, Dorsoduro.* ☎ *041-5235404. www.hotelsalute.com. 58 units. Doubles 90€–100€. AE, MC, V. Vaporetto: Salute. Map p 133.*

★★★ **Al Ponte Mocenigo** SAN POLO Open the gate, cross a canal on a private marble bridge, enter the pretty courtyard, and then step into this enchanting little palazzo, where large and atmospheric rooms are complemented by modern amenities that include a steam room—as well as a great deal of old-fashioned hospitality from the friendly and helpful owners. *Fondamenta Rimpetto Mocenigo, San Polo.* ☎ *041-5244797. www.alponte mocenigo.com. 10 units. Doubles 95€–145€. AE, MC, V. Vaporetto: San Stae. Map p 134.*

★ **Antica Locanda Montin** DOR-SODURO A pretty garden; a homey, low-key atmosphere; a downstairs trattoria; and even views of a small canal—along with bargain prices for the location—compensate for the worn decor and fairly spartan amenities. *Fondamenta Eremite, Dorsoduro.* ☎ *041-5227151. www.locanda montin.com. 12 units. Doubles*

A Price for All Seasons

Accommodations in Venice are never inexpensive, but at some times of the year they are especially expensive. May and June, September and October, Christmas and New Year's holidays, and Carnevale are unofficially high season, when rates can double or even triple those of other times of the year. Prices fluctuate wildly, though—if a hotel has vacancies, no matter what the season, prices might come down.

A spacious duplex suite at the Bauer Palladio.

85€–110€. AE, MC, V. Vaporetto: Accademia. Map p 133.

★★ Antica Locanda Sturion
SAN POLO   Two large rooms overlooking the Grand Canal are the top choices in this 13th-century inn that's just steps from the Rialto bridge, but all the accommodations are loaded with character and the breakfast room enjoys the knockout view, too. Some of the rooms nicely accommodate families, and the kids come in handy when it's time to carry bags up and down the many flights of stairs. *Calle del Sturion, San Polo.* ☎ 041-5236243. www.locandasturion.com. 11 units. Doubles 120€–135€. AE,

MC, V. Vaporetto: San Silvestro. Map p 134.

★★ Bauer/Bauer Il Palazzo/ Bauer Palladio SAN MARCO
Choose between an 18th-century palazzo on the Grand Canal, a 1950s addition, or the converted convent of La Zitelle on Giudecca. Rooms vary from grandiose antique-filled suites to some in the San Marco annex that look like Hollywood movie sets from the 1930s. Guests in San Marco enjoy a stunning rooftop terrace, while the Giudecca outpost is backed by an enormous and luxuriant garden. A solar-powered craft ferries guests between the San Marco and Giudecca properties. *Campo San Moisè, San Marco; or Fondamenta delle Zitelle, Giudecca.* ☎ 041-5207022. www.bauervenezia.it. 227 units. Doubles 400€–550€. MC, V. Vaporetto: San Marco/Vallaresso or Zitelle. Map p 131.

★★★ Ca' della Corte DORSO-
DURO   Behind a welcoming entrance court is one of Venice's most charming small inns, with extremely comfortable character-filled rooms, a roof terrace, and a garden. Several apartments are also available. *Corte Surion, Dorsoduro.* ☎ 041-715877. www.cadellacorte. com. 7 units. Doubles 110€–125€. MC, V. Vaporetto: Piazzale Roma. Map p 134.

Location, Location, Location

Getting lost in Venice can be a pleasure, but not when you're dragging luggage over bridges and up and down stairs as you look for your hotel. When booking, find out exactly *where* your hotel is, *where* the nearest vaporetto stop is, and the easiest way to get from the stop to the hotel. Many hotels print maps on their websites. If in doubt, you may want to treat yourself to an expensive but practical luxury and arrive at your hotel in a water taxi.

The waterside restaurant of the Cipriani hotel (p 138).

★★★ Ca' Maria Adele DORSODURO

Hip has arrived in Venice with a bang—a tasteful bang. Be it contemporary or antique, 1950s style or Moroccan, the eclectic decor in the public spaces and themed guest rooms here is elegant and rather exciting, sometimes over the top, but always with an eye toward comfort. *Rio Terà dei Catacumeni, Dorsoduro.* ☎ *041-5203078. www.camariaadele.it. 12 units. Doubles 250€–450€. MC, V. Vaporetto: Salute. Map p 133.*

★★★ Ca' Pisani DORSODURO

A 16th-century palazzo, art moderne furnishings, and wonderful contemporary artwork blend harmoniously in this high-design, high-chic, and extremely comfortable hostelry. But some traditional elements, such as the quiet neighborhood and proximity to the Accademia, are also part of the appeal. *Rio Terrà Antonio Foscarini 979a, Dorsoduro.* ☎ *041-2401411. www.capisanihotel.it. 29 units. Doubles 213€–435€. MC, V. Vaporetto: Accademia. Map p 133.*

★★ Casa Bocassini CANNAREGIO

A little oasis tucked away on the back streets of one of the quietest quarters of Venice offers pleasant, comfortable rooms surrounding an enchanting little garden. *Calle del Volto, Cannaregio.* ☎ *041-5236877. www.hotelboccassini.com. 10 units. Doubles 70€–100€. MC, V. Vaporetto: Fondamenta Nuove. Map p 132.*

★★ Casa Fontana CASTELLO

The Stainer family has been welcoming guests to their convent-turned-hotel for 40 years. It's a snug retreat from the hustle and bustle of nearby San Marco. The reassuringly old-fashioned rooms have updated bathrooms and overlook Campo San Provolo or Campo San Zaccaria and its stunning church; two rooms have private terraces. *Campo San Provolo, Castello.* ☎ *041-5220579. www.hotelfontana.com. 16 units. Doubles 85€–180€. AE, MC, V. Vaporetto: San Zaccaria. Map p 131.*

★ Casa Querini CASTELLO

This old palazzo in the quiet Campo San Giovanni Novo square seems miles from San Marco, when it's actually just a few minutes away. A small terrace on the campo is a nice place to watch the neighborhood comings and goings, and the rooms upstairs are unusually spacious and pleasantly decorated in the ubiquitous hotel "Venetian antique" style. *Campo San*

Giovanni Novo, Castello. ☎ 041-2411294. www.locandaquerini.com. 11 units. Doubles 110€–200€. AE, MC, V. Vaporetto: San Zaccaria. Map p 131.

★★★ **Cipriani** GIUDECCA This getaway reached by private launch pampers guests with luxurious accommodations in a cluster of centuries-old buildings and with such amenities as a gorgeous swimming pool, a spa, tennis courts, lush gardens, and waterside bars and restaurants. *Giudecca 10.* ☎ *041-5207744. www.hotelcipriani.it. 96 units. Doubles 625€–815€. MC, V. Closed Nov–Mar. Vaporetto: Zitelle. Map p 133.*

★★★ **Danieli** SAN MARCO A marble-clad entrance to a 13th-century doge's palace wins the prize for the best lobby in Venice, and the rooms upstairs in what is one of the finest hotels anywhere are no less opulent—even those in the "new" adjoining 19th- and 20th-century wings. *Riva Degli Schiavoni, Castello.* ☎ *041-5226480. www.starwood.com/luxury. 235 units. Doubles 410€–650€. AE, DC, MC, V. Vaporetto: San Zaccaria. Map p 131.*

★★★ **DD.724** DORSODURO A contemporary, sophisticated style pervades this chic little inn, tucked away near the museums, Salute, and other prime Dorsoduro sights. Some rooms and the lounge overlook a small garden. *Rio Terrà Antonio Foscarini, Dorsoduro.* ☎ *041-2770262. www.dd724.it. 8 units. Doubles 280€–400€. MC, V. Vaporetto: Accademia. Map p 133.*

★★★ **Domus Ciliota** SAN MARCO The modern rooms in this former monastery are small and utilitarian, but they surround a flower-filled cloister and are an extremely good value. *Calle delle Muneghe, San Marco.* ☎ *041-5204989. www.ciliota.it. 51 units. Doubles 90€–140€. MC, V. Vaporetto: San Samuele. Map p 131.*

★★★ **Excelsior** LIDO This exotic palace by the sea, one of Europe's grandest hotels, has all the resort amenities—private beach, swimming pool, golf privileges, tennis courts—you could ever want or need. But you may choose never to leave the sumptuous Moorish-themed rooms, many with sitting alcoves and all with a view of the sea, lagoon, or lush gardens. *Lungomare Gugliemo Marconi 41, Lido.* ☎ *041-5260201. www.starwood.com/westin. 195 units. Doubles 450€–700€. AE, DC, MC, V. Closed Nov–Mar. Vaporetto: Terrazza, Tropicana. Map p 133.*

The Danieli hotel's extravagant lobby.

The marbled lobby bar in the Gritti Palace.

★ **Florida** CANNAREGIO   If you have an early morning train to catch, these sparkling-clean and comfortable faux-antique-furnished rooms are worth considering—not just because of the convenience, but also because they're a real bargain, and offer air-conditioning and other amenities not usually found in this price range. *Calle Priuli dei Cavaletti, Cannaregio.* ☎ *041-715253. www.hotel-florida.com. 24 units. Doubles 90€–145€. AE, MC, V. Vaporetto: Ferrovia. Map p 132.*

★ **Fujiyama Bed and Breakfast** DORSODURO   An air of calm pervades these four attractive rooms, each named after the well-traveled owners' favorite cities (Tokyo, Harbin, Shanghai, and Paris). Venice's only Japanese tea room is downstairs, and a lovely rear garden and a sunny terrace are among the many other amenities. *Calle Lunga San Barnaba, Dorsoduro.* ☎ *041-7241042. www.bedandbreakfast-fujiyama.it. 4 units. Doubles 72€–160€. AE, MC, V. Vaporetto: Ferrovia. Map p 133.*

★★★ **Gritti Palace** SAN MARCO   Doge Andrea Gritti built this palazzo in 1525, and the sheen of luxury hasn't faded since—making the Gritti a top choice for guests who expect to be pampered amid all the trappings of grandeur. Immense rooms and suites groan under the weight of swags, ornate mirrors, and Venetian antiques, and many overlook the Grand Canal. *Campo Santa Maria del Giglio, San Marco.* ☎ *041-794611. www.starwood.com/luxury. 91 units. Doubles 550€–850€. AE, DC, MC, V. Vaporetto: San Zaccaria. Map p 131.*

★★★ **Hotel Ai Due Fanali** SANTA CROCE   A 14th-cenurty building that was once part of the nearby church of San Simeone Profeta Campo is still graced with enough frescoes, paneling, and antiques (the check-in desk is an old altar) to lend a wonderfully quirky old-world air to the place, and the top-floor breakfast room and roof terrace are a delight. The train station is just across the Grand Canal, but the quiet corner of Santa Croce seems far removed from the fray. *San Simeone Profeta, Santa Croce.* ☎ *041-718490. www.aiduefanali.com. 16 units. Doubles 93€–220€. AE, MC, V. Vaporetto: Riva di Biasio. Map p 134.*

★★★ **Hotel Ai Mori d'Oriente** CANNAREGIO   A house once occupied by Turkish traders still exudes an exotic air, with Turkish carpets and furnishings setting the guest rooms apart from the ordinary. *Fondamenta della Sensa, Cannaregio.* ☎ *041-711001. www.morihotel.*

A charming room, with balcony, in the Hotel American.

com. 55 units. Doubles 250€–410€. MC, V. Vaporetto: Orto. Map p 132.

★★★ Hotel Al Piave CASTELLO

Who says you have to pay high prices for high style? Tastefully appointed rooms combine luxurious fabrics and furnishings with wooden beams, polished tile floors, and other architectural features to provide the sort of comfortable lodgings in which you'll actually want to spend time. *Ruga Giuffa, Castello.* ☎ *041-5285174. www.piave.hotelinvenice.com. 13 units. Doubles 110€–170€. AE, MC, V. Vaporetto: San Zaccaria. Map p 131.*

The Belle Epoque Hotel des Bains, the setting for Mann's Death in Venice.

★★ Hotel Al Sole SANTA CROCE

Palazzi-turned-hotels are hardly a rarity in Venice, but this one stands out with its lovely location on a canal, close to the Frari, San Rocco, and the lively Campo Santa Margherita. Guest rooms are cozily adorned with the occasional beamed ceiling and antique furnishings, and most have pleasant views onto the palace's own garden or the neighboring rooftops. *Fondamenta Minotto, Santa Croce.* ☎ *041-2440328. www.alsolehotels. com. 62 units. Doubles 120€–180€. AE, DC, MC, V. Vaporetto: Piazzale Roma. Map p 134.*

★★★ Hotel American DORSO-

DURO   Large rooms furnished in antique Venetian style and a lovely terrace provide just the right atmosphere for a retreat in this quiet corner of the Dorsoduro neighborhood. In some rooms, flower-filled balconies overlooking a small canal add an extra dose of charm. *Fondamenta Bragadin, Dorsoduro.* ☎ *041-5204733. www.hotelamerican.com. 30 units. Doubles 80€–310€. AE, MC, V. Vaporetto: Accademia. Map p 133.*

★★★ Hotel Bel Sito SAN MARCO

There's an air of quiet elegance to this small hotel, in which reproduction antiques and tasteful fabrics make the cozy rooms unusually pleasant and restful. The neighborhood is quiet but within an easy walk of both the Accademia and San Marco. *Campo Santa Maria del Giglio, San Marco.* ☎ *041-5223365. 34 units. Doubles 150€–235€. AE, MC, V. Vaporetto: Giglio. Map p 131.*

★★★ Hotel des Bains LIDO

The beach, pools, tennis courts, and other amenities provide all you'll need for a complete vacation at this Art Nouveau resort hotel where Thomas Mann wrote and set *Death in Venice*. The place still sets the gold standard for an old-world pampered retreat. The large rooms and lounges have stylishly retained their century-old glamour, and there's just enough of a whiff of decadence to satisfy fans of the novel and film. *Lungomare Marconi 17, Lido.* ☎ *041-5265921. www.starwood.com. 191 units. Doubles 300€–450€. AE, DC, MC, V. Closed Nov–Mar. Vaporetto: Lido. Map p 133.*

★★★ Hotel Galleria DORSODURO

One of the biggest bargains in Venice is this pleasant little *pensione* right on the Grand Canal. Rooms have been pleasantly redone in traditional Venetian style, though some still

The tree-shaded pool at the Hotel des Bains.

share bathrooms—but all you'll really care about is the captivating waterway beneath your window. *Rio Terrà Antonio Foscarini, Dorsoduro.* ☎ *041-5232489. www.hotelgalleria.it. 34 units. Doubles 115€–140€. AE, MC, V. Vaporetto: Accademia. Map p 133.*

★★ Hotel Pausania DORSODURO

The entrance to this 14th-century palazzo is through a stunning courtyard with a well and an exterior stone staircase. Guest rooms are a bit less atmospheric, but have benefited from a thorough renovation, and the verandah and garden are as lovely as ever. *Fondamenta Gerardini, Dorsoduro.* ☎ *041-5222083. www.hotel pausania.it. 24 units. Doubles 110€–150€. AE, DC, MC, V. Vaporetto: Ca' Rezzonico. Map p 133.*

★★ Hotel San Cassiano/Ca' Favretto SAN POLO

A small palazzo on the Grand Canal, home to 19th-century painter Giacomo Favretto and other notable Venetians, now houses romantically furnished and delightful rooms, some facing the famous waterway. The colorful scene can also be enjoyed from the waterside terrace. *Calle della Rosa, San Polo.* ☎ *041-5241768. www.sancassiano.it. 35 units. Doubles 179€–239€. MC, V. Vaporetto: San Stae. Map p 134.*

A room at the simple, small, and beautiful Hotel San Cassiano.

The Best Lodging

★★★ Hotel San Geremia

CANNAREGIO   The location on a small campo just off the well-worn path from the train station toward the Rialto is one of many attributes of this pleasant little hotel. Others are the bright rooms sponge-painted in soothing earth tones and nicely done up with contemporary furnishings. Ask for a room facing the campo, or, if you don't mind climbing stairs, one of the top-floor units with terraces. *Campo San Geremia, Cannaregio.* ☎ *041-716245.* www.sangeremia.com. *20 units. Doubles 110€–150€. AE, DC, MC, V. Vaporetto: Ferrovia. Map p 132.*

★★ Hotel San Sebastiano Garden

DORSODURO   Everything about this palazzo seems outsized, from the commodious standard rooms to the enormous suites and parklike secret garden with splashing fountain. Furnishings are a surprisingly successful blend of traditional grandiosity and the chicly contemporary. *Fondamenta San Sebastiano, Dorsoduro.* ☎ *041-5231233.* www.

La Calcina's quiet terrace, perfect for lounging.

hotelsansebastianogarden.com. *16 units. Doubles 210€–250€. AE, DC, MC, V. Vaporetto: San Basilio. Map p 133.*

★★★ Hotel Saturnia and International

SAN MARCO   What looks like another standard big hotel on the well-trodden path between San Marco and the Rialto is full of surprises. A 14th-century palazzo and newer wings house a delightful warren of large and individually decorated rooms that blend traditional Venetian, Art Deco, and contemporary decor, and a garden and roof terrace are welcome retreats from the busy neighborhood. *Via XXII Marzo, San Marco.* ☎ *041-5208377.* www.hotelsaturnia.it. *93 units. Doubles: 140€–240€. AE, MC, V. Vaporetto: San Marco/Vallaresso. Map p 131.*

★★ Hotel Villa Mabapa

LIDO   An Art Nouveau villa and two adjoining houses, just steps from the beach and set in a large, leafy garden, provide a nice way to enjoy the Lido without having to pay the higher cost of one of the more posh resorts. All of the large guest rooms are different, and many retain 1930s-style furnishings. *Riviera San Nicolò, Lido.* ☎ *041-5260590.* www.mabapa.it. *71 units. Doubles 150€–230€. AE, MC, V. Vaporetto: Lido. Map p 133.*

★★★ La Calcina

DORSODURO   British essayist John Ruskin wrote part of *The Stones of Venice* here, and the years have been kind to this pleasantly old-fashioned hotel overlooking the Giudecca Canal. Recent renovations have buffed up the parquet floors and put a shine on the comfortable old furniture. *Fondamenta Zattere ai Geuati, Dorsoduro.* ☎ *041-5206466.* www.lacalcina.com. *29 units. Doubles 99€–158€. MC, V. Vaporetto: Zattere or Accademia. Map p 133.*

The 15th-century pensione *La Residenza.*

★★ La Fenice et des Artistes
SAN MARCO This old-fashioned favorite with opera buffs and stars from the nearby Fenice theater encompasses two 19th-century palaces and offers homey, comfortable rooms (all with new bathrooms), rather grand public areas, and even a pretty little garden. *Campiello della Fenice, San Marco.* ☎ *041-5232333. www.fenicehotels.it. 70 units. Doubles 150€–280€. AE, DC, MC, V. Vaporetto: Santa Maria del Giglio. Map p 131.*

★★★ La Residenza CASTELLO
Top prize for palatial and atmospheric lodgings at a good price goes to this old-fashioned *pensione* that occupies the 15th-century Palazzo Gritti Badoer. The lobby is a period piece of polished wood, chandeliers, and oil paintings, while the large high-ceiling guest rooms have all been beautifully refurbished with reproduction antiques that do justice to the lovely surroundings. *Campo Bandiera e Moro, Castello.* ☎ *041-5285315. www.veniceresidenza.com. 14 units. Doubles 80€–180€. AE, MC, V. Vaporetto: Arsenale. Map p 131.*

★★ La Villeggiatura SAN POLO
What must be the most off-putting entryway to any Venetian hotel takes you through a dank hall into a courtyard and up a series of external staircases. At the top: A wonderfully airy and stylish retreat tucked under the heavily beamed ceilings of the top floors of a medieval palace. *Calle dei Botteri, San Polo.* ☎ *041-5244673. www.lavilleggiatura.com. 6 units. Doubles 140€–180€. MC, V. Vaporetto: Rialto. Map p 134.*

★★ Locanda Antico Fiore SAN
MARCO The large, tasteful, but no-frills rooms are a relative bargain, and the location—in a quiet corner of town just steps from the Grand Canal and Accademia bridge—is superb. *Corte Lucatello, San Marco.* ☎ *041-5227941. www.anticofiore.com. 33 units. Doubles 110€–150€. MC, V. Vaporetto: San Samuele. Map p 131.*

★★ Locanda Ca' Zose DORSO-
DURO A quiet and sunny corner just steps from Salute, the Centro d'Arte Contemporana, and the Guggenheim offers a pretty lounge/breakfast room, large attractive guest rooms, and attentive service from the charming Campanati sisters. *Calle del Bastion, Dorsoduro.* ☎ *041-5226635. www.hotelcazose.com. 12 units. Doubles 85€–155€. MC, V. Vaporetto: Salute. Map p 133.*

★★★ Locanda Cipriani TORCELLO
A much-touted celebrity retreat lives up to its rep as a haven of casual elegance. Guests are cosseted by such homey amenities as plush armchairs and excellent beds, a lovely garden, and a noted restaurant (p 108). Best of all, guests have the enchanting island almost to themselves when the day-trippers leave. *Piazza Santa Fosca 29, Torcello.* ☎ *041-730150. www.locandacipriani.com. 6 units. Doubles 240€–340€. AE, DC, MC, V. Vaporetto: Torcello. Map p 132.*

★★ Locanda Fiorita SAN MARCO
The shiny bathrooms, handsome furnishings, and wisteria-shaded terrace overlooking the *campiello* provide a

★★★ Locanda La Corte

CASTELLO The eponymous court-yard—most welcome after a summer's day of exploring—along with exposed beams, polished floors, and plenty of other 16th-century embellishments, make this small palazzo a cozy and stylish retreat in a pretty backwater of the city. *Calle Bressana, Castello.* ☎ *041-2411300. www.locandalacorte.it. 16 units. Doubles 90€–180€. AE, MC, V. Vaporetto: Fondamenta Nuove. Map p 131.*

★★★ Locanda San Barnaba

DORSODURO The pretty garden and sunny roof terrace make it difficult to spend too much time indoors, but the guest rooms in this fine old palazzo are delightful—crisscrossed by ancient timbers and nicely done up with Turkish carpets, painted bureaus, plump armchairs, and other comfy trappings. The two-level junior suites are especially handy for travelers with kids in tow. *Calle del Traghetto, Dorsoduro.* ☎ *041-2411233. www.locanda-sanbarnaba.com. 13 units. Doubles 120€–170€. AE, MC, V. Vaporetto: Ca' Rezzonico. Map p 133.*

The smart Locanda Cipriani (p 143), on the island of Torcello.

welcoming, old-fashioned air. Some rooms are situated in a nearby annex, Ca' Morosini, but opt for one in the palazzo. *Campiello Nuovo, San Marco.* ☎ *041-5234754. www.locandafiorita.com. 16 units. Doubles 110€–130€. AE, MC, V. Vaporetto: San Samuele. Map p 131.*

The courtyard cafe of the Locanda La Corte palazzo hotel.

The facade of the Pensione Accademia/Villa Maravege.

★★★ Londra Palace CASTELLO

This 19th-cenutry neo-Gothic palace laden with oil paintings and antiques inspired Tchaikovsky to write his fourth symphony—but it's quite alright if you're moved to do nothing more than enjoy the water views from one of the sumptuous guest rooms or the airy roof terrace. **Do Leoni**, one of Venice's best restaurants, is on the premises. *Riva degli Schiavoni, Castello.* ☎ *041-5200533. www.hotellondra.it. 53 units. Doubles 265€–399€. AE, DC, MC, V. Vaporetto: San Zaccaria. Map p 131.*

★★ Messner DORSODURO

Guest rooms are spread throughout three nearby buildings, and while the decor is fairly standard "hotel modern" throughout, those in the 14th-century palazzo enjoy high ceilings, tall windows, and other old-world touches. Some rooms overlook a delightful garden and others a canal, and the glorious waterfront around Salute is just steps away. *Fondamenta Ca' Balà, Dorsoduro.* ☎ *041-5227443. www.hotelmessner.it. 33 units.*

Doubles 100€–14€. AE, MC, V. Vaporetto: Salute. Map p 133.

★★ Metropole CASTELLO

Venice's own master of Baroque music, Antonio Vivaldi, once lived in this palazzo, and the maestro might still feel right at home amid the bric-a-brac and swirls of fabric. Rooms vary widely in decor (a few are almost contemporary in feel) and in outlook, but most have a view—be it of the Bacino San Marco, a side canal, or the lovely rear garden and pool. *Riva degli Schiavoni, Castello.* ☎ *041-5205044. www.hotelmetropole.com. 72 units. Doubles 150€–600€. AE, MC, V. Vaporetto: San Zaccaria. Map p 131.*

★★ Oltre il Giardino SAN POLO

The former home of Gustav Mahler's widow is tucked into a luxuriant garden next to a canal and provides the aura of a country retreat—not dispelled by the handsome and beautifully furnished rooms and suites and excellent service. *Fondamenta Contarini, San Polo.* ☎ *041-2750015. www.oltreilgiardino-venezia.com.*

The serene garden atmosphere at Oltre il Giardino.

9 units. Doubles 150€–250€. AE, MC, V. Vaporetto: San Tomà. Map p 134.

★ **Pantalon** DORSODURO The basic rooms decorated in faux Venetian antique furnishings are perfectly comfortable and the service is commendable, but this hotel's best assets are the sunny roof terrace and the lively neighborhood scene. *Crosera San Pantalon, Dorsoduro.* ☎ *041-718683. www.hotel pantalon.com. 24 units. Doubles 100€–150€. AE, MC, V. Vaporetto: San Tomà. Map p 133.*

★★★ **Pensione Accademia/ Villa Maravege** DORSODURO A patrician villa that served as the Russian consulate until the 1930s still exudes the air of a private home, with comfortable lounges, antique-filled rooms, and two large gardens. If the place looks familiar, there's good reason: It's the charming spot where Katharine Hepburn's character stayed in the David Lean movie *Summertime. Fondamenta Bollani, Dorsoduro.* ☎ *041-5210188. www. pensioneaccademia.it. 27 units. Doubles 140€–250€. AE, MC, V. Vaporetto: Accademia. Map p 133.*

★★ **Pensione Guerrato** SAN POLO Staying smack in the middle of the Rialto market area can be a heady but tiring experience, and these old-fashioned, high-ceilinged rooms in a former convent, furnished with an eclectic mix of antiques, provide a welcome retreat. A choice few have partial views of the Grand Canal. *Calle Drio la Scimia, San Polo.* ☎ *041-5285927. http://web.tiscali.it/ pensioneguerrato. 14 units. Doubles 95€–145€. AE, MC, V. Vaporetto: Rialto. Map p 134.*

★★★ **Pensione Seguso** DORSO-DURO Many of the guests have stayed here many times before, and it's easy to see the appeal of the homey, old-fashioned ambience, stunning views of the Giudecca canal, and waterside terrace. *Fondamenta Zattere ai Geuati, Dorsoduro.* ☎ *041-5222340. www.pensioneseguso venice.com. 34 units. Doubles 124€–180€. AE, MC, V. Vaporetto: Zattere or Accademia. Map p 133.* ●

The Pensione Seguso's waterside terrace.

10 The Best Day Trips & Excursions

Padua (Padova)

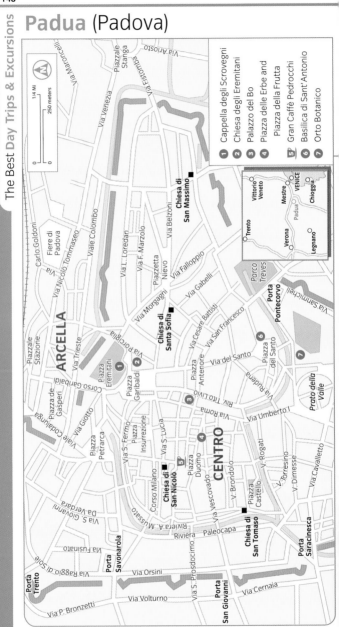

1 Cappella degli Scrovegni
2 Chiesa degli Eremitani
3 Palazzo del Bo
4 Piazza delle Erbe and Piazza della Frutta
5 Gran Caffè Pedrocchi
6 Basilica di Sant'Antonio
7 Orto Botanico

Previous page: The riverfront in Verona at dusk.

Proud Padua seems content to take a backseat to Venice, though it has plenty of treasures of its own. These include one of Europe's oldest universities, a stunning fresco cycle by Giotto, and a medieval botanical garden. START: **Padua is only 30 minutes from Venice by train, with departures about every 15 minutes. By car, take the A4 Autostrada. The tourist information office in the train station dispenses maps and other information. From the train station, follow Corso di Popolo and Corso Garibaldi toward Piazza delle Erbe and the city center; the route will take you to all the major sights. You can easily tour the city on foot, and buses from the station go to the sights as well.**

1 ★★★ Cappella degli Scrovegni.

One of the world's great painting cycles, by Giotto (1267–1337), covers the walls of what was once the chapel of the palace of the Scrovegni family. The magnificent frescoes are, in effect, atonement for the ill-gotten gains the family acquired through usury. The frescoes have been restored and are painstakingly maintained—visitors are even required to enter through a decontamination chamber. Giotto painted the frescoes from 1303 to 1305, and in these scenes of the life of the Virgin Mary and Christ he introduced the concept of naturalism to Western painting. Biblical scenes such as Judas's betrayal of Christ with a kiss and the flight into Egypt are depicted with humanity and emotion that bring

A Giotto fresco in the Cappella degli Scrovegni.

A spectacular Giotto cycle lines the interior of the Cappella degli Scrovegni.

the paintings to life. Off the adjacent cloisters, the **Museo Civico Eremitani** houses ancient artifacts, as well works by Tintoretto and other Venetian artists. ⏱ *Visits to chapel restricted to 15 min. Piazza Eremitani 8, off Corso Garibaldi.* ☎ *049-2010020. www.cappelladegli scrovegni.it. 11€ plus 1.15€ booking fee. Tickets must be booked in advance by going online, calling the number above, or at Padua tourist offices. Mon–Fri 9am–7pm, Sat 9am–1pm. Bus: 3, 8, 10, or 12 from train station.*

2 ★★ Chiesa degli Eremitani.

What's most moving about this beautifully restored 13th-century Romanesque Church of the Hermits is what's missing—the bulk of a fresco cycle, *Life and Martyrdom of St. James and St. Christopher,*

The 16th-century anatomical theater in the Palazzo del Bo.

painted by Padua-born Andrea Mantegna from 1454 to 1457. The church was leveled in a German air raid in 1944; fortunately, two of the panels had been removed for safekeeping and two others were salvaged from the rubble. ⏱ *15 min. Piazza Eremitani.* ☎ *049-8756410. Daily 8:30am–12:30pm, 4:30–7pm. Bus: 3, 8, 10, or 12 from train station.*

③ **★★ Palazzo del Bo.** Italy's second-oldest university, founded in 1222, has drawn such scholars as Dante, Copernicus, and Oliver Goldsmith, and was Europe's first institution of higher learning to graduate a female, Elena Lucrezia Corner

The lively markets of the Piazza delle Erbe and Piazza della Frutta.

Piscopia (in 1678). Guided tours of the palazzo, named for a medieval inn frequented by students and now the center of the university, show off such features as the anatomical theater from 1594 and the battered lectern from which Galileo Galilei lectured from 1592 to 1610. ⏱ *1 hr. Via VIII Febbraio.* ☎ *049-8275111. 3€. Open by guided tour Mar–Oct Mon, Wed, and Fri 3, 4, and 5pm; Tues and Thurs, Sat 9, 10, and 11am. Nov–Feb Mon, Wed, and Fri 3 and 4pm; Tues, Thurs, and Sat 10 and 11am. Bus: 3, 8, or 12 from train station.*

④ **★★ Piazza delle Erbe & Piazza della Frutta.** These two adjoining squares in the city center house one of Italy's largest and liveliest markets; produce is on offer in Piazza delle Erbe, and clothing and housewares in Piazza della Frutta. The building with the loggia rising above the market stalls is the **Palazzo della Ragione,** built in the 13th century, rebuilt in the 15th century, and once home to the law courts. ⏱ *30 min. Piazza delle Erbe & Piazza della Frutta. Market Mon–Sat 8am–1:30pm. Bus: 3, 5, 8, 9, 10, 11, or 12 from train station.*

⑤ **Gran Caffè Pedrocchi.** One of Europe's legendary grand cafes, recently restored to its 19th-century grandeur, is almost a mandatory stop for a cup of coffee and panino or pastry. For an extra 3€, you can step upstairs to tour the bizarre theme rooms—but spend the euros on another cappuccino instead. *Piazzetta Pedrocchi.* ☎ *049-8781231. Sun–Tues 9am–9pm; Wed–Sat 9am–midnight. Bus: 3, 8, 12, 16, 18, or 22 from train station.*

6 ★★ Basilica di Sant'Antonio. Padua is a famous pilgrimage city, and the faithful flock to this 13th-century "Il Santo" church to honor Anthony, a Portuguese Franciscan friar who came to Padua around 1230 to preach against usury. Ironically, the city's other great shrine, the Cappella degli Scrovegni (p 149), was funded by the gains of money-lending. Anthony's body rests in the Cappella d'Arca, surrounded by nine marble bas-reliefs depicting scenes from his life by Renaissance artists. The saint's tongue is housed separately, in the reliquary, and has been all the more appreciated since its recent theft and recovery. ⏱ *45 min. Piazza del Santo.* ☎ *049-8789722. www.basilica delsanto.org. Late Oct to Apr daily 9am–1pm, 2–6pm; May to late Oct*

The ornate door of the 13th-century Basilica di Sant'Antonio.

daily 8:30am–1pm, 2–6:30pm. Bus: 3, 8, 12, or 18 from train station.

7 ★★ Orto Botanico. The oldest botanical garden in Europe was founded in 1540 to provide medicinal herbs and plants to the university. At the center of the garden, the original design can still be seen: Flower beds are planted in a circle, representing the earth, surrounded by water. Some specimens include a palm planted in 1585. ⏱ *30 min. Via Orto Botanico 15.* ☎ *049-656614. Apr–Oct daily 9am–1pm, 3–6pm. Bus: 3, 8, 12, or 18 from train station.*

"Il Santo," otherwise known as the Basilica di Sant'Antonio.

Verona

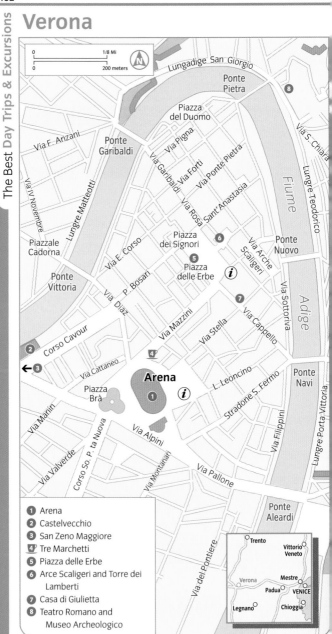

1 Arena
2 Castelvecchio
3 San Zeno Maggiore
4 Tre Marchetti
5 Piazza delle Erbe
6 Arce Scaligeri and Torre dei Lamberti
7 Casa di Giulietta
8 Teatro Romano and Museo Archeologico

This handsome city on the River Adige was founded by the Romans in the 1st century A.D., flourished in the Middle Ages, and was a part of the Venetian empire. Traces of its long history are much in evidence in the Roman arena, fine churches, and piazzas and palazzi, and no small part of the city's allure is the star-crossed romance of its two most famous citizens, Romeo and Juliet. START: **Verona is about 1½ to 2 hours from Venice by train, with departures about every hour. By car, take the A4 Autostrada. The tourist information office near the arena in Piazza Brà dispenses maps and other information. From Verona's train station, it is about a 10-minute walk down Corso Porta Nuova to Piazza Bra and the arena, and from there, Via Mazzini leads the short distance to Piazza delle Erbe and the other sites of the old city.**

① ★★ **Arena.** The best-preserved Roman arena in the world still commands the center of town. When the arena was built in the 1st century A.D., the entire population of Verona could squeeze in for gladiator shows and mock naval battles. The amphitheater is still filled to its 20,000-person capacity when operas are performed on summer evenings—a must for anyone visiting Verona at this time. ⏱ *30 min. Piazza Brà.* ☎ *045-8003204 or 045-8077500 (for information on opera performances). Mon 1:45–7:30pm, Tues–Sun 8:30am–7:30pm. 3.10€. www.arena.it. Tickets 20€–150€. Bus: 11, 12, or 13 from train station.*

② ★★ **Castelvecchio.** The castle of the Della Scala family, medieval rulers of Verona, looms over the River Adige. The interior was rebuilt in the 1960s by Venetian architect Carlo Scarpa, and stunning galleries house a collection of paintings by Tintoretto, Tieopolo, Guardi, and other artists whose works are usually associated with Venice. ⏱ *1 hr. Corso Castelvecchio 2.* ☎ *045-594734. 3.10€. Mon 1:45–7:30pm, Tues–Sun 8:30am–7:30pm. Bus: 11, 12, or 13 from train station.*

③ ★★★ **San Zeno Maggiore.** One of Italy's finest Romanesque churches was built in the 12th

Verona's 1st-century Roman Arena.

century as a shrine to San Zeno, the first bishop of Verona and the city's beloved patron saint. Zeno's remains are enshrined behind a magnificent facade on which 12th-century sculptors Nicolò and Guglielmo portray scenes from the Bible, a theme that is carried over to the church's bronze doors. Inside, a triptych of the *Madonna and Child* by Andrea Mantegna graces the altar, and Zeno comes to life in a marble likeness that breaks the mold of religious statuary to show the famously good-natured saint chuckling. ⏱ *45 min. Piazza San Zeno.* ☎ *045-592813. 3€. Mon–Sat 8:30am–6pm, Sun 1–6pm. Bus: 31 or 32 from train station.*

4 🍴 **Tre Marchetti.** Before heading to other sights, linger over pasta or *baccala* (salt cod, a house specialty) in atmospheric surroundings that are truly old—meals have been served here since 1291. *Vicolo Tre Marchetti.* ☎ *045-8030463.*

The Romanesque church of San Zeno Maggiore in Verona.

The much-photographed balcony at Casa di Giulietta (Juliet's House).

5 ★ **Piazza delle Erbe.** The site of the Roman Forum is now Verona's central square, surrounded by palazzi and the venue for a daily market. Many of the wares on offer are of the ho-hum T-shirt variety, but enough fresh produce from the Veneto is on sale to lend an air of authenticity to the marketplace. ⏱ *30 min. Piazza delle Erbe. Market Mon–Sun 8:30am–7:30pm. Bus: 11, 12, or 13 from train station.*

6 ★★ **Arce Scaligeri & Torre dei Lamberti.** The tombs of the Della Scala family that ruled Verona for most of the 13th and 14th centuries are masterpieces of medieval stone work. What also becomes apparent is the family's taste for bestowing canine names on other members of the family, from Mastino I (Big Mastiff, founder of the dynasty) to Cansignorio (Lord Dog, one of the last of the clan). Cangrande (Big Dog) was a patron and protector of Dante. You can see the tombs at any time through the fence without paying admission, but if you do pay for a close-up look, the same ticket allows you to ascend the nearby "Tower of the Lamberti," a medieval hulk that rises 84m (275 ft.) and affords stunning views. ⏱ *30 min. Via Santa Maria in Chiavica. 2.60€ for tombs and tower (elevator); 2.10€ for tombs and tower (stairs). Courtyard open for close-up viewing June–Aug Mon 1:45–7:30pm, Tues–Sun 8:30am–7:30pm. Bus: 11, 12, or 13 from train station.*

7 ★ **Casa di Giulietta.** Juliet's House, Verona's shrine to love, is a lovely medieval home . . . and there any authentic association with Shakespeare's heroine aside. Most shameless is the balcony from which the doomed maiden allegedly hailed Romeo—it's a 1920s addition built to capitalize on romantic appeal. ⏱ *15 min. Via Cappello 23. ☎ 045-8034303. 3.10€. Mon 1:30–7:30pm; Tues–Sun 8:30am–7:30pm. Bus: 11, 12, or 13 from train station.*

8 ★★ **Teatro Romano & Museo Archeologico.** Verona's Roman theater dates from the 1st century B.C., when the outpost was an important crossroads between Rome and the northern colonies. The stone seats are built into the side of a hill, and the old city across the River Adige provides a stunning backdrop for Verona's summer festival of drama, music, and dance. An elevator ascends from the theater grounds to the cliff-top monastery that now houses the archaeological museum's small collection of statuary and other artifacts; the real draw, though, is the view over the city. ⏱ *45 min. Rigaste Redentore 2. ☎ 045-8000360 or 045-8066485 (for information on the festival). www.estateteatraleveronese.it. 2.60€. Theater Tues–Sun 9am–7pm; museum Mon 1:30–6:45pm, Tues–Sun 8:30am–6:45pm. Bus: 31, 32, 33, or 73 from train station.*

Cafe tables overlooking Verona's ancient 20,000-seat Arena (p 153).

Ravenna

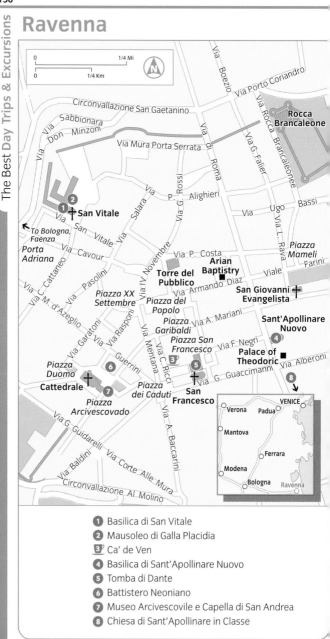

1. Basilica di San Vitale
2. Mausoleo di Galla Placidia
3. Ca' de Ven
4. Basilica di Sant'Apollinare Nuovo
5. Tomba di Dante
6. Battistero Neoniano
7. Museo Arcivescovile e Capella di San Andrea
8. Chiesa di Sant'Apollinare in Classe

For 2 brief centuries, before the Lombards invaded in 750, Ravenna flourished as the seat of the Byzantine empire. The most striking evidence of the city's former power are the brilliant mosaics that shine within Ravenna's churches and other landmarks, which will captivate travelers who have been smitten with the mosaics of San Marco. START: **Ravenna is about 3 hours by train from Venice, usually with a change in Ferrara. The trip by bus is faster, a little less than 2 hours, as is the car trip down the coast to Ferrara, a delightful stop, and from there on SS16. From Ravenna's train and bus stations, it is about a 10-minute walk down Via Farini to Piazza del Popolo, an elegant, 16th-century square from the city's days under Venetian rule. The Basilica di San Vitale and Mausoleo di Galla Placidia are a few blocks to the north of the square, and the Basilica di Sant' Apollinare Nuovo is a few blocks to the south.**

❶ ★★★ Basilica di San Vitale.

The octagonal church that the Emperor Justinian completed in 540 as a symbol of his earthly might is covered in mosaics that say much about the power structure of the 6th century: Christ oversees his earthly creatures from his perch on a celestial orb, and next to him is Justinian, endowed with a halo and a crown to indicate his role as head of church and state. Justinian's two most important mortal adjuncts, Theodora (his courtesan and later empress) and a bald Maximian

(bishop of Ravenna), look on. *Note:* A **Visit Card** allows entry to the Basilica di San Vitale, Mausoleo di Galla Placidia, and Basilica di Sant'Apollinare Nuovo and can be purchased at each location; you cannot pay for separate admissions to these sights. ⏱ *30 min. Via San Vitale. Visit Card 9.50€ Mar to mid-Jun, 7.50€ Jun–Feb. ☎ 0544-219518. Open Apr–Sept daily 10am–7pm; Oct and Mar daily 10am–5:30pm; Nov–Feb daily 9:30am–4:30pm.*

Intricate mosaics adorn the ceiling of the Basilica di San Vitale.

2 ★★★ **Mausoleo di Galla Placidia.** The tomb of the sister of the Roman emperor Honorius, who moved the capital to Ravenna in 402, is all the more moving for its simplicity and the touching symbolism of the mosaics. Doves drink from fountains as the faithful are nourished by God, and Christ is clad in a brilliant purple robe and surrounded by lambs, the faithful. Soft light, filtering through alabaster panels, bathes the depictions in an otherworldly glow. *Via San Vitale, next to Basilica di San Vitale.* ☎ *0544-541688. Visit Card 9.50€ Mar to mid-Jun, 7.50€ Jun–Feb. Apr–Sept daily 10am–7pm; Oct and Mar daily 10am–5:30pm; Nov–Feb daily 9:30am–4:30pm.*

3 **Ca' de Ven.** Almost as enticing as the mosaics is this atmospheric 16th-century wine cellar just off Piazza del Popolo. Patrons sit at long communal tables to enjoy *piadina,* a local flatbread, served with cheese and prosciutto and washed down with white wine. The *torta di marzipan,* a house specialty, is a memorable follow-up. *Via C. Ricci.* ☎ *0544-30163.*

4 ★★★ **Basilica di Sant'Apollinare Nuovo.** In this simple 6th-century church, lustrous mosaics preserve a swirl of motion for the ages. On the left side of the church, once reserved for women, 22 virgins approach Mary and the Christ child with gifts; on the right side, 26 martyrs proceed toward an enthroned Christ surrounded by angels. *Via Roma.* ☎ *0544-219518. Visit Card 9.50€ Mar to mid-Jun, 7.50€ Jun–Feb. May–Sept daily 10am–7pm; Oct–Apr daily 10am–5pm.*

5 ★★ **Tomba di Dante.** The author of the *Divine Comedy* died in exile in Ravenna in 1321. Dante's native Florence has been clamoring for the remains of the greatest mind of the early Renaissance for centuries, but for the time being visitors to Ravenna can pay homage at the simple tomb and in a small museum. *Via Dante Alighieri.* ☎ *0544-30252. Free admission. Tomb daily 9am–noon, 2–5pm; museum Tues–Sun 9am–noon.*

6 **Battistero Neoniano.** In this small, enchanting octagonal baptistery built in the early sixth century, a sea of intensely colored blue and gold mosaics on the dome depict the baptism of Christ by John the Baptist, while the twelve apostles, carrying crowns as a sign of celestial glory, look on. The prophets make an appearance on reliefs on the arches supporting the rotunda. ⏱ *15 min. Piazza del Duomo.* ☎ *0544-215201. 7.50€ (includes admission to the Museo Arcivescovile). Apr–Sept daily 9am–7pm; Mar and Oct daily 9am–5:30pm; Nov–Feb daily 9:30am–4:30pm.*

A mosaic of the empress Theodora, in the Basilica di San Vitale (p 157).

The Basilica di Sant'Apollinare Nuovo's mosaic work leads to the altar.

7 Museo Arcivescovile e Capella di San Andrea.

Ravenna's sixth-century Archbishop's Palace, itself a monument, houses another sixth-century treasure, the richly carved ivory throne of Maximian, a bishop of Ravenna during the reign of Justinian. 🕐 *15 min. Piazza Arcivescovado.* ☎ *0544-215201. 7.50€ (includes admission to the Battistero Neoniano). Apr–Sept daily 9am–7pm; Mar and Oct daily 9am–5:30pm; Nov–Feb daily 9:30am–4:30pm.*

8 ★★★ Chiesa di Sant'Apollinare in Classe.

The size of this austere structure bespeaks its former dominance at the center of Classe, once the busy port for landlocked Ravenna—briefly the most important city in the Western world. Mosaics here depict Christ in *Judgment* and Sant'Apollinare, a bishop of Ravenna, but most engaging is a *Transfiguration* set against a field of brilliantly green grass where colorful flowers bloom and charming animals roam. *Via Romea Sud, Classe,* about 5km (3 miles) south of city center. ☎ *0544-473569. 2€. Daily 9am–5:30pm. From the train station and Piazza Cadutti (near Dante's tomb), take bus 4 or 44.*

The imposing door to the Tomba di Dante.

The Brenta Canal

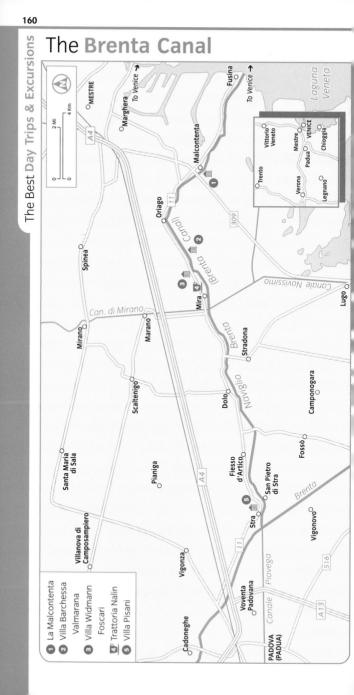

1 La Malcontenta
2 Villa Barchessa Valmarana
3 Villa Widmann Foscari
4 Trattoria Nalin
5 Villa Pisani

In the 17th and 18th centuries, Venetians of wealth and standing built summer villas along the banks of the Brenta Canal, on the mainland just west of the lagoon. Several dozen of these magnificent structures still stand on the green banks of the placid canal, and some are open to the public. Visiting them is like stepping into the grandeur of the last days of the Venetian Republic. ***Tip:*** Bus schedules make it difficult to see more than a few villas on a day trip—settle for a jaunt to La Malcontenta, or, if you're really ambitious, continue on from there to the village of Mira and its two nearby villas, Villa Barchessa Valmarana and Villa Widmann Foscari.

START: **Begin at La Malcontenta; following Rte. S 11 by car or by bus from Venice's Piazzale Roma.**

① ★★★ La Malcontenta. Modeled after an ancient temple, with a classical portico that rises above the flat, grassy lowlands on a bend of the canal, Malcontenta is the most famous villa on the Brenta and one of the best-known works of the architect Andrea Palladio. (See p 46, ① and ②, for other examples of this master's work.) Inside are frescoes by Giambattista Zelotti and Battista Franco. The house is also known as **Villa Foscari**, for the family of doges who commissioned a country retreat in the 16th century; their descendants still come here in summers. According to romantic lore, the more poetic name derives from a malcontent Foscari wife exiled to the villa for an adulterous affair; more prosaically, the entire neighborhood came to be known as Malcontenta during the controversial excavation of a canal, the *fossa dei malcontenti,* in the 15th century. ⏱ *1 hr. Via dei Turisti, Malcontenta.* ☎ *041-5470012. 10€. May–Oct Tues and Sat 9am–noon; open other times for groups. Bus: 53 ATVO or ACTV from Piazzale Roma to Padua.*

② ★★ Villa Barchessa Valmarana. The Valmaranas tore down their villa in the 19th century to avoid paying taxes, but the remaining *barchessa,* an outbuilding converted to a residence, is quite grand. The house sits amid beautiful formal gardens on the banks of the canal and houses fine furnishings and frescoes by a student of Tiepolo. ⏱ *1 hr.* ☎ *041-4266387.*

One of Palladio's architectural masterpieces, La Malcontenta, on the Brenta Canal.

Cruising the Brenta

The easiest way to see the Brenta is on a cruise. *Il Burchiello*, operated by the regional tourism office of Padua, Via Orlandini 3 (☎ 049-8206910; www.ilburchiello.it), stops at Villa Pisani, Barchessa Valmarana, or Villa Widmann, as well as Malcontenta, and pulls in for a lunch stop (the meal costs extra) at the village of Mira. The price—71€ for a full day; 44€ for a half-day—includes transportation by bus back to Venice from Padua. The boat departs Venice from the Pieta dock on Riva degli Schiavoni.

www.villavalmarana.net. 6€. Mar–Oct Tues–Sun 10am–6pm; Nov–Feb Sat–Sun 10am–6pm. Bus: 53 ATVO or ACTV from Piazzale Roma to Padua.

3 ★★ Villa Widmann Foscari. Carlo Goldoni, Igor Stravinksy, and Gabriele D'Annunzio are among the illustrious visitors to this rococo villa. They may well have enjoyed the two-story ballroom, with a minstrel's gallery and frescoes glorifying the Widman clan. ⏱ *1 hr.* ☎ *041-424973. 5€. Mar–Apr Tues–Sun 10am–5pm; May–Sept Tues–Sun 10am–6pm; Oct Tues–Sat 10am–5pm; Nov–Mar Sat–Sun 10am–5pm. Bus: 53 ATVO or ACTV from Piazzale Roma to Padua.*

4 Trattoria Nalin. Enjoying a dish of risotto with scampi and a glass of crisp white from the Veneto vineyards on the flowery terrace is a perfect way to take a pause from villa viewing. *Via Nuovissimo 29, Mira.* ☎ *041-420083.*

5 ★★ Villa Pisani. The doge Alvise Pisani built this grandiose villa to impress, a function it still fulfills. By far the grandest house on the Brenta, the villa has 114 rooms (Pisani was the 114th doge), extensive grounds, and a grand ballroom frescoed by Tiepolo; not too surprisingly, the master glorifies the Pisani family. Napoleon, who could not have been unaware of the Villa Pisani's resemblance to a French château, bought the house from the Pisani clan in 1807. Hitler and Mussolini found the villa to be a suitable venue for their first meeting, in 1939. ⏱ *1 hr.* ☎ *049-502074. 5€. Apr–Sept Tues–Sat 9am–7pm; Oct–Mar Tues–Sat 9am–4pm. Bus: 53 ATVO or ACTV from Piazzale Roma to Padua.* ●

The grand Villa Widmann Foscari in the town of Mira.

The **Savvy Traveler**

Before You Go

Italian Government Tourist Board Offices

In the U.S.: New York: 630 Fifth Ave., Suite 1565, New York, NY 10111 (☎ 212/245-4822; fax 212/586-9249). Chicago: 500 N. Michigan Ave., Suite 2240, Chicago, IL 60611 (☎ 312/644-0996; fax 312/644-3019). Los Angeles: 12400 Wilshire Blvd., Suite 550, Los Angeles, CA 90025 (☎ 310/820-1898; fax 310/820-6367; www.italiantourism. com). **In Canada:** 175 Bloor St. E., Suite 907, South Tower, Toronto, Ontario M4W 3R8, Canada (☎ 416/925-4882; fax 416/925-4799; www. italiantourism.com). **In the U.K.:** 1 Princes St., London W1B 2AY (☎ 020/7408-1254 or 090/6550-8925, calls are charged at £1 per minute; fax 020/7399-3567; www. italiantourism.com). **In Australia:** Level 4, 46 Market St., Sydney, NSW 2000 (☎ 0612/9262-1666; fax 0612/9262-1677; www.italian tourism.com).

The Best Times to Go

Try to avoid **July and August,** and August especially, when the heat and humidity can be oppressive and many restaurants and other businesses close for vacation; on the other hand, hotels rates come down in July and August. The best times weather-wise are **April and May** or **September and October.** You may or may not want to be in Venice during **Carnevale,** depending on your taste for crowds and drunken revelry.

Festivals & Special Events

FEBRUARY **Carnevale** (p 125), Venice's most famous festival, brings revelry to Venice for the 10 days before Ash Wednesday, when Lent begins. Festivities include masked processions, contests for best costumes, and fireworks.

MAY **Festa e Regata della Sensa,** a ceremony at San Nicolo on the Lido in which the mayor throws a laurel wreath into the sea, renews the Marriage of Venice to the Sea; a regatta follows. For the **Vogalonga** (p 126), the first Sunday after the feast of the Ascension, Venetians take to sea in all kinds of craft and row to Burano and back; anyone can participate.

JUNE TO NOVEMBER **Biennale D'Arte Contemporanea e Architettura** (p 125) features art in odd years (mid-June to Nov) and architecture in even years (Sept–Oct).

JULY The **Festa del Redentore** (p 125), on the third weekend of the month, commemorates the end of the plague outbreak of 1576.

AUGUST TO SEPTEMBER For the **Regata Storica** (p 126), festooned boats with crews in period costumes make their way down the Grand Canal on the first Sunday of the month. **Mostra Internazionale d'Arte Cinematografica** (the Venice International Film Festival; p 125) is one of the world's most important and longest-running showcases for international films.

NOVEMBER **Opera season** begins at the recently rebuilt La Fenice. During the **Festa della Madonna della Salute** (p 125), on November 21, religious processions cross a pontoon bridge over the Grand Canal to the church of Santa Maria della Salute.

The Weather

May, June, September, and early October are the most pleasant

Previous page: The Piazza San Marco from above.

VENICE'S AVERAGE DAILY TEMPERATURE & MONTHLY RAINFALL

	JAN	FEB	MAR	APR	MAY	JUNE
Temp (°F)	43	48	53	60	67	72
Temp (°C)	6	9	12	16	19	22
Rainfall (in.)	2.3	1.5	2.9	3	2.8	2.9
Rainfall (cm)	5.8	3.8	7.4	7.6	7.1	7.4

	JULY	AUG	SEPT	OCT	NOV	DEC
Temp (°F)	77	74	68	60	54	44
Temp (°C)	25	23	29	16	12	7
Rainfall (in.)	1.5	1.9	2.9	2.6	3	2.1
Rainfall (cm)	3.8	4.8	7.4	6.6	7.6	5.3

months. July and August can be hot and humid, and the late fall and winter can be rainy (Nov and Mar are especially wet). Damp chill can make winter months seems especially cold. *Acqua alta* (high-water) tides briefly flood low-lying areas in the fall and winter months; the Piazza San Marco is one of the first areas to be submerged. When the flooding comes, the city constructs raised walkways along major routes. (*Note:* Venetians wait patiently for their turn to pass along on the walkways, and it's considered extremely rude to push ahead.) Many natives wear high rubber boots when the waters hit; if you find the weather is curtailing your explorations, invest in a pair. Count on having soggy feet for just a short while: The waters usually recede in 2 or 3 hours.

Useful Websites
Venice's official tourist board site is **www.turismovenezia.it**; the city government site is **www.comune. venezia.it**. Other useful addresses are **www.italiantourism.com** and **www.veniceworld.com**, a handy compilation of Venice-related links.

How to Get the Best Airfare
Online services such as **www.travel ocity.com**, **www.expedia.com**, **www.orbitz.com**, and **www. cheaptickets.com** make it easy to search for low airfares. The site **www.hotwire.com** provides especially low fares but with the proviso that you don't know the time of departure or routing until you book and pay. On **www.priceline.com**, you can name your own price for a ticket, but if your bid is accepted, you are committed to the purchase. In the U.K., **www.opodo.com**, **www.lastminute.com**, and **www.discount-tickets.com** offer some of the best prices on flights. Increasingly, airlines also offer discounted fares on their websites; when traveling to Venice, for example, check out fares at **www. alitalia.com**, **www.britishairways. com**, and **www.delta.com**. Sunday travel sections in most newspapers also have special deals on travel, often from large travel agencies and consolidators, and some flights may be surprisingly inexpensive. Wherever you find a fare, you will get the best deal if you are flexible about the date and time of day you want to fly.

How to Get the Best Hotel Deals
Many of the websites mentioned above under "How to Get the Best Airfare" also offer reasonably priced hotel rooms, as does **www.hotels. com**. Keep in mind that most of these services require you to pay in full upfront, so you may be stuck

with a room you don't like. (But if you don't like it when you arrive, always ask to change rooms!) Also, check with hotels to see what sort of special offers might be available directly from them. (These usually appear on the hotel's website.) If you see an offer on another website, call or write the hotel, mention the offer you've seen, and ask if the hotel will match it or do better—this way you will be dealing with the hotel, can request the sort of room you want, and won't be locked into a prepaid arrangement. Bargaining is a respected skill in Venice, so never be afraid to ask if a hotel can provide a more favorable rate.

Cell (Mobile) Phones

Cellphones can save you quite a bit of money, since they allow you to avoid high hotel phone charges. To use your cellphone in Italy, you must have a **GSM (Global System for Mobiles)** cellphone with a 900 GSM frequency; this allows you to make calls anywhere in the world, though it can be expensive. It may be less expensive to rent a cellphone from an Italian provider at the airport or to purchase a prepaid phone SIM card to use in your phone. To rent a phone outfitted for use in Italy in advance of your trip, check **www.roadpost.com** or **www.intouchglobal.com**.

Getting **There**

By Plane

Venice's **Marco Polo Airport** is 10km (6½ miles) north of the city on the mainland. From **North America,** Alitalia and Delta fly nonstop to Venice from New York's John F. Kennedy airport. Other flights from North America usually go through Milan or Rome, where they connect with flights to Venice. Travel time is about 9 hours, longer, of course, when it's necessary to make a connection. From the **U.K.,** British Airways flies nonstop to Venice from London and Manchester. Flying time is about 2½ hours.

The **ATVO airport shuttle bus** (☎ 042-1383671; www.atvo.it) connects Marco Polo Airport with Piazzale Roma, not far from Venice's Santa Lucia train station. Buses leave from the airport about every half hour, and the trip costs 3€ and takes 20 minutes. Buy tickets at the newsstand just inside the terminal. You can get to other parts of Venice by **vaporetto** from the Piazzale Roma stop.

Taxis are also available in front of the terminal building and the trip to Piazzale Roma costs about 30€.

The **Cooperative San Marco/Alilaguna** (☎ 041-5235775; www.alilaguna.it) operates a large *motoscafo* (shuttle-boat) service from the airport with stops at Murano and the Lido before arriving after about 1 hour in Piazza San Marco; the trip costs 10€. The fee for a **private water taxi** is a legal minimum of 55€, but the fare is usually closer to 75€ for 2 to 4 passengers with few bags; water taxis are usually available at the landing outside the airport or contact the **Corsorzio Motoscafi Venezia** (☎ 041-5222303; www.motoscafi venezia.it).

By Car

Large car parks at the entrance to the city include the **Garage San Marco,** Piazzale Roma (☎ 041-5232213), about 26€ for 24 hours, and **Isola del Tronchetto** (☎ 041-5207555), about 18€ a day. It is less expensive to park on the mainland at Mestre for about 4.50€ a day, where options include **Parking Stazione** (☎ 041-938021), and take the train from there.

By Train
Stazione Venezia–Santa Lucia, Venice's train station, is 4½ hours from Rome, 2½ hours from Florence, 2½ hours from Milan, and 1½ hours from Bologna. The Ferrovia vaporetto stop is on the Grand Canal in front of the station.

By Bus
Buses arrive at the **Piazzale Roma** station. For schedules, call ☎ 041-5287886.

Getting **Around**

By Vaporetto
Vaporetti (water buses) connect points along the Grand Canal, other areas of the city, and islands. Boats run every 10 or 15 minutes from 7am to midnight, and once an hour after midnight until morning. An *accelerato* makes every stop; a *diretto* makes express stops. *Vaporetti* may well provide the most costly form of public transportation in the world: A single fare is 6.50€ and is valid for 60 minutes. You must stamp your ticket in one of the machines at each stop. Travel cards are available for 12 hours for 14€, 24 hours for 16€, 36 hours for 21€, 48 hours for 26€, and 72 hours for 31€. Tickets are available at stops, from newsstands and tobacco shops, and from ACTV and VeLa (see below); travel cards are sold at the tourist offices (see below); you may also purchase single fares on the boat. Do pay—if you're caught without a ticket the fine is a steep 21€. For information, contact **ACTV (Azienda del Consorzio Trasporti Veneziano),** Calle Fuseri 1810, off the Frezzeria in San Marco (☎ 041-5287886, www.actv.it; Mon–Sat 7:30am–7pm), or **VeLa,** Piazzale Roma (☎ 041-2722249; www.velaspa.com; daily 7:30am–8pm).

By Traghetti
Traghetti are large, unadorned gondolas rowed by standing gondoliers across the Grand Canal. The ride is reasonably priced at .50€, but if you do as the Venetians do and stand as you are ferried across the water, it can be a bit of a challenge. Some popular *traghetti* crossings are between Fondamente del Vin to Riva del Carbòn (Mon–Sat 8am–2pm) and the Pescaria and Santa Sofia (Mon–Sat 7:30am–8:30pm; Sun 8am–7pm), both near the Rialto. An especially scenic ride is that between San Marco and the Dogana (daily 9am–noon, 2–6pm).

By Water Taxi
Taxi acquei (water taxis) are expensive: 8.70€ fixed rate from departure and 1.30€ for each 60-second period thereafter. Each bag over 50 centimeters (20 in.) long costs 1.50€, plus there's a 5.50€ supplement for service from 10pm to 7am and a 5.90€ surcharge for travel on holidays. These rates are for four people; add 1.60€ for each extra passenger. You'll find water-taxi stations at the Ferrovia (☎ 041-716286); Piazzale Roma (☎ 041-716922); the Rialto Bridge (☎ 041-5230575 or 041-723112); Piazza San Marco (☎ 041-5229750); the Lido (☎ 041-5260059); and Marco Polo Airport (☎ 041-5415084). Call **Radio**

Taxi (☎ 041-5222303 or 041-723112) for a pickup anywhere in the city; a surcharge of 4.15€ is added.

By Gondola

If your fantasies involve hearing "'O Sole Mio" as you float down the Grand Canal, expect to pay 80€ for up to 40 minutes (100€, 8pm–8am), with up to six passengers, and 40€ for each additional 20 minutes (50€, 8pm–8am). There are 11 gondola stations around the city, including those at Piazzale Roma, the train station, the Rialto Bridge, and Piazza San Marco. Gondolas are regulated by the **Ente Gondola** (☎ 041-5285075; www.gondolavenezia.it). Negotiate a fee before you step into the craft, and be prepared—no self-respecting gondolier is going to let passengers disembark without trying to persuade them to take a longer ride.

On Foot

Walking is the only way to explore Venice, and a delightful experience. Throngs of tourists crowd San Marco, but you may get the impression that few venture beyond it. Yellow signs direct you to the major city points. Carry a detailed *pianta della città* (map of the city) with a thorough street index. One of the most detailed is published by Strade Demetra and can be purchased at newsstands and bookstores. No matter how carefully you follow a map, time after time you'll find yourself lost—enjoy the experience of simply wandering. Venetians are extremely polite when asked for directions, so if you become worrisomely lost, ask for help: *"Mi scusi, siamo perduti. Desideriamo andare a . . ."* ("Excuse me, we're lost. We want to go to . . .").

Fast **Facts**

AMERICAN EXPRESS The main office is on Salizzada San Moisè, just west of Piazza San Marco (☎ 041-5200844). Summer hours are Monday to Saturday 8am to 8pm for banking, 9am to 5:30pm for other services; in winter, all services are Monday to Friday 9am to 5:30pm and Saturday 9am to noon.

APARTMENT RENTALS Resources for apartment rentals of a week or more are **www.veniceapartment.com** and **www.interflats.it**.

ATMS ATMs (automated teller machines) are located throughout the city. Italy uses four-digit PINs; if you have a six-digit number, change it at your bank before you leave.

BABYSITTING Ask your hotel to help you arrange a babysitter.

BANKING HOURS Banks are open Monday to Friday 8:30am to 1:30pm and 2:35 to 3:35pm.

BIKE RENTALS Venice is not for cyclists—in fact, biking is forbidden for adults in the city. However, bikes are available on the Lido through **Bruno Lazzari,** Gran Viale 21B, Lido (☎ 041-5268019), open March to September daily 8am to 8pm; October to February daily 8:30am to 1pm and 3 to 7:30pm.

BUSINESS HOURS Shops are open Monday to Saturday, 9am to 12:30pm and 3 to 7:30pm, though some that have a lively tourist trade remain open throughout the day. Most businesses that do not cater to tourists are closed on Sunday; in winter they close on Monday morning, and in summer usually on Saturday afternoon. Grocers are usually closed on Wednesday afternoons. Most restaurants close at least one day a week and many close on holidays, sometime in July or August for vacation, frequently over Christmas, and often for a week or so in January before Carnevale.

CONSULATES **U.S.:** In Milan, Largo Donegani 1 (☎ 02-290351; Mon–Fri 9am–noon for visas, Mon–Fri 2–4pm for telephone info). **U.K:** In Mestre, Piazzale Sangue (☎ 041-5055990).

CREDIT CARDS Visa and MasterCard are widely accepted; many businesses do not accept American Express. You may be able to have a PIN assigned by your bank so that you can use your card at ATMs.

CUSTOMS Citizens of non-EU countries are allowed to bring the following into Italy duty-free: 200 cigarettes or 50 cigars or 250 grams of tobacco; 1 liter of spirits or 2 liters of wine; 50 grams of perfume. On leaving Italy, U.S. citizens who have been abroad for at least 48 hours are entitled to bring home $400 worth of duty-free merchandise. Be sure to keep receipts of all your purchases. Citizens of other EU countries do not need to declare goods.

DENTISTS & DOCTORS Check with the consulate of the United States or the United Kingdom, the American Express office, or your hotel.

DISCOUNTS **VeniceCard Orange** provides unlimited travel on public transportation, entry to many museums, use of public toilets, and discounts in some shops; it's available for 59€ for 3 days or 77€ for 7 days. **VeniceCard Blue** provides entry to museums and costs 37.50€ for 3 days, 58€ for 7 days. Both are available at tourist offices and other outlets; for more information contact ☎ 041-2424 or go to www.hellovenezia.com. The **Chorus** card provides entry to 16 participating churches and costs 9€ and is valid for 1 year. It's available at churches and tourist offices or by calling ☎ 041-2750462 or visiting www.chorusvenezia.org.

DRESS Legs and shoulders should be covered when entering churches. Women may want to carry a scarf to cover their heads.

DRUGSTORES Regular hours are Monday to Friday 9am to 12:30pm and 3:45 to 7:30pm; Saturday 9am to 12:45pm. At least one pharmacy in each *sestiere* (district) is open all night on a rotating basis; the tourist office keeps a list and a sign posted outside all pharmacies indicating which pharmacy is currently remaining open.

ELECTRICITY Electrical current is 220V AC, with two- or three-pronged plugs. You will need a transformer for most electrical appliances you bring with you, and also an adapter for electrical outlets.

EMERGENCIES Dial ☎ 113 to reach the police, ☎ 115 to report a fire, and ☎ 118 to summon an ambulance and/or emergency medical assistance.

HOLIDAYS Offices, shops, and many restaurants are closed on the following holidays: January 1, New Year's Day; Easter Monday; April 25, Liberation Day and the feast day of Saint Mark, the city's patron; May 1, Labor Day; August 15, Assumption of the Virgin; November 1, All Saints Day; December 8, Feast of the Immaculate Conception; December 25, Christmas; and December 26, feast day of Saint Stephen.

HOSPITALS **Ospedale Civile Santi Giovanni e Paolo,** on Campo Santi Giovanni e Paolo, has Englishspeaking staff and provides emergency service 24 hours a day (☎ 041-785111; vaporetto: San Tomà). For an ambulance and emergency medical aid, dial ☎ 118.

INSURANCE Check with you health insurance plan to see if you are covered while traveling abroad. If not, you can purchase travel insurance policies that cover health care abroad and often transportation back home if necessary.

INTERNET ACCESS Internet access can be surprisingly difficult in Venice. The city and hotels have been slow to adopt Wi-Fi, and Internet cafes are not as widespread as they are in other cities. Among them are **Internet Point,** Calle della Sacrista (☎ 041-5284871; daily 10am–11pm; 6€ an hour; vaporetto: San Zaccaria); and **Venetian Navigator,** Calle delle Bande, between San Marco and Campo Santa Maria Formosa (☎ 041-5226084; May–Oct daily 10am–10pm; Nov–Apr daily 10am–1pm, 2:30–8:30pm; 6€ an hour; vaporetto: Rialto).

LOST & FOUND The central **Ufficio Oggetti Rinvenuti (Lost and Found office)** is in the annex to the *Municipio* (City Hall) on Calle Piscopia o Loredan, just off Riva del Carbon on the Grand Canal, near the Rialto Bridge (☎ 041-788225; Mon, Wed, and Fri 9:30am–12:30pm; vaporetto: Rialto).

MAIL You can buy *francobolli* (stamps) at *tabacchi* (tobacconists). The **central post office** is on the San Marco side of the Rialto Bridge at Rialto in the Fondaco dei Tedeschi building (☎ 041-2717111 or 041-5285813; stamps available Mon–Sat 8:30am–6:30pm, other services Mon–Sat 8:10am–1:30pm; vaporetto: Rialto). Postal services are also available near Piazza San Marco on Calle Larga dell'Ascensione and near Piazzale Roma on Fondamenta Santa Chiara (Mon–Fri 8:30am–2pm; Sat 8:30am–1pm).

MONEY The euro is Italy's official currency. Euro banknotes come in denominations of 5€, 10€, 20€, 100€, 200€, and 500€, and coins of .2€, .5€, .10€, .20€, .50€, 1€, and 2€.

POLICE In an emergency, dial ☎ 112 or ☎ 113.

SAFETY Venice is one of Italy's safest cities. Beware, however, of pickpockets in crowds in the streets or on the *vaporetti,* and of occasional thievery at night in the dark backstreets. As is the case anywhere, common sense is your best protection.

SENIOR TRAVELERS Members of **AARP (American Association of Retired Persons),** 601 E. St., NW, Washington, DC 20049 (☎ 800/424-3410; www.aarp.org) are often eligible for discounts on airfare, hotels, and car rentals. If you are 50 or older, consider becoming a member before traveling. Many seniors also enjoy tours with **Elderhostel,** 11 Avenue de Lafayette, Boston, MA 02111 (☎ 877/426-8056; www.elderhostel.org), which provides escorted tours with an emphasis on lectures and field trips, is relatively inexpensive, and provides an excellent opportunity to meet like-minded travelers.

SMOKING Smoking is prohibited in all buildings with public access, including restaurants and bars, and on public transportation.

TAXES Like all members of the European Union, Italy has a value-added tax (VAT), called **IVA.** On your hotel bills, the IVA will range from 9% to 19%, depending on whether your room is first or second class or luxury. IVA is automatically included in the cost of goods you buy. If you are from a non-European Union country and spend more than 150€ in a store, you are entitled to reimbursement of the IVA. Ask for an invoice at the store, then take it to the customs office at the airport and have it stamped while you are still in Italy. Once home, send the vendor the stamped invoice. Eventually he or she will send you your refund. Be sure to make a copy of the invoice before you mail it. If you made your purchase with a credit card, you can ask that the card be credited. Many stores now belong to a "Tax Free for Tourists" plan (look for stickers in the window) and will issue a check when you pay for your purchase. At the airport, have the check validated by customs, then cash the check in the Tax Free booth. You can also mail it back within 60 days.

TELEPHONES   Most public phones in Venice require that you use a *schede telefoniche* (phone card), available at newsstands, bars, and elsewhere. To make a call, tear off one corner of the card as indicated and insert it in the appropriate slot. Even when calling within Venice, you will need to dial the prefix, 041. You can also purchase phone cards for *schede telefoniche internazionali* (international calls). When making international calls, dial 00, the country code, the area code (without the initial zero), and then the number. Some country codes are: Australia, 61; New Zealand, 64; U.K., 44; U.S., 1. You can also make international calls using phone cards provided by AT&T and other providers. To do so, dial the card access number, the country code, the area code and number, and your calling-card number. Avoid making calls from your hotel room, as these can be quite expensive. Access numbers for some common providers are: AT&T (☎ 172-1011), MCI (☎ 172-1022), and Sprint (☎ 172-1877).

TIPPING   In restaurants, a 15% *servizio incluso* (service charge) is typically included on your bill, but leave a little extra (a euro or two) if the service has been especially good. Give checkroom attendants .75€ and washroom attendants .25€ to .35€. A service charge is also included in your hotel bill, but give the chambermaid 1€ for each day of your stay and the porter 1.50€ to 2.50€ for carrying your

bags. A concierge expects tips for any extra service he or she provides.

TOILETS   Public toilets are marked by blue and green WC signs. There is a fee of about .50€ to 1€. *Signori* means men; *signore,* women; when looking for a toilet, ask for *"il bagno."*

TOURIST OFFICES IN VENICE   The government-run **APT,** Piazza San Marco (☎ 041-5298711), has offices throughout the city. Staffs tend to be extremely helpful and supply free maps, as well as information on sights concerts, exhibitions, and other events. Tourist offices also provide hotel listings. Offices are in the Piazza San Marco, Giardinetti Reali, the train station, the arrival halls at the airport, Piazzale Roma, on the Lido at GranViale 6a (high season only), and in Mestre at Corso del Popolo 65. Hours vary (and are subject to change): The San Marco office is open daily 9am to 3:30pm, and the offices around the corner in the Giardinetti and in the train station are open daily 8am to 6:30pm (vaporetto for the two San Marco offices: San Marco/Vallaresso).

TRAVELERS WITH DISABILITIES   Venice, city of bridges and stairs, can be difficult for almost anyone to navigate, especially those with physical disabilities. Some of the city's 400 bridges have been outfitted with mechanized lifts for wheelchairs, but most still involve a climb up and down steps at either end or navigating a steep incline. Italian law has done much to regulate wheelchair accessibility to hotels, restrooms, restaurants, and museums, but not all are wheelchair accessible; it's essential that you call ahead of time to verify accessibility. *Vaporetti* provide relatively easy access for wheelchairs. The tourist office provides a free map showing wheelchair-accessible sights, and an excellent resource is **Accessible Venice** (☎ 041-2748144;

www.comune.venezia.it/handicap), which provides accessibility information, barrier-free itineraries, and other information.

TRAVELER'S CHECKS ATMs have made traveler's checks a bit of an anachronism, but if you want to use them, call **American Express** (☎ 800/721-9768 in the U.S. and Canada; www.americanexpress.com); **Thomas Cook** (☎ 800/223-7373 in the U.S. and Canada, or 44/1733-318-950 from anywhere else collect;

www.thomascook.com); **Visa** (☎ 800/227-6811 in the U.S. and Canada, or 44/0207-937-8091 from anywhere else collect; www.visa.com); or **Citicorp** (☎ 800/645-6556 in the U.S. and Canada, or 813/623-1709 from anywhere else collect). To report lost or stolen traveler's checks in Italy, call toll-free: American Express (☎ 800/872-000); Thomas Cook (☎ 800/872-050); or Visa (☎ 800/874-155).

A Brief **History**

A.D. 400–600 Refugees flee barbarians on mainland to islands in lagoon.

421 According to tradition, Venice was founded on April 25, feast day of Saint Mark, patron saint of Venice.

639 Building on Torcello's cathedral begun.

697 According to legend, first doge elected.

729 Doge attempts to form hereditary monarchy. Civil war ensues, until doge is murdered.

814 Building of first Palazzo Ducale begun.

828 Body of Saint Mark stolen from Alexandria.

834 Building of first Basilica di San Marco begun.

867 Torcello's cathedral rebuilt.

1000 Venice begins to become maritime power.

1008 Torcello's cathedral rebuilt again.

1094 Basilica di San Marco consecrated.

1095 Venice furnishes ships and supplies for first Crusade.

1171 The six districts of Venice are established.

1173 First Rialto bridge built.

1204 The Sack of Constantinople. Venice's booty includes four bronze horses now in Basilica di San Marco.

1255 War with Genoa.

1309 Building of current Palazzo Ducale begun.

1310 Venetian Constitution is passed; Council of Ten instituted.

1348–49 The plague (Black Death) cuts city's population in half.

1380 Venice wins maritime supremacy over the Mediterranean and Adriatic.

1453 Venice's empire reaches its peak after Constantinople falls to the Turks; Venice's power then begins to wane.

1489 Venice conquers Cyprus.

1514 Fire destroys Rialto bridge.

1516 Ghetto founded.

1630 Black Death strikes again, reducing population to its smallest in 250 years.

1718 Venetian maritime empire ends.

1792 La Fenice opera house opens.

1797 Napoleon invades the Veneto; Venetian republic ends.

1798 Napoleon gives Venice to Austria.

1804 Napoleon crowned king of Italy.

1848 Venice revolts against Austria.

1849 Venetian troops surrender.

1866 Venice freed from Austrian rule; united with kingdom of Italy.

1870–1900 Industry grows; railway bridge linking Venice to mainland built; tourism begins to flourish.

1895 First Biennale D'Arte.

1902 Campanile in Piazza San Marco collapses.

1966 Venice devastated by floods; discussions on how to save the fragile city become heated.

1996 La Fenice destroyed by fire.

2002 Mobile tide barriers to control tidal damage completed.

2003 La Fenice reopens.

Venetian Art & Architecture

Venice has inspired artists since the city's earliest beginnings. Their works fill churches, *scuole* (guildhalls), and museums, and to spend time in front of these works is reason alone to come to Venice.

The Byzantine Era

Founded in the 7th century, rebuilt in the 9th, and altered in the 11th, the **Basilica di Santa Maria Assunta** on Torcello still stands as the best example of the city's Byzantine past. A Greek-cross plan, covered porch, marble columns, splendid mosaics, and other telltale signs of the Byzantine are much in evidence here and in the adjoining church of **Santa Fosca**. The interior of the **Basilica di San Marco** was decorated with brilliant Byzantine mosaics in the 12th century. Even though many of the original tiles have been replaced or badly restored over the years, enough remain to create a magical, ever-changing environment.

The Gothic Period

The **Palazzo Ducale,** begun in the 14th century and built over several centuries, beautifully exemplifies the hallmark Gothic elements: pointed arches, skillful ornament and tracery, pierced quatrefoil decoration, and capitals atop the columns. Venice's fine Venetian-Gothic palaces also include the **Ca' d'Oro,** which architect **Bartolomeo Bon** (1374–1464) imbued with elegant tracery, opulent detail, color, and a richly decorated facade.

The Renaissance

Balance and symmetry, hallmarks of Renaissance painting and architecture, are in many ways antithetical to the Venetian love of color and ornamentation. The exquisite church of **Santa Maria dei Miracoli** is a good example of how architect **Pietro Lombardo** (1435–1515) balanced the two sensibilities. Panels of richly colored marble glisten in the Venetian light and tie the church to the Gothic style, but classical rounded arches, beautifully balanced proportions, and a soaring dome are perfectly in keeping with Renaissance ideals.

The great architect **Andrea Palladio** (1508–80) spent several years in Rome studying its ruins, and classical elements—balance, proportion, and harmony—are much in evidence in two of Venice's finest churches, **San Giorgio Maggiore** and **Il Redentore.** More Palladian classicism graces the shores of the Brenta Canal, where the villas he built for Venetian aristocracy resemble temples. **Sansovino** (1486–1570) fled to Venice after the sack of Rome, bringing with him an appreciation of the classical that appears in the Marciana Library and other buildings around the **Piazza San Marco.**

Venetian art made a great step forward when the **Coronation of the Virgin** (in the Accademia) and other works by **Paolo Veneziano** (active 1320–65) appeared, displaying fluid lines, a lack of strict formality in the composition, and bright, opulent colors, all marking a move away from the Byzantine.

Giovanni Bellini (1430–1516) brought Venetian painting to the threshold of the Renaissance, and the step forward is especially noteworthy in **Madonna with Saints** in the church of San Zaccaria. The colors are mellow and rich, and light illuminates the figures, which stand out as individuals rather than stock decoration.

When you enter Room 5 in the Accademia and see the **Tempest,** one of the most mysterious paintings in Western art, you move into another world—and understand why **Giorgione** (1477–1510) is considered to be the first modern artist. A storm approaches, a sensuous, lyrical mood pervades, color and light fill the painting, and landscape and drama take center stage.

It is said that **Titian** (1485?–1576) was so highly regarded that when Charles V visited his studio and the artist dropped his brush, the emperor picked it up. During his long career, Titian made breakthroughs in color and light, created dazzling, luminous effects with glazes, and experimented with composition. All these elements are evident in **Madonna with Saints and Members of the Pesaro Family** in the Scuole Santa Maria Gloriosa dei Frari. Here, Titian takes a conventional subject and turns it upside down, moving the Madonna from the center of the composition to the upper right side of the painting; other figures form a strong diagonal moving toward her, and brilliant light and color envelop the entire painting.

Tintoretto (1518–94), a native Venetian, worked passionately, using a wide brush and priming the canvases with dark tones, then bringing out the lights. In his **Last Supper** in San Giorgio Maggiore, you see Tintoretto's use of light and his focus on everyday scenes.

In the Venetian world of **Paolo Veronese** (1528–88), robust men and women dressed in sumptuous clothing move about in marble settings, obviously enjoying life and awash in bright blues and yellows and violets and pinks. Typical is **Feast in the House of Levi** in the Accademia, in which a holy event is depicted as a secular scene—to such an extent that this painting of the Last Supper was considered to be blasphemous.

The Baroque Period

Baldassare Longhena (1598–1682) is Venice's master of the baroque, and he described his greatest creation, the church of **Santa Maria della Salute,** as "strange, worthy, and beautiful."

The church is massive, topped by domes inspired by Saint Peter's in Rome. The theatrical exterior is decorated with sculpture, and the octagonal form creates an exuberant and dynamic pattern; the interior is remarkable for its huge central space.

Religious zeal hit a new height in such works of art as **Giambattista Piazzetta's** (1682–1754) *Glorification of Saint Dominic* in the church of Santi Giovanni e Paolo, in which figures ascend into the swirling heavens.

Giambattista Tiepolo (1696–1770), the master of the Venetian baroque, is best known for his colorful frescoes in **Palazzo Labia** and other Venetian churches and palaces.

Canaletto (1697–1768), **Pietro Longhi** (1702–58), and **Francesco Guardi** (1712–93) shifted the focus from religion to secular, even everyday, subjects. Canaletto's views of the Grand Canal, Longhi's scenes of balls and other social gatherings, and Guardi's paintings of the Lagoon hang in the Museo del Settecento Veneziano.

Useful **Phrases & Menu Terms**

Phrases

ENGLISH	ITALIAN	PRONUNCIATION
Thank you	Grazie	*graht*-tzee-ay
Please	Per favore	*pehr*-fah-*vohr*-eh
Yes	Si	*see*
No	No	*noh*
Good morning	Buongiorno	bwahn-*djor*-noh
Good evening	Buona sera	*bwahn*-oh *serr*-ah
How are you?	Come sta?	koh-may-*stah*?
I'm well	Molto bene	*mohl*-toh-*bhen*-eh
Excuse me	Scusi	*skoo*-zee
Where is . . .	Dovè . . .	doh-*veh* . . .
a hotel	un albergo	oon ahl-*behr*-goh
a restaurant	un ristorante	oon reest-ohr-*ahnt*-ey
the bathroom	il bagno	eel *bahn*-nyah
To the right	A destra	ah *dehy*-stra
To the left	A sinistra	ah see-*nees*-tra
Straight ahead	Avanti	ahv-*vahn*-tee
Good	Buono	*bwoh*-noh
Bad	Cattivo	ka-*tee*-voh
Open	Aperto	ah-*pair*-toh
Closed	Chiuso	kee-*oo*-soh
Hot	Caldo	*kahl*-doh
Cold	Freddo	*fray*-doh
Big	Grande	*gran*-day
Expensive	Caro	*kahr*-roh
Cheap	A buon prezza	ah bwon *pretz*-so
Small	Piccolo	*pee*-koh-loh
I'm sorry	Mi dispiace	*mee* dis-*pach*-e-ray

Do you speak English?	Parla inglese?	*par*-la in-*glay*-say?
I would like	Vorrei	*vor*-ray
How much does it cost?	Quanto costa?	*kwan*-to *kos*-ta?
Help!	Aiuto!	eye-*yooh*-toh!
Call . . .	Chiama . . .	kee-*ah*-mah . . .
the police	la polizia	lah poh-*lee*-tsee-ah
a doctor	un medico	oon *meh*-dee-koh
an ambulance	un ambulanza	oon am-boo-*lehn*-tsah
First course	Il primo	eel *pree*-moh
Main course	Il secondo	eel seh-*kon*-doh
The bill please	Il conto, per favore	eel kon-toh *pehr* fah-*vohr*-eh

Numbers

ENGLISH	ITALIAN	PRONUNCIATION
1	Uno	*oo*-noh
2	Due	*doo*-ay
3	Tre	*tray*
4	Quattro	*kwah*-troh
5	Cinque	*ceen*-kway
6	Sei	*say*
7	Sette	*set*-tay
8	Otto	*oh*-toh
9	Nove	*noh*-vay
10	Dieci	dee-*ay*-chee
11	Undici	*oon*-dee-chee
12	Dodici	*do*-dee-chee
13	Tredici	*tray*-dee-chee
14	Quattordici	kwah-troh-*dee*-chee
15	Quindici	*kwin*-dee-cee
16	Sedici	*say*-dee-cee
17	Diciassette	dee-cee-a-*set*-tay
18	Diciotto	dee-cee-ah-*oh*-toh
19	Diciannove	dee-cee-ah-*noh*-vay
20	Venti	*vehn*-tee
30	Trenta	*treyn*-tah
40	Quaranta	kwah-*rahn*-tah
50	Cinquanta	cheen-*kwan*-tah
60	Sessanta	sehs-*sahn*-tah
70	Settanta	seht-*tahn*-tah
80	Ottanta	oht-*tan*-tah
90	Novanta	noh-*vahnt*-tah
100	Cento	*chen*-toh
1000	Mille	*mee*-lay

Menu Items

ENGLISH	ITALIAN	PRONUNCIATION
Anchovies	Acciughe	ah-*choo*-gay
Artichokes	Carciofi	kar-*chof*-fee
Beans	Fagioli	fah-*joh*-lee
Beef	Manzo	*man*-zoh
Butter	Burro	*boor*-roh
Cheeses	Formaggi	for-*mahd*-jee
Chicken	Pollo	*po*-lo
Clams	Vongole	*vahn*-goh-lee
Consomme	Brodo	*bro*-doh
Desserts	Dolci	*dol*-chee
Eggplant	Melanzana	meh-lan-*tsah*-nee
Eggs	Uova	*woh*-vah
Fish	Pesce	*pech*-ay
Lamb	Agnello	ahn-*yell*-oh
Liver	Fegato	fay-*gah*-toh
Meat sauce	Ragu	rah-*goo*
Mushrooms	Funghi	*foon*-gee
Nuts	Noci	*no*-chee
Pork	Maiale	may-*ah*-lay
Rice	Riso	*ree*-so
Sardines	Sarde	*sar*-day
Sauce	Salsa	*sahl*-sa
Sausages	Salsiccie	sahl-see-*chee*-ay
Shrimp	Gamberoni	gam-ber-*oh*-nee
Snails	Lumache	loo-*mah*-chay
Soup	Zuppa	*zoo*-pah
Steak	Bistecca	*bee*-stek-kah
Tomatoes	Pomodori	poh-mo-*dor*-ee
Veal	Vitello	vi-*tell*-oh
Vegetables	Contorni	kan-*tor*-nee
Vinegar	Aceto	ah-*chay*-toh

Index

Photo **Credits**

184